ABOUT THE AUTHOR

Itty Abraham was trained in economics at Loyola College, Madras and received his Ph.D. in political science from the University of Illinois at Urbana-Champaign. He spent the academic year 1995–96 as a post-doctoral fellow at the Center for International Security and Arms Control, Stanford University. He is currently Program Director for South Asia and Southeast Asia at the Social Science Research Council in New York. He is the coeditor of *Southeast Asian Diasporas*, a special issue of *Sojourn: Journal of Social Issues in Southeast Asia*. This is his first book.

POSTCOLONIAL ENCOUNTERS

A Zed Books series in association with the International Centre for Contemporary Cultural Research (ICCCR)

Series editors: Richard Werbner and Pnina Werbner

This series debates the making of contemporary culture and politics in a postcolonial world. Volumes explore the impact of colonial legacies, precolonial traditions and current global and imperial forces on the everyday lives of citizens. Reaching beyond postcolonial countries to the formation of external ethnic and migrant diasporas, the series critically theorises:

- the active engagement of people themselves in the creation of their own political and cultural agendas;
- the emerging predicaments of local, national and transnational identities and subjectivities;
- the indigenous roots of nationalism, communalism, state violence and political terror;
- the cultural and religious counter-movements for or against emancipation and modernity;
- the social struggles over the imperatives of human and citizenship rights within the moral and political economy.

Arising from the analysis of decolonisation and recolonisation, the series opens out a significant space in a growing interdisciplinary literature. The convergence of interest is very broad, from anthropology, cultural studies, social history, comparative literature, development, sociology, law and political theory. No single theoretical orientation provides the dominant thrust. Instead the series responds to the challenge of a commitment to empirical, in-depth research as the motivation for critical theory.

Other titles in the series:

Richard Werbner and Terence Ranger, eds, *Postcolonial Identities in Africa* (1996).

Pnina Werbner and Tariq Modood, eds, *Debating Cultural Hybridity: Multi-Cultural Identities and the Politics of Anti-Racism* (1997).

Tariq Modood and Pnina Werbner, eds, *The Politics of Multiculturalism in the New Europe: Racism, Identity and Community* (1997).

Richard Werbner, ed., *Memory and the Postcolony: African Anthropology and the Critique of Power* (1998).

THE MAKING OF THE INDIAN ATOMIC BOMB

SCIENCE, SECRECY AND THE POSTCOLONIAL STATE

ITTY ABRAHAM

ZED BOOKS

London & New York

The Making of the Indian Atomic Bomb was first published by
Zed Books Ltd, 7 Cynthia Street, London N1 9JF, UK,
and Room 400, 175 Fifth Avenue, New York, NY 10010, USA,
in 1998.

Designed and typeset in Monotype Bembo by
Lucy Morton & Robin Gable, Grosmont
Printed and bound in the United Kingdom by Biddles Ltd,
Guildford and King's Lynn

A catalogue record for this book is available from the British Library

Library of Congress Cataloging-in-Publication Data
Abraham, Itty, 1960–
    The making of the Indian atomic bomb : science, secrecy and the
postcolonial state / Itty Abraham.
        p.   cm. — (Postcolonial encounters)
    Includes bibliographical references and index.
    ISBN 1–85649–629–5 (hb). — ISBN 1–85649–630–9 (pb)
    1. Atomic bomb—India—History. 2. Nuclear weapons—India.
    3. Nuclear proliferation—India. 4. Nuclear weapons—Testing—Law and
Legislation—India. I. Title. II Series.
    QC773.A27   1998
    355.8'25119'0954—dc21   98–27616
                                                                 CIP

Distributed exclusively in the USA by St Martin's Press,
175 Fifth Avenue, New York, NY 10010, USA.

ISBN 1 85649 629 5 (Hb)
ISBN 1 85649 630 9 (Pb)

CONTENTS

ACKNOWLEDGEMENTS

I have a number of individuals and institutions to thank for allowing me to complete this work. The bulk of it was written at the Center for International Security and Arms Control (CISAC) at Stanford University in 1995–96, a perfect setting for this kind of project. The Center is particularly interested in the intersection of science and politics, and seeks to generate conversations between visiting scientists and social scientists across their respective specialisations. For a scientific novice like me to be able to walk down the corridor and talk to experts in nuclear physics about the most trivial of physical problems aided my work in so many ways. I know this would have been a very different book without the generosity of my fellow residents at Galvez House. I have particularly to thank Scott Sagan, who first invited me to spend a year at the Center, and who was the most gracious of hosts at a time when he had so many other important issues making demands on his time. Gabrielle Hecht was kind enough to share her knowledge of the French nuclear industry and a lot of her ongoing work with me. My thanks also to CISAC's former director, David Holloway, and also to Lynn Eden and Dean Wilkening for asking tough questions, keeping me on track, and for putting up with a 'postie' in a place where there had been none before. Two presidents of the Social Science Research Council, David Featherman and Kenneth Prewitt, were kind enough to grant me an unusually long study leave to allow me to spend nine months in Palo Alto. Without their generosity, completing this book would not have been possible.

I want to record my appreciation to the following institutions: the Carnegie Corporation, for providing the funds that supported me at CISAC; the Social Science Research Council; and the MacArthur Foundation, who paid for my first foray into the arcane world of nuclear politics as a graduate student at the University of Illinois, when I first began to think through a number of the issues that appear in this work. My thanks to Virendra Singh, Govind Swarup, and Ravinder Kumar for generosity at short notice. Lorna Arnold saved me months of effort as she helped me find my way through the British archives. Thanks also to the staff at the many libraries and archives who helped me and granted permission to use their materials. These include the Niels Bohr Library at the American Institute of Physics (formerly in New York City, now in Maryland); Columbia University libraries; Hoover Institution archives in Stanford, California; Bancroft Library at the University of California, Berkeley; Stanford University libraries; Library of Congress; US National Archives; National Security Archive, Washington DC; UK Public Records Office, Kew Gardens; India Office Library, London; Royal Society of Great Britain, London; Tata Institute of Fundamental Research library, Bombay; Tata Archives, Bombay; and the Nehru Memorial Museum and Library, Delhi. My thanks also to the editors at Zed Books, Robert Molteno and Louise Murray, for all their help.

Bits and pieces of this work have been presented at seminars over the last two years. I learnt a lot while being grilled at the Center for Cultural Studies at the University of California, Santa Cruz, South Asia/Middle East seminar at the University of Chicago, South Asia seminar at Cornell University, political science department at the University of Hawai'i, School of International Studies at Jawaharlal Nehru University, CISAC Wednesday seminar at Stanford University, the Rethinking South Asia conference at Tufts University, and of course at the annual South Asia conferences at the University of Wisconsin at Madison. My deep gratitude to Anna Tsing, Susanne and Lloyd Rudolph, Shelley Feldman, Sankaran Krishna, Kanti Bajpai, Lynn Eden, and Sugata Bose for inviting me to present my ideas and for the many conversations with participants at these seminars who unfortunately are too numerous to name.

A number of individuals have been crucial in shaping the way the arguments here have been formed, strengthened, and sometimes completely revamped. In many ways, Ashis Nandy is responsible for making me think about this problem and for showing me how to proceed, often through the provocation of just a sentence in one of his many essays on science and modernity. David Ludden and Arun Elhance led me to think very differently about space. Gyan Prakash has been a great help in talking through the complications of poststructural theory and science in colonial India. Ron Suny was always willing to stop and talk about nationalism in all its guises and the follies of the postcolonial. Anna Tsing took a great interest in a subject far from her own specialisation and made me think through issues I had taken for granted. The first draft of this work was read and commented upon by Amrita Basu, Stephen P. Cohen, and

Sankaran Krishna, who gave me reams of excellent advice, which I have done my best to incorporate and respond to in a manner consistent with the quality of their suggestions. David Lelyveld, apart from making it possible for me to take a year off by agreeing to take over my job, gave me the benefit of his extraordinary knowledge of India and cultural history in his detailed reading of my original manuscript. I can only hope that what finally appears will come close to meeting their rigorous standards of scholarship. Sankaran Krishna and I have engaged in an open-ended conversation about the state, national security, and the nature of the postcolonial for so long that his ideas are scattered all over this book. His help and support have been invaluable. And finally, for introducing me to new ways of thinking about culture and politics, for never letting me get away with a half-baked idea, for reading and re-reading this manuscript from beginning to end, for putting up with all the trials of a book in process in three different cities for four years, and for always being there, Lalitha Gopalan. The best parts of this book are as much hers as they are mine, though its inadequacies must remain mine alone.

PREFACE

THE PROBLEM

Over the course of a week in May 1998, to the surprise and horror of the world, India conducted five nuclear tests. Its prime minister, Atal Behari Vajpayee of the right wing Bharatiya Janata Party (BJP), announced to the world that India was now a full-fledged nuclear power, and that it has a 'big bomb'. Domestic public reaction to this event was enormously positive, at least in the big cities. Practically all political parties signed up to the general euphoria, some even noting that this event was long overdue. It is striking how similar public opinion in 1998 was to the reaction in 1974, when India set off its first underground 'peaceful' nuclear explosion at its Pokhran test site. We hear very different voices repeat the same refrain, addressed to the same audience. Raj Thapar, long a political insider but by then a bitter critic of the government, had this to say in her memoirs: 'What did I really feel [about the 1974 nuclear explosion]? Hate as I did every bit of nuclear experimentation, convinced that it was a sad and cruel waste for starving countries such as ours, I couldn't escape the current of glee that streaked through me at the thought of what other nations would say – they wouldn't be able to kick us around as before.'[1] Raja Ramanna, architect of the 1974 explosion wrote:

> [The 1974 explosion] came as a surprise to the world. They hadn't expected such an achievement from a developing country ... their criterion for measuring success was different in the sense that they judged the success of a country by its material acquisitions and its overt proof of development ... India didn't conform to any of these, and in this context alone it seemed somewhat relevant when the Western world expressed bewilderment, coupled with fear and panic at the success of Pokhran.[2]

To be in New Delhi during that week in May 1998, or in summer 1996 when the Comprehensive Test Ban Treaty (CTBT) was being discussed, was to see intellectuals from across the political landscape joining in almost unanimous agreement that India's actions were completely justified. For those on the left, this defiance seemed to hark back to the days when Indian rhetoric at the United Nations and other international meetings sparkled with the possibilities of new alliances across the South, of changing the norms of international society through progressive ideals and sheer numbers. For those on the right, especially those who had been calling for some years for India officially to announce its nuclear status, the international response to these explosions confirmed why it was needed in the first place: to get the attention and grudging respect of the major nuclear powers. All in all, it was a rare voice indeed that noted the narrowness of the debate, and questioned its premises in relation to its avowed goals.

India's position is all the more ironic because it was India's first prime minister, Jawaharlal Nehru, who had proposed a complete nuclear weapons test ban in the first place. In Geneva, before the United Nations nearly forty years before, Nehru had proposed what then must have seemed a quixotic and impossible step toward disarmament. The proposal was rejected summarily at the time, but never quite went away. In the 1960s, an international treaty went into effect banning nuclear tests underwater, on the ground, and in the atmosphere: the 'partial' test ban. And as recently as 1993, the United States and India jointly sponsored a resolution in the United Nations proposing a comprehensive test ban. Just three years later, India would be noticeably absent from the near universal acceptance of this treaty; not only that but at various points in the negotiations, India had seemed to take steps to scuttle the process entirely.

Historical ironies aside, what caused India's *volte face*? Praful Bidwai and Achin Vanaik assert that, starting in 1994, a campaign led by 'pro-nuclear advocates' in the Indian security community began the process of rethinking India's historic stance on the test-ban treaty for two related reasons.[3] First, achieving international consensus on the CTBT suddenly appeared to be a real possibility, and, second, signing the treaty at this point would, for Indian hawks, 'formalise the nuclear asymmetry between India and China'. As Bidwai and Vanaik note, taking this step to deny the asymmetry between India and China is more symbolic than meaningful. China is so far ahead of India in the nuclear game that it would take many decades for India even to be able to redress the present imbalance. However, to assert the importance of China in the Indian strategic calculus is to provide an ostensible reason for India to acquire nuclear weapons.

But India's stance at these negotiations marks a sea change in its self-representation. The Indian diplomatic position, which once claimed to be based on peaceful coexistence and a 'third path' in international relations, has now merged into identity with the discourse adopted by the great powers. For the first time, the universal goals of disarmament and world peace that it had once stood for were being sidelined in favour of a realist argument that prioritised India's 'sovereign national interests'. In some respects, signs of a shift had been visible since 1995, when the 25-year-old nuclear non-proliferation treaty (NNPT) was extended indefinitely. India had always refused to sign the treaty, as it appeared to endorse the possession of nuclear weapons by some countries while it permanently denied them to others. It has always said that it took this position not because it wanted to develop its own weapons but because the treaty was discriminatory, creating two tiers of states in the international system. Its rejection of the NNPT was a position taken in the name of all the second-tier countries, the nuclear have-nots, a position that was based on its sense of leadership and influence among third world nations. What came as a complete shock to Indian foreign policy makers at the NNPT negotiations in 1995 was how far away from the international consensus the Indian position now was. If, at one time, taking a stand 'for the third world' was popular, even principled, by 1995 international opinions about atomic energy had shifted so much that India's stated reasons for opposing the treaty no longer seemed valid. In many observers' eyes, Indian rejection of the NNPT now looked like nothing more than the actions of a country that wanted to have nuclear weapons and that would not sign a treaty that might obstruct that goal. That feeling was furthered by India's response to the CTBT, and finally confirmed by its actions in May 1998. But is this the correct frame with which to understand India's affair with nuclear power?

For me the problem begins with questions generated by the wholly enthusiastic domestic Indian response to the May 1998 explosions, the 1996 CTBT negotiations, and the underground test of 1974, but it cannot stop there. In all these cases, the intensity of the response of the Indian intelligentsia and urban public points to a deep and disturbing relation to nuclear power, which says much about the nature of Indian political culture and raises profound questions about the Indian state. Uncovering that relation in all its complexity, I argue, helps explain not only the Indian nuclear programme in a distinctly new way, it also moves us toward a better understanding of the postcolonial state's project of modernity. These dual objectives are what this book is about.

PROBLEMS OF STUDYING THE INDIAN
NUCLEAR ESTABLISHMENT

Why has it taken so long for a detailed critical study of India's flirtation with nuclear weapons to be written? The most obvious reason is simply one of access. The Indian government has been quite unwilling to allow scholars full and unfettered access to the official records of the nuclear complex, on the dubious grounds that questions of national security are at stake. What the state has done is put out a sanitised official narrative of scientific and peaceful progress, a narrative produced through glossy publications like *Nuclear India*, published by the Indian department of atomic energy, through memoirs which bear heavily on a selective recall of events and causes, and, most important, through the creation of an official myth around the figure of Homi Jehangir Bhabha, the first leader of India's nuclear establishment.[4] This seamless narrative of science for the nation's development is interspersed with the diplomatic feats of non-aligned and non-nuclear India, and it is through this lens that the academic discourse on nuclear India has been positioned. In spite of the attention, whether critical or supportive, on diplomatic and strategic histories of India's nuclear policy, the conditions and events of her nuclear *practice* have scarcely been scrutinised. That is the starting point for this book.

I soon grew to appreciate the difficulty of retelling this story. When asked detailed questions about the history of the nuclear programme, so many senior individuals in the Indian scientific and nuclear policy community would simply repeat to me what I had already learned from an examination of the available documents. This made me realise that owing to the weight of the official state narrative and the centralisation of decision making being in the hands of so few people, most individuals one would have expected to be in a position to know something had replaced their own recollections with the official version of what happened, had never been in a position to know what had transpired at key moments, or just would not talk on the record for various reasons, including fear. Because of the official secrecy that cloaks this programme in India, and the notorious unreliability of memories of events from 40 and 50 years ago, I decided early on that I would forgo interviews completely. I decided that, especially given the secretive nature of the Indian nuclear establishment and the potentially controversial nature of some of my conclusions, I would use only public sources, in order to allow interested parties to retrace my arguments if they so choose. Fortunately, much of the relevant official records of the United Kingdom and the United States are open to researchers, as are some private archives in those countries and in India. I began five years ago to search state archives for official records and private archives for letters and other unpublished materials that provided insights into the events, steps not taken, and decision making related to the Indian nuclear programme. That effort led to the present work and helps explain its one apparent shortcoming, namely that it does not, unlike similar studies of the UK, USSR, France, and the United States, use the official records of the country being studied.[5] At one level, then, this is an interpretive study that provides a critical retelling of how India 'grew to love the Bomb', using a wide range of relevant evidence – but it does not stop there. The story of atomic energy is also the story of postcolonial India. Coming to terms with the promises, hopes, and disappointments of that greater project is the other purpose of this book.

Itty Abraham
New York City

NOTES

1. Raj Thapar, *All These Years* (Delhi: Penguin, 1991), p. 379.
2. Raja Ramanna, *Years of Pilgrimage* (Delhi: Viking, 1991), pp. 92–3.
3. Bidwai and Vanaik, 'Testing Times', especially pp. 59–68.
4. For a discussion of official narratives and their relation to national security, see my 'Toward a reflexive South Asian security studies'. in M.G. Weinbaum and Chetan Kumar, eds., *South Asia Approaches the Millennium: Re-examining national security*, Boulder, Colo., Westview, 1995. *Nuclear India* is published by the Department of Atomic Energy; memoirs include Ramanna's *Years of Pilgrimage*; the myth around Bhabha is one of the themes of this book.
5. Students of the Chinese nuclear experience have a similar problem, but at least they have the official documentary history of the Chinese programme to use as a point of departure. See John W. Lewis and Xue Litai, *China Builds the Bomb*, Stanford, Stanford University Press, 1988.

INTRODUCTION

ATOMIC ENERGY AS A
WORLD HISTORICAL MOMENT

On 2 December 1942, James B. Conant of Harvard University received a cryptic telephone message from Chicago, 'The Italian navigator has reached the New World.' [1] Conant asked in response, 'And how did he find the natives?' 'Very friendly' was the reply.[2] This coded statement meant that three years after its theoretical possibility had been established, the 'Italian navigator', Enrico Fermi, had experimentally confirmed the possibility of a controlled nuclear chain reaction. The world's first atomic pile had been built in an abandoned squash court at the University of Chicago using a uranium metal and uranium oxide core and graphite moderator. From these prosaic beginnings would eventually come a new post-Columbian era – the Manhattan Project and the building of the world's first atomic bombs.

Following the massive destruction of Hiroshima and Nagasaki in the Second World War, the atom was universally taken to be the primary symbol of the new era, the so-called 'atomic age', a prototypical modern conjuncture forever oscillating between the agonies of mass death and standardised terror, and the euphoria of tremendous economic trans-formation through the permanent resolution of the ever increasing need for electrical energy at little or no cost. What is extraordinary today, more than half a century later, is not only that the significance of the times was recognised, but that attempts to understand it gave rise to near-religious passion.[3] It is a singular moment indeed when a historical period is named by those participating in it. Attempts to label our contemporary moment in the same way – postmodern, information age, late industrial, global anarchy, the end of history – points to the difficulty even of finding enough common ground to begin to pose the question. After 1945, the destroyed city of Hiroshima became the metonymic label for an entire historical period, though not all remembered equally or in the same way the horror of the 'noiseless flash' over Hiroshima.[4]

From this self-conscious beginning, it became impossible to contain atomic energy. The symbolic meaning and presence of the atom crossed and recrossed the lines between popular culture, lived experience, political protest, strategic discourse, modern design, industry, medicine, and agriculture, so much that it truly became an 'atomic age' whether one was in the US, France, China, or anywhere else. The Indian political classes soaked up the historicity and passion of the moment. For more spiritually minded Indian nationalists, the temporal coincidence of India's independence in 1947 and the sudden possibility of access to enormous and cheap sources of energy seemed too good to be true – it had to be divinely ordained. For more hard-headed state intellectuals, atomic energy was an opportunity that could not be missed, both for its tremendous power potential and because it was one area where the most developed and the least developed states would be beginning on relatively even footing. This split response would be replicated across the world.[5]

We realise immediately that for all its multiple avatars, atomic energy had a particular presence around representations of the state and nation, reflecting its origins in the modern meeting of science and war. In some cases, particularly the United States, the Soviet Union, and China, the nuclear issue was from the outset a question of the bomb. For the United States, building the bomb moved seamlessly from being a part of the war effort to defeat the Axis powers to being a central element of winning the Cold War against its new adversary, the USSR, once an ally against German aggression.[6] The Soviet Union followed a similar path. Stalin became obsessed with building atomic weapons once he realised what they meant in the new calculus of world power, and his scientists had little choice but to follow the dictates of the state.[7] In China, for all Mao's initial posturing about nuclear weapons being 'paper tigers', he was not averse to accepting help from the Soviets to build bombs. When that help dissipated, he ensured that Chinese scientists continued the process that would eventually lead them to an atomic test in 1964.[8] In all these cases, the perception of a military threat – whether that threat was real or imagined – governed practice. The state needed a bomb and in due course scientists delivered.

The British and French were in a more ambivalent situation. While scientists from both countries had played a considerable part in creating the scientific preconditions for building atomic bombs, and small numbers of them had taken part in the US Manhattan Project, after the war they had a choice. Atomic energy did not have to be used for weapons alone, and in the post-war period there was time to reflect and to think about the massive state resources necessary for a weapons programme. At the same time, both France and Britain were states with extensive colonial possessions and scarcely dented ambitions to greatness, though relatively weak in terms of the new international context. Under these conditions, they hedged: peaceful nuclear programmes did begin, cheek by jowl with military programmes, often as a result of scientists calling the shots in the absence of strong political direction. In other words, all the acknowledged nuclear weapons states had military objectives for their nuclear programmes from the outset. This stands in contrast to the second generation of nuclear powers, where the movement from established civilian programmes to covert military programmes would be more typical.

The relationship of atomic weapons programmes to civilian energy programmes is, however, not the whole story. Due to the significance of atomic energy in defining an entire historical moment, deeply contested questions around definitions of the nation were also played out in these early years of nuclear decision making. The most direct conflict was around the role and importance of public and private participation in the nuclear programme. In the Communist states, for obvious reasons, and in Great Britain, with its latent socialism and would-be aristocratic distrust of private enterprise, this was not an issue, but in France and the United States it was. It must be remembered that in the early post-war years there was far less anxiety about public projects for national development than is the case today. The war years, with virtual central planning in the United States, and the proven effectiveness of Keynesian fiscal economic prescriptions in ending the Great Depression, defined a context where the state was considered to have an important role to play in stabilising, directing, and even participating in the capitalist economy. Notwithstanding, the question of who would control atomic energy immediately became a political issue in France and the United States. In the US a workable solution was found with the state subsidising private enterprise through the direct and often free transfer of technology and expertise for the production of electricity, while the state built a complex of laboratories and fissile material production sites for their military programme.[9] In France, a similar tension led first to the removal of Communist Frédéric Joliot-Curie from leadership of the atomic energy commission (CEA), and then to an institutional split between the pro-private-sector CEA, which would pursue military goals, and the leftist, state-owned electricity production corporation, oriented toward the civilian sector.[10]

Defining nuclear programmes also generated divisions about autonomy and national independence. In most cases it was assumed that nuclear programmes would be independent national products for two reasons: first because of the efforts of the United States in trying, unsuccessfully as it would turn out, to control the spread of expertise on and materials for producing nuclear energy,[11] and second, because it was widely assumed that knowledge about atomic energy was so vital to national security that no country would share it anyway. National independence, one would imagine, would have to be the default option, even if unwillingly, as the official history of the British nuclear programme makes so clear.[12] Yet we find that, notwithstanding the rhetoric, practically no state travelled alone. While a case could be made for the initial autonomy of nuclear programmes, best exemplified by the often markedly different style of reactor design, from the mid-1950s onward a regular exchange of information about nuclear matters ensued under the aegis of a series of UN-sponsored international conferences. The Soviet Union was extremely important in the early years of the Chinese nuclear programme, while the Americans trained nuclear scientists from around the world in their universities. Perhaps this was nothing more than an unconscious recognition of external help in the superpowers' own nuclear histories, namely the international cast of scientists who built the US bomb and the spies who helped speed along the Soviet effort. However, the assumption of independent national programmes, which was more true for some countries than for others, led to considerable anxiety among the public and political classes when it appeared that one country's programme was moving along faster than another's. The usual measures of such advancement were nearly always military − usually a nuclear test in some place far away from the metropolis. The anxiety of being left behind was closely related to an expression of national pride in being able to be a part of this 'race', and took expression in the numbers of ways in which national programmes could find points of uniqueness, whether real or feigned.

With nations turning so often to the past to authenticate themselves, incorporating the hyper-modernity of this technology into existing national discourse was often a complex feat of rhetorical shifts. The aesthetics of nuclear energy and its artefacts had to be acknowledged, and in many cases visitors could not but draw contrasts between the stark lines of nuclear reactors and their pristine surroundings. The contrasts of modernity and tradition, however defined, find frequent mention in France, for example, where reference would be made to nuclear reactors in terms of past technological marvels like the Eiffel Tower, the Arc de Triomphe and even the cathedral of Notre Dame![13] In the United States and the Soviet Union it was little different; for all the contrast in their political systems, one can easily see in both a similar aesthetic of triumphant rationalism in which atomic energy was the proof of the relative superiority of their own ideology.[14]

Finally, the atomic complexes of the world were united in their common disregard for the environment and the civil and political rights of national subjects.[15] Inevitably, these megatechnologies, whether in the West, East or South, would, in the course of their normal functioning, lay waste large areas of land, pollute water tables and agricultural lands, destroy the livelihoods of hundreds and thousands of nearby residents, and poison the air and water with radioactive wastes – and this is to speak only of the reactor systems. Individuals within these complexes, completely insulated by the security apparatus of the state, have performed medical experiments on unwilling and unknowing subjects, have sometimes deliberately, sometimes with indifference and sometimes in ignorance exposed soldiers and citizens to huge amounts of radiation, have, through commission and omission, caused the deaths of individuals, have waged public relations campaigns and carried out a wide range of subversive practices against their enemies, and have in general caused and endorsed the loss of rights for vast numbers of their people. All of this is in the normal course of their functioning.

As we shall see, India was little different in this regard. Self-reliance and autonomy were watchwords of the nuclear programme, but only in name: the atomic energy complex drew heavily on Western help, especially from Britain and Canada, but also the United States and France, for expertise and designs to build its reactors. On the question of ownership, the Indians took their cue from their former colonial masters and kept the atomic complex in state hands with minimal private participation. Symbolically, the hyper-traditional met the hyper-modern in the shape of the atomic reactors, the most modern of objects so similar to the *lingams* found in countless Shiva temples across the country. Finally, the land, water and air around the atomic complexes would be despoiled, the rights of citizens flouted and the lives and health of thousands of individuals marked permanently in the normal course of its functioning. The one apparent difference of the Indian programme was the constant reiteration of its entirely peaceful nature, but this too would not last. In the end the political class came back to a simple but powerful dichotomy to guide their rhetoric and actions: atomic energy in the form of a power reactor would be a crucial source of electrical energy for Indian development, while nuclear power in the form of its explosive potential could safeguard the security of the state in an anarchic world.

NATIONAL DEVELOPMENT AND
NATIONAL SECURITY

Atomic energy can be and has been used with equal ease to invoke economic progress or military supremacy. The question is whether this shift from development to security is primarily driven by the possibilities inherent in atomic energy, or is only the clearest manifestation of a more basic modern ambivalence that cannot distinguish between these twin goals of state action.

One of the more unexpected occurrences of the late 1980s and early 1990s was the renunciation by three countries, in two separate regions of the world, of their respective desires to produce nuclear weapons: Brazil and Argentina in South America, and the Republic of South Africa. They had quite dissimilar domestic reasons for deciding that nuclear weapons were no longer necessary for their security, and the acts of renunciation took many observers of nuclear issues by surprise.[16] The surprise emerges because ingrained in the narrative of nuclearisation is the irreversibility of the act. Not only are all states alleged to want to have nuclear weapons, but once they have them they never give them up. Nothing, in other words, can compensate for nuclear weapons. This view is empirically incorrect, not only because of these recent revocations, but because most scholars and policy makers have also forgotten the number of countries that gave up their nuclear programmes in the 1950s, for example Sweden and Australia, and that some countries with active nuclear programmes consciously and deliberately rejected the option of weapons acquisition in the first place, most notably Japan and Germany.

The last 50 years show that the move from a civilian nuclear energy programme to a nuclear weapons programme, while easy to do from a technical standpoint, firstly, is less than common, secondly, can be reversed, and thirdly, demands an act of political will to come about. Equally common is the move from a nuclear weapons programme to a programme of civilian nuclear energy, as in the case of all the acknowledged nuclear powers. The option that it is the possibilities inherent in atomic energy that drive the shift proves to be empirically ambiguous on the basis of this brief examination of the evidence.

This leaves us with the posited similarity between national development and national security. The idea of 'national development' in the form we are most familiar with is a post-Second World War construction.[17] Development was the name given to a wide range of practices that took as their object the 'third' world of newly independent nations. These practices sought especially to improve economic growth as measured through GDP statistics;[18] saw economic change as something that could be induced from without, relying on strengthening the state and using Keynesian fiscal policy;[19] and were based on a selective and partial reading of Western experiences in the 18th and 19th centuries to reify a normalised trajectory of historical change.[20] This was a modernist project, deeply influenced by the Enlightenment's values of secularism, faith in science, exploitation of nature, and, above all, optimism for the future that transmutes into hubris about what is possible through the application of these values.[21] These ideas and practices were institutionalised as the ideology of modernisation, its 'house name' being development studies.

The model of national development is foreshadowed in the writings of Friedrich List in 19th-century Germany and Alexander Hamilton in late 18th-century America. For these thinkers, and basic to the ideology of modernisation, are the ideas of the national state as the engine of economic takeoff and mercantilism as a strategy for strengthening the national state. The state was counterpoised to the private sector, members of which were either too venal or too weak to promote large-scale economic change. The initial goals of development were to improve national capabilities through industrialisation and overall self-sufficiency – the mercantilist strategy.[22] The seductiveness of this vision is shown in the hugely popular strategy of import-substituting industrialisation which flourished in the decade after the Second World War in countries as different as Indonesia, Brazil, Egypt, and India. The often unstated but easily understood outcome of a strong, balance-of-trade–obsessed state was an increase in national power, which in turn was measured as a function of the state's wealth and economic production capacity. In short, and in the full recognition that these are simplifications, net increases in national wealth and by extension, national power, were the dual goals of 'national development'. Under these circumstances, and following the logic of dominant ideas, national development and national power became coterminous. But when 'national power' as an outcome is invoked, what must be presupposed is a world already filled with states, against and in relation to whom national power is a meaningful category. National power thus *follows* from the idea of an international system made up of states, even though it is considered a foundational category in modern theories of international politics. When seen in this light, national power discursively mutates into the other prime rationale of state behaviour, 'national security'.

National security, which officially takes as its purpose the strengthening of the military might of the state, the protection of the territories claimed in its name, and the conservation of the way of life identified as the cultural norm,[23] is as much a time-dependent and place-specific ideology as national development. Again a post-War phenomenon, national security has a number of genealogies, but is probably most influenced by the histories of the United States, aptly symbolised by the translation of the Department of War into the Department of Defense in 1947. National security in this mode can be summarised as a totalising condition of civilian militarisation beyond simply border defence or even inter-state war,[24] the indistinguishability of war and peace in relation to the practices of state security institutions and the panoply of legal instruments that support their activities,[25] the militarisation of information and the enormous growth in intelligence agencies, related to which can be observed ever increasing degrees of state surveillance, deeply dependent on technology, which identify social threats to established order both within and without the formal territories of the state,[26] and the increasing scientisation of the practices of war to such an extent that the battlefield has become increasingly a virtual space.[27] In short, 'national security' expresses the paranoias of the modern state; it remains a major contradiction within democratic states; indeed the extent of the technological penetration of society by the national security apparatus is usually in direct proportion to the wealth of the state.

While national security can be said to be a truly global phenomenon at this point, the modular form was imported into the third world along with national development in the early post-War period, which gives this combination a distinct history from that moment on. This particularly modern mode of conceptualising the political became internalised in academic fields such as development studies and political development under the rubric of modernisation theory, was transmitted and reproduced through bilateral training and exchange programmes like the US International Military Education Training (IMET), and was imposed and strengthened through selective actions and policies of multilateral financial institutions and also through multilateral scientific development institutions like the UNDP, the International Rice Research Institute and the World Health Organisation; the twinned discourse of national security and development came to set the conceptual limits to national 'pathways to progress'.

Most important, both national development and national security converged around the state as the pre-eminent ideologies of modernisation. The two were usually institutionalised in complementary ways, with the military often represented as the most modern of institutions, capable of taking over the state in order to ensure development, and the national development apparatus using militarised forms of strategic intervention, for example in controlling epidemics or forcing reproductive management on national publics. The official lines between security and development are fuzzy in most settings; perhaps the apogee was reached in Brazil where, under the military regimes of the 1960s and 1970s, the official slogan *segurança e desenvolvimento* (security and development) tersely encapsulated their inseparability.

The link between security and development is state power, its form the iterative effort towards its enhancement. State power, like all modernist fictions, is directed toward ensuring the fixity and permanence of boundaries, establishing irrevocable difference between inside and outside, and its total sovereignty over what is within.[28] The process is endless: boundaries are always in flux, undermined by history and geography, constantly in a state of reinterpretation, and undone by globalisation and economic processes which demonstrate daily the limits of the state's actual control. There is an iterative dynamic here which for all its variation sets up one constant: the search for state power. Atomic energy is, in this sense, no different from many projects of the modern state. Its particular form, split between the twin objectives of state action, development and security, makes it perfectly suited to be the epitome of the modern state's will to power.

INTERNATIONAL RELATIONS THEORY AND PROLIFERATION STUDIES

One might expect mainstream international relations (IR) theory to be attentive to the issue of countries acquiring nuclear weapons, given their importance within the dominant 'neo-realist' approach.[29] Instead we find that theorising on this issue is too wrapped up in the particular interests of the status quo power(s) to be of much analytic use. The issue of countries developing nuclear weapons is usually termed nuclear 'proliferation' in IR discourse. I am not the first to point to the peculiar historical reasoning that defines 1964, the year that China conducted its first test, as the watershed date that makes a country acquiring nuclear capabilities after that moment an official proliferator, but not those quicker off the nuclear mark. France, Britain, the former Soviet Union, and the one that started it all off, the United States, all countries that conducted their first nuclear tests before that date, are not proliferators: they, along with China, are permanent members of the UN Security Council. This tacit distinction suggests there is something altogether different about post-1964 proliferators: somehow they are seen to embody a distinct threat to the prevailing order, a threat that cannot always be specified, but whose existence is accepted without question in academic prose. Even among the potential proliferators post-1964, some states are treated differently than others. Countries like Japan and Germany have both the means and, some would argue, the desire to develop nuclear weapons, but are not classified on the checklist of suspected proliferators. North Korea, Iran, Libya – countries with considerably different abilities and resources which have yet to take the final step toward nuclearisation – are habitual members of the suspected proliferator family.

Given these systematic asymmetries, the term 'proliferation' must give up any pretence to being an objective, analytic concept. 'Proliferation' must be located within a political lexicon of IR and its use understood as *political language*: in this case a discourse which denotes the concern of some (states, intellectuals, media) with others' possession of nuclear weapons because of those others' alleged unwillingness to play by the 'rules of the game'.[30] If this was all that was at stake in the problem of proliferation, continued semantic clarification would be all that was necessary. But the problem is deeper than that.

In the IR frame, the logic of proliferation is allegedly based on a latent or structural desire to acquire nuclear weapons, a desire basic to the states of the international system. The argument flows easily from the precepts of realism. Within this body of theory, the search for national security is negative-sum for the international system; it is argued that efforts to enhance one state's security leads inevitably to the decline in another state's security, the outcome harming both and making the international system worse off (more insecure) than before. Nuclear weapons are privileged in this scheme as the ultimate source of national security. States, defined as insecure at the outset and seeking to alleviate this condition, will logically move from one level of destructive capacity to the next, ending only when they have sufficient nuclear weapons to sustain a 'minimum deterrent' capability or when they have indirectly acquired weapons by making an alliance with a nuclear power who can guarantee absolute nuclear protection.[31] The search for security thus leads 'naturally' to the acquisition of weapons of greater destructive capacity. Each action in this direction leads to greater threat to all, creating a vicious spiral of international insecurity and legitimising the enormous arsenals of the superpowers.

Given the apparent common sense of this argument, rather than examine more closely the assumptions that underlie neo-realism, the bulk of Western analytic effort has been devoted to a US foreign policy issue: what Scott Sagan calls the 'supply' question of how to restrict nuclear weapons technology from reaching suspected proliferators.[32] As Sagan notes, any *theory* of proliferation would have to explain not only why states seek weapons, but also why some states give them up – something the literature is a long way from doing. For 40 years, the logic of the desire to arm made so much sense that little effort was made to question it or look more carefully at the factors which led states to develop nuclear weapons. As a result, we are faced with a condition where little historical detail is known about the nuclear pasts of most states other than the pre-1964 proliferators.

These mis-formulations all come to the fore in the case of India. The realist IR case for India is conveniently summarised as the combination of a cause – the decision by China, India's neighbour and rival, to become a nuclear power; an event – the 1974 nuclear explosion followed by the 1998 tests; and the consequences of that understanding – a willingness to absorb many costs, including a general deterioration of the security of India's neighbourhood, the breakdown of relations with so many countries, and the international distrust of Indian motives and statements that followed. Completely inconsistent with this explanatory schema, however, is the timing of the explosion, and India's reaction (and inaction) following the 1974 explosion and its multiple effects.[33] If India was responding to China, why did it wait until 1974 to demonstrate nuclear capability when it could have done so much earlier?[34] Contemporary accounts remind us of the surprise that political leaders felt at the hostile international reaction, especially Canada's, following news of the nuclear explosion. If India intended to use the nuclear test of 1974 as a signal that it was a nuclear power, why did it not follow through with further tests at once, leading to the deployment of nuclear weapons? Why did it not behave as we have grown to expect of nuclear states, such as China or France, both of which followed their first fission bomb tests with thermonuclear explosions a few years later, leading finally to the deployment of these weapons? Clearly the Indian case does not fit conventional understandings of the nature of nuclear proliferation.[35]

Other explanations do exist in the literature. Most do not question the argument that nuclear weapons build security, nor do they embed their explanatory factor within a larger theory of state and society. These explanations seek to add a new variable to explain the Indian case, namely, political leadership, or more precisely, the exigencies of politics combined with the personality of then Indian prime minister, Indira Gandhi. The standard explanation is as follows: Indira Gandhi, following a huge electoral victory in March 1971, and the prosecution of a successful war against Pakistan later that year, was facing considerable internal unrest and dissatisfaction by 1973–74. She decided, in a series of secret meetings with senior members of the Indian bureaucracy, to conduct a nuclear test to restore faith in her leadership and the nation more generally. While the historical evidence might bear out the accuracy of this rendition up to a point, it leaves more analytic questions open than it resolves. While this explanation partly helps to address the question as to why 1974, it does not offer any counterfactual explanation of why the same event could not have happened earlier. Indira Gandhi was even more desperate for political support in the late 1960s, when she was battling the 'syndicate' of regional political leaders, and when the economy was in shreds, but from what we know this option was never on the cards. In the early 1970s, after her massive election triumph and a victorious war against Pakistan, it could be argued that she had achieved the pinnacle of her personal power: retrospectively we know she would never be as unchallenged again. In other words, it is equally possible to argue that the 1974 explosion was an expression of power rather than weakness, especially when we recall that the decision to conduct the explosion was taken nearly two years before the actual event.[36]

If we leave these particular details aside, since most of the arguments that use the 'domestic factors' explanation must resort to speculation in the absence of conclusive evidence, a far more interesting question emerges. Regardless of timing, why would a nuclear explosion be the means by which a political leader seeks to bolster sagging support? Nobody seems to question the *means* by which this leader, and a quarter of a century later the BJP government, would seek to assert the nation's strength: what was so compelling about a nuclear explosion that would give a government the popular legitimacy it sought? This question moves the analysis away from quotidian political struggles and abstract strategic gaming into other realms – political culture, the power of ideas, and, most important, the knotty relationship between events, histories and conjunctures.

KEYS TO THE ARGUMENT: CONJUNCTURE, POSTCOLONIAL, FETISH

This section outlines three conceptual and methodological elements that recur in this book. I have suggested that India's response to nuclear power represents a puzzle both from the point of view of its own history and in relation to traditional international relations theories. Focusing on the semiotics of one event, the 'peaceful nuclear explosion' of 1974, I argue for a turn in attention to political culture, the meanings and values attributed to political actions and the role of politics as a mass cultural form. To establish this thesis and follow through its implications, I make the following arguments, encapsulated as the *why* and the *how* of atomic energy. In order to explain *why* atomic energy became such a powerful force and figure in the constitution of the newly independent state, for the remainder of this chapter I evaluate current theories of the Indian state and offer another interpretation of the balance of political forces at the moment of independence. This allows us to see how atomic energy filled a discursive vacuum in the production of the postcolonial state and met the strategic needs of India's first prime minister, Jawaharlal Nehru. The *how* of atomic energy's location within the state apparatus is addressed in the following chapter, which deals largely with the person and politics of a nuclear physicist, Homi Jehangir Bhabha, and how he became the founder of the Indian atomic energy programme. Separating the why and the how through a careful recounting of the multiple histories that go into the meeting of atomic energy and the Indian state makes it quite clear that this outcome was in no way predetermined. Over and over again, we see the importance of historical *conjuncture*, not only in relation to Indian political forces, but also in the interplay of the domestic and the international realms. After the fact, the relationship between atomic energy and India may seem preordained, but in its early years success in this enterprise was by no means apparent, especially to the main figures involved in its establishment. Conjuncture likewise plays an important part in the later history of the atomic energy agency. As we shall see in the third and fourth chapters, which trace the institutional development of the atomic energy agency through the decades of the 1950s and 1960s and up to 1974, we find that there were always a number of potential outcomes and great uncertainty about which would emerge dominant at moments retrospectively seen to be critical. By the end of this recounting, we are in a position to understand how the 1974 nuclear explosion came about, the subject of the final chapter, which allows me also to suggest what we should make of that explosion.

The term 'postcolonial' is now common parlance in the overlapping worlds of cultural studies, history, and literary studies, and even sometimes in the social sciences. Its overuse and underspecification have led many to reject it as a viable concept of analysis, a feeling that is probably reaffirmed by the many recent attacks on postcolonial scholars and scholarship from a variety of political, cultural and epistemological standpoints.[37] I have no interest in recapitulating these often vituperative arguments, but since the term is a central element of my own argument I have to say something about what I mean. In this work, the postcolonial is not understood as a chronological condition; thus after Indian independence the state does not automatically become a postcolonial state by virtue of having been prior to that time a colonial state; rather, the postcolonial is seen as a specific moment of a global condition of modernity. If the project of modernity was at its best deeply secular, committed to the application of science for the betterment of the human condition, and committed to rationality in ordering human affairs, these were exactly the goals of the postcolonial project.[38] But the *condition* of the postcolonial emerges from its moment in world space and time, into a world whose dominant rules and values appear already defined.

The gap between the condition and the project of modernity, the split between being and becoming, is seen as the problem. Outside the West, 'modernity' was seen to have a different meaning. Through the development of colonialism and the working of a global world system of capitalism, a particular kind of modernity was made modular.[39] Notwithstanding its foreignness to and historical and geographical alienation from the third world, modernity-as-a-Western-thing was immensely powerful through its identity with the 'true' definition of the historical moment, and as such was both deeply desirable and impossible to escape. In other words, the postcolonial project became the means by which the condition of modernity would be engendered as an indigenous, naturalised state of being. In a typically modern way, while the postcolonial was the desire to become modern, it was, in the same instance, the recognition of modernity's absence. The shroud of postcolonial modernity defined the ambitions and fears of a dependent political class trying to come to terms with a global condition where the rules were set by someone else.[40]

Like any modern moment, the postcolonial modern was thus marked by a particular experience of time and practice of space. Postcolonial time is always a time-in-waiting, of being able to see the future in the present through knowledge of conditions prevalent in advanced states, yet of always being behind them in terms of one's own development. Postcolonial time is always incomplete, lagged, but drives state action in an endless search for 'modernisation' and 'development'. Hence the postcolonial anxiety about world rankings and never 'catching up' while endlessly projecting the moment when it might happen. Postcolonial space is obsessed with boundaries. Reflecting again the condition of being born into a world where the rules of political subjectivity, of statehood and sovereignty, are already defined, the mimetic practices of postcolonial space are always about trying to establish beyond doubt where national space begins and ends. Thanks to the histories of imperial cartography, neither blood nor land is singular enough to resolve the difference between nationality and citizenship; the postcolonial nation can never be contained within the territorial limits of the state. Thus the obsession with boundaries. The clearest way to resolve these intrinsic doubts is through state violence: as Max Weber puts it bluntly, 'the decisive means for politics is violence'.[41] As a result, the potential for state violence is never restricted to the realm of the outside, as the precepts of international relations would have it, but must spill into the borders of the country in the process of making them.[42] In what follows, we draw out the particular time/space dynamic that emerges from an examination of

the nuclear complex. The third chapter in particular is structured the-
matically by one experience of postcolonial time, which I term *urgency*,
while in the fourth and fifth chapters I address the particular practice of
postcolonial space made visible through the histories of the atomic energy establishment, namely *secrecy*.

Finally, 'fetish'. Science and technology, both as desired forms of
modern practice and as privileged instruments ensuring fundamental
change, are central to an understanding of the postcolonial condition.
But while science as practice and technology as instrument of change
may have been equally privileged, they cannot be co-ordinated and
directed with the same degree of control. For the Indian citizen to
become truly modern, s/he would need to internalise the norms of
science, the so-called 'scientific temper' much beloved by Nehru, but
this was obviously less amenable to state dictates. What the state could
do was install massive, modern, awesome technological artefacts – dams,
steel mills, new cities, nuclear reactors – objects embodying a different
rationality, which would transform traditional landscapes through their
sheer power; the hope was that the technological artefact would stand in
relation to the people as a modern *fetish*.

The idea of the fetish runs through Marxism, psychoanalysis, and
anthropology. What I am most concerned with is the idea that the fetish
embodies both a unique historical object and a certain fixity of place in
order to appear to stand independent of social relations. The process of
fetishisation, the modernisation of everyday life in this case, is the
'transition of the general form into a universal form, its modal shift from
existence and possibility to necessity.... Arising as the real representation
of material social relations, [fetishes] exist as material objects; they are
fetishes insofar as they have become necessary functional parts that are
privileged command–control points of a working system of social reproduction.... These causally effective representational forms are "universals"
that incorporate the particular social processes that produce them and
which they thereby alter.' [43] The state's objective was eventually to transform the landscape of traditional India through the power of modern
technology, to erase all signs of what had been there before, so much so
that the modern technological artefact would become the naturalised
expression of what remained: the postcolonial. Equally natural to this
new landscape would be the political subject who took these 'functional
parts' as intrinsic to his own modern constitution, existing prior to and
independent of everyday social relations.

The technological devices that the postcolonial state would create,
nearly always in alliance with different foreign agencies – the steel mills
of Durgapur (British), the Indian Institutes of Technology (British, West

German, US, Soviet), or the city of Chandigarh (French) – would each, in their own way, become fetishised as pure expressions of the post-colonial state, offering both a relief from prior modes of being through a direct application of science and technology, and invoking, in their rationality, size and scale, the new state which was their object. A socialist-realist style of monumentality was crucial: the repeated representation of these objects through official state instruments (including photographs, radio, and documentary cinema) stressed the height of the object, the number of tons of steel used or produced, the enormity of displacement of people and nature, always while asserting the indigenous character of the fetish. I argue that building nuclear reactors, like dams and steel mills, belongs to a domain of activity marking out a postcolonial national space, even as these objects had narrow economic functions. Within these new spaces, a logic different from the representations of India as 'tradi-tional' was meant to operate. These new spaces would be rationalised, scientifically ordered spaces filled with individuals who, having shed pre-rational religious or sectarian loyalties would identify primarily as modern men – in a word, 'Indian'. But can one fetishise an explosion?

AUTONOMY, CRISIS AND LEGITIMACY IN THE POSTCOLONIAL STATE

The first step toward a new understanding of Indian nuclear history is to outline the context within which it all happened. We especially need to understand the nature of the newly independent state and the political demands made upon it, and to appreciate the unique position of atomic energy as a strategic condition that helped define this state and which would help resolve its particular contradictions. First some definitions: following Jessop and Poulantzas, I define state power as a 'complex social relation' comprising a hybrid 'institutional complex of forms of repre-sentation and intervention'.[45] Economic, political, social, and ideological forces shape the structural ensemble of the state and are in turn shaped by it: the traditional state–society dichotomy does not have any analytic purchase here. Even as we can distinguish specific social forces (rural peasantry, regional capitalists) from institutional components of the state (national bureaucracy, military), we do not attribute interests to these forces based on their putative social character. These social formations are mutually constitutive of the other at all times, thus, 'state' and 'social' power do not exist in a vacuum but are a complex *outcome* of the inter-play of multiple social forces which must be contextually defined and historically derived. I recognise that a purely relational definition could be taken to mean the collapse of the state into society, making it appear as just another social actor, but that is not my intent. I seek to retain an analytic appreciation of the institutional components of the state apparatus in order to understand the strength or weakness of the state as a material force in society, while at the same time arguing for an understanding of the State as an ensemble of relations that (seeks to) stand independent of social forces and that (seeks to) give identity, ascribe values, and adjudicate conflict to the entire social ensemble as a coherent entity. In other words, the State is also, always, an *ideological* relation.

By ideology we mean neither a distorted refraction (false consciousness) nor a political legerdemain of the strong over the weak. According to Lefort, 'we can define [ideology] only by recognising the attempt, peculiar to modern society, to conceal the enigma of its political form, to cancel out the effects of social and temporal division which are produced therein, to re-establish the "real" [as if it were natural and not mediated through social relations and language]'.[45] He argues that ideology emerges in capitalist society from the process of the broadening of capitalist relations to include an entire society even as it disaggregates that society into two social classes. The attempt of the dominant class, the bourgeoisie, to represent as universal their particular class point of view – what Gramsci has called the establishment of hegemony – is the origin of ideology. But the process of ideological formation is always haunted by the contradiction that emerges from its operation: if it were to represent the entirety of the social formation it would have to expose its own contingent nature, thereby denying the possibility of the 'true' representation of the universal. As a result, ideology ends up being fragmentary and partial, always cycling back on itself to cover up the traces of its own presence.

The preceding definitions are situated at a level of generality that while useful as a starting point, need to be specified against concrete historical conditions. Two themes predominate in the literature on the Indian state: the first is its 'relative' autonomy, the second is the related 'crisis' of the state. The autonomy debate, which helps to establish the nature of state power, was set off in its present form by Pranab Bardhan.[46] Bardhan argues that the post-independence Indian state was characterised by a high degree of 'functional' autonomy, with its own corporate interests 'fuelled not only by motives of self-aggrandisement but quite often also by … its conception of the national interest'. Functional autonomy is possible, he argues, on the basis of state capabilities, that is, the Indian state's ownership and control of a vast array of instruments of material production, namely, the public sector. Achin Vanaik, in response, agrees broadly with the characterisation of the Indian state as autonomous (though he is careful to point out that it is 'relatively' rather than 'functionally' autonomous). He notes, in the first decades after 1947, the personnel of the state elite enjoyed an independent authority and prestige that made them both the main actors in and principal directors of the unfolding socio-economic drama of Indian development, though class constraints existed. Over time, however, with the strengthening of the main proprietary classes (the industrial and agrarian bourgeoisie) the autonomous behaviour of the state became confined more and more to its 'regulatory' rather than to its 'developmental' functions.[47]

This passage describes a 'night-watchman' state, which controls power as long as the bourgeoisie is weak, and steps aside when they have an independent power base. The state backs away, it is assumed, because it no longer serves capital's interests, which can now be served by private (foreign or domestic) capital. The move to 'regulatory' from 'developmental' functions suggests a relative decline in the state's control over the means of production: its capabilities. Whether or not this is accurate is an empirical question (and many would dispute it), but regardless of the answer, we see that state autonomy is seen to vary on the basis of the condition of state capabilities. But an argument based on capabilities cannot lead to any conclusions about in whose interests the state might act, nor does it tell us anything about political relations within the state. State capabilities or institutional resources cannot, of themselves, amount to the state's relative autonomy – after all, the ability of the state to appear relatively autonomous is an ideological relation.

Far more pertinent to the autonomy issue is the state elite's 'independent authority and prestige'. Vanaik suggests that this condition existed prior to independence, a condition allowing state managers their privileged position as 'actors' and 'directors' of the 'drama' of development. Likewise, Bardhan argues for the existence of a 'national interest' that structured the acquisition and character of state power. In these articulations we step away from the state's autonomy as capabilities, and render autonomy within a discourse of political legitimacy that emerges from the dominant *representation* of the state, a state with authority, prestige, and interests. But if we are not to assume that the state has always had these characteristics, where do these relations come from? Rather than take the approach that attributes to the state inherent essential characteristics or alleged respect as an outcome of state capabilities, I suggest that these characteristics need to be explained. If relative autonomy is an ideological relation, we cannot identify the existence of autonomy as the reflection of pre-existing categories, it must emerge from the interplay of specified historical and social relations. The autonomy of the state is built upon the successful imposition of social and political values on the society (itself an ideological formation).

The strength of the autonomy argument in the Indian case, especially the idea that it existed fully blown at the moment of independence, is closely related to arguments about state crisis. Many scholars argue that a 'crisis of legitimation' is considered to have emerged in the mid-1970s as the result of, variously, the ongoing radicalisation of political rhetoric and the institutional decline of the Congress party as a means of expressing political demands; worsening economic performance and malaise as a result of two decades of slow growth and maldistribution; the rise of organised political dissent through new social movements led by Jayaprakash Narayan, combined with increased frequency of political cycles.[48]

The most common explanations for the crisis of the 1970s find their expression in the move from regime failure to state weakness. The decline of governmental authority comes as a result of factors such as the economy, political movements, and social factors, but especially as a result of the decay of leadership. This focus on leadership is always a contrast between father and daughter, between Jawaharlal Nehru, India's first prime minister, and Indira Gandhi, its third. The degree of consensus about Indira Gandhi's disastrous effect on political institutions is mirrored by the agreement that her father was a very different kind of leader. Not only this, but the objective conditions of his rule allowed him, it is argued, to be different. These objective conditions are nothing other than the same factors that allow the easy assertions of state autonomy at the moment of and in the years following independence, namely, strong state capabilities. In other words, there is a symptomatic relationship between the assertion of state autonomy and state crisis, both depending on the alleged degree of independent power retained by the state at the moment of independence and, as we shall see, a selective blindness to the conditions and centrifugal forces in play at the moment of independence.

I would like to turn this argument on its head and suggest that, rather than being autonomous, the Indian state was in a crisis of authority *at the moment of its creation as an independent state*. Autonomy from social forces was the condition the state wanted to achieve: not in the sense of a balance of material power, but as an ideological condition, the investment of the state with legitimate political authority. The existence of a crisis can be argued on a number of fronts. For our purposes, the crucial issue is the legitimacy of political authority.

We often take it for granted that since the Congress coalition had fought a successful battle against the colonial state for independence, this relative success translated into the legitimacy of the postcolonial state. Why? We know only too well that the question of 'what' was going to become free was highly contested. The partition of India and Pakistan, at the moment of independence, at the very least points to an élite division along lines of politico-religious identity. But the tragedy of massive communal riots resulting from contestations underlying the separation of India and Pakistan is only part of the story. For instance, the work of Ritu Menon and Kamla Bhasin on the return of 'abducted women' points to the deep anxieties entailed in the efforts to re-establish and assert patriarchal authority in the name of the new Indian state.[49] The new leadership's conservative response to the Royal Indian Navy mutiny of 1946, seemingly an act anti-colonial nationalists should have greeted with joy, makes it clear that Nehru was not going to risk the potential future loss of civilian authority over the armed forces in favour of additional support for the Congress movement.[50]

Further, the new state managers had more than the former British India to contend with. Over 500 small and large principalities had to be integrated into and administered by the new state, and in three of those cases, Hyderabad, Kashmir, and Junagadh, accession to India was possible only as a result of armed force. The case of Kashmir, half a century later, is still far from resolved. The problem of asserting sovereignty over and integrating former European colonies like Goa and Pondicherry had their own dynamic and took nearly two decades to be resolved to the satisfaction of the Indian state, if not of those living there. Various communities in British India were under the impression that they would be allowed to become free when the British left: parts of the north-east of India still bear the scars of being brought by force, again and again, into the Indian state. In the Telengana district of Hyderabad state, a rural insurrection broke out which was suppressed only by the induction of large numbers of Indian troops. It is difficult, quite apart from the India–Pakistan split, to make a credible case for the new government being acknowledged as a legitimate political entity at the moment of its independence, regardless of the history of the Indian National Congress as an anti-colonial force.

A different order of crisis can be discerned within the new Indian state. The former colonial bureaucracy, the Indian Civil Service (ICS), had to be made a part of the new Indian state. While getting rid of them completely might have been a desirable option for those who argued for a clean break with the past, political exigency demanded that they be retained to help manage the ongoing series of conflicts and breakdowns. Conflicts over the status and entitlements of the ICS reflected deeper strains within the Congress leadership.[51] Whether indicated by battles within the Constituent Assembly or over the ideological direction of the Congress, Nehru's control over the party was far from complete. Even after the death of his main rival, Sardar Vallabhai Patel, disputes over the control of the Congress party were resolved only by a greater centralisation of power in Nehru's hands.[52]

These multiple conditions constraining the acceptance of the legitimacy of the new state result from the continued structural existence of the colonial state, albeit in new garb. Partha Chatterjee recognises the continuation of colonial relations in the social order even after independence when he notes, 'But if the ordinary functions of civil and criminal administration were to continue within forms of rationality that the new state had not given to itself, how was it to claim its legitimacy as an authority that was specifically different from the old regime?' He identifies the attempt to transform colonial social relations through the bureaucratic production of the discourse of 'development'. In his words, 'it was in the universal function of "development" of national society as a whole that the postcolonial state would find its distinctive content'.[53] The project of a new state ideology can be seen in materialist terms as an attempt to resolve the contradiction emerging upon independence: the institutions of political liberalism being forced to work through an unchanged colonial state apparatus marked by coercion and dominance. What emerges is a postcolonial state, with an independent ideological justification, existing at the same time as a colonial state apparatus. The former cannot supplant the latter all at once; given the political compromises of the dominant social classes, the coercive apparatus of the colonial state continues to play an important role in the maintenance of the status quo. The new institutional formation seeks to resolve latent and manifest social cleavages by inaugurating a new form of modernity and creating a new political subject.

POSTCOLONIAL VISIONS AND SCIENCE

The postcolonial vision of India, summarised by Chatterjee as the 'discourse of development', was crucially dependent for its articulation on the idea of science. The idea of science, epitome of and metaphor for the modern, was a recurrent theme in anti-colonial nationalist thought as well, especially as it grappled with the seemingly opposed categories of 'tradition' (the authentic present) and 'modernity' (the desired future) while seeking to remain 'Indian'. Gyan Prakash notes how nationalist élites had sought to construct an image of modern India through an appropriation of ancient 'Hindu' science. Hindu revivalist groups, such as the Arya Samaj, re-read Hindu scriptures, for example the Vedas, with an eye to extracting information that could be represented as continuous with modern scientific knowledge. Thus Swami Dayanand could argue that, 'God made the world out of Nature or atoms, which are the material cause of the universe. The Vedas and the profane sciences prove the matter or the aggregate of atoms to be the primary or the eternal substance of the phenomenal world.'[54] Others, like the chemist P.C. Ray in his two-volume *History of Hindu Chemistry* (1902–9) sought to recover the memory of scientific practices that might be described as consistent with modern scientific knowledge. In general, their effort was to show that Hinduism was based on scientific principles, a claim that permitted modern India to be situated in sympathetic relation to its own past, and also to establish Vedic Hinduism as the pre-eminent definition of Indian traditions.

Yet there were other voices discussing science in colonial India, in discussions that began to evoke an understanding of science in relation to other objects, especially the state.[55] While similar to the position outlined above, these debates drew on world, rather than Indian, history in order to argue for an instrumentalist vision of science. Modernity no longer appeared in mere juxtaposition to science, but as the outcome of the application of science to all aspects of social life. This view is especially vivid in a popular science journal published in English in Calcutta, *Science and Culture*. Started by Meghnad Saha, Palit Professor of Physics at Calcutta University, in 1935, the first lines of the editorial in the first issue read as follows:

> The call that brings 'Science and Culture' into existence is truly the call of the times. For it is obvious to every thinking man that India is now passing through a critical stage in her history, when over the cultural foundations of her ancient and variegated civilisation, structures of a modern design are being built. It is necessary that at such a juncture the possible effects of the increasing application of discoveries in science to our national and social life should receive very careful attention; for if the present is the child of the past, it may with equal emphasis be said that the future will be the child of the present. The present generation by its policy and action will shape the course of the future.[56]

While 'India' is by no means absent from these lines, 'she' appears in a very different way. India is positioned in relation to her past akin to the nationalist discourse above, but also in relation to her future. Science appears as a crucial intermediary and instrument, making the present and thereby linking present and future. The 'call' of the editorial is to a social vanguard in the making, namely, all 'thinking' men, who have the responsibility of building India's future through the 'increasing application' of science to India. The tropes of science's instrumentality and the vanguard of thinking men mark the shift to a new discourse of Indian modernity, which abjures a discussion of the anxieties of nationhood in favour of voicing desire for a more active agency of Indian statehood.

These alternate conceptions of science and nation, the first where modern science is appropriated to authenticate the Indian nation, the other where science makes the Indian nation modern, come together in the Constituent Assembly debates on atomic energy in 1948. In these debates, assembly delegates feel obliged to demonstrate their under-standing of science wherever possible, and to articulate its preferred relation to atomic energy and national development. One of these del-egates, H.V. Kamath, summarises the nationalist view when he states,

> our seers and sages, four thousand years ago, perhaps in 2000 BC, said some-thing about [atomic] energy which scientists today are propounding in 2000 AD. [Freely translating a Sanskrit verse, he goes on] In the infinitesimal as well as the infinite, in the atom as well as the universe resides the one *shakti* [...] the shakti of the atom and the shakti of the *atman* are same shakti [... and, in sum] The analytic methods of science will bring us to the same view as was arrived at by the synthetic processes of our sages and seers.[57]

This reading of the relation of science to nation was completely at odds with the interpretation of Jawaharlal Nehru, who sponsored the Atomic Energy Bill. Nehru's argument for the acceptance of this new legislation relies on a different trajectory for Indian history. For Nehru, the scientific object, the atom, is the sign of a new era of human civilisation.

> But we are on the verge I think of a tremendous development in some direction of the human race. Consider the past few hundred years of human history: the world developed a new source of power, that is steam – the steam engine and the like – and the industrial age came in. India with all her many virtues did not develop that source of power. *It became a backward country because of that.* The steam age and the industrial age were followed by the electrical age which gradually crept in, and most of us were hardly aware of the change. But enor-mous new power came in. Now we are facing the atomic age; we are on the verge of it. And this is something infinitely more powerful than either steam or electricity.[58]

The contrast between these two interpretations is even more marked than their historical antecedents above. From the writing of an authentic Indian/Hindu nation through science in Kamath, the discursive register has shifted, in Nehru, to a displacement of the subject 'India' to an abstract humanist understanding of world history. This is an understanding of human evolution, first as dependent on the exploitation of matter, and second, which allows progress to be demonstrated tangibly and 'objective-ly' through an examination of a society's primary source of energy. India is mapped on a world scale and the progressive transformation of this world depends on access to newer and more developed sources of energy.

Another way of distinguishing these views is through the registers of time and space. For Kamath, it is necessary to show that time collapses in the writing of the Indian nation. The past and the present meet each other in his argument through the identical scientific knowledge held by both Indian sages and Western scientists, authenticating the nation by domesticating science. Nehru rejects 'nation-time'. He is arguing for the existence of a 'world-time', a time that is marked by the material form of energy that societies use. In Nehru's argument, India has moved from being the only measure of the passage of time to being located in a world-historical space, where it is one among many, and where the historical epoch is marked by a non-human entity – the atom.

The power of Nehru's interpretation lies also in the explanation he provides for why India became colonised in the first place: 'it became backward because of that'. Rather than the perfidy of competing Indian élites or the skill and intrigue of Western conquerors, India became colonised because of its lack of technological sophistication. Technology is presented as devoid of adjective: it did not belong to someone, as in 'Western' technology, hence it was available for India's development. This argument makes colonisation an objective condition that could have been prevented, and can yet be overcome through an appropriation of the modern object – science. As a rhetorical device, given that this is a parliamentary debate, this is a powerful move. One cannot argue with the forces of history, especially if they are legitimised in scientific terms. In talking of atomic energy in relation to world history, Nehru implies there can be no other option but for India to adopt this technology if universal development is to come about. Dissenters are thus made to appear anti-modern and even unpatriotic. The logic of the argument implies that those who disagree are opposed to national progress. The position associated with Mohandas Karamchand Gandhi, which questioned the efficacy of modern techniques in a context like India, is thus also put in its place – far from the imperatives of *raison d'état*.

Nehru's evocation of international historic time and a world space filled by other states is nothing short of the shift from 'narrating' a nation through science to 'producing' a state through technology. Central to this production is the atom and the scientific knowledge necessary to transform the independent nation to a modern state. Bringing together the ideas of instrumental science and the historical era of the atomic age are Nehru's distinctive contribution to this discourse: a discourse founded less on the endless iteration of writing the nation than of transforming a territory, a state-in-the-making. There is a price to pay, however, for this interpretation. Nationalist thought had deployed its weight around the creation of 'India', a construct that had mobilised science to frame selectively its vision of modernity. Now an argument was being made that would take away what was 'Indian' about science by locating it within world time. Could 'India' sustain this loss? Could a new state in the process of constituting its own legitimacy independent of a colonial past afford to marginalise representations of the nation?

NOTES

1. Conant, a chemist, long-serving president of Harvard University, and member of the wartime National Defense and Research Committee was, along with Vannevar Bush, a key figure in the nexus of science and statecraft in the United States. On the other end of the phone was Arthur B. Compton, brother of Karl Compton, another key player in the meeting of science and the state.

2. Quoted in Laura Fermi, *Atoms in the Family* (Albuquerque: University of New Mexico Press, 1954), p. 198.

3. From Robert Oppenheimer's self-described invocation of the Bhagvad Gita in Alamogordo, 'I am become Death, the Shatterer of Worlds', to Churchill's 'This revelation of the secrets of nature, long mercifully withheld from man, should arouse the most solemn reflection in the mind and conscience of every human being capable of comprehension', religious imagery surrounding the first use of atomic explosives has been rampant. Notwithstanding the pride of achievement of much of the official and mass media rhetoric, fear of its meaning is never far away. Quotes taken from Paul Chilton, 'Nukespeak: nuclear language, culture and propaganda', in *Nukespeak: The media and the bomb* (London: Comedia, 1982). Gandhi was showed no ambivalence at all in decrying the bomb as an abomination. 'I regard the employment of the atom bomb for the wholescale destruction of men, women, and children as the most diabolical use of science' *Harijan* (New Delhi), 29 September 1946, quoted in Abha Dixit, 'Status Quo: Maintaining nuclear ambiguity', in David Cortright and Amitabh Mattoo, eds., *India and the Bomb: Public Opinion and Nuclear Options* (Notre Dame: University of Notre Dame Press, 1996).

4. John Hersey reminds us in his classic essay *Hiroshima* that none of the survivors of the atomic blast remembers hearing anything at the moment of impact, only of seeing a 'sheet of light' covering the sky (original 1946, New York: Vintage, 1985).

5. In what follows I draw particularly on Margaret Gowing, *Independence and Deterrence, vol. 1, Policy Making* (New York: St. Martin's Press [1964], 1974); Robert Jungk, *Brighter than a Thousand Suns* (New York: Harcourt Brace, Jovanovitch, 1956); Robert Rhodes, *The Making of the Atomic Bomb* (New York: Simon and Schuster, 1986); David Holloway, *Stalin and the Bomb* (New Haven: Yale University Press, 1994); John P. Lewis and Xue Litai, *China Builds the Bomb* (Stanford: Stanford University Press, 1988); Bertrand Goldschmidt, *The Atomic Complex* (La Grange Park, Ill: American Nuclear Society, 1982).

6. For the role of scientists in this move see Daniel Kevles, *The Physicists* (Cambridge, Mass.: Harvard University Press, [1971], 1995), especially chapter 21; and David Dickson, *The New Politics of Science* (Chicago: University of Chicago Press, 1984), especially chapter 3.

7. Holloway, *Stalin and the Bomb*, chapters 4–6.

8. Lewis and Xue, *China Builds the Bomb*, chapter 3.

9. Kevles, *The Physicists*, chapter 22.

10. Gabrielle Hecht, 'Political Designs: Nuclear reactors and national policy in postwar France', *Technology and Culture* 35, 4, (1994).

11. Barton J. Bernstein, 'The Quest for Security: American foreign policy and international control of atomic energy, 1942–1946', *Journal of American History*, 60 (March 1974).

12. Gowing's argument in *Independence and Deterrence* is that American refusal to cooperate after the war was a major factor in the creation of the British programme.

13. Gabrielle Hecht, 'Peasants, Engineers, and Atomic Cathedrals: Narrating modernization in postwar provincial France', (forthcoming in *French Historical Studies*), typescript, p. 5.

14. See Spencer R. Weart, *Nuclear Fear: A History of Images* (Cambridge, Mass.: Harvard University Press, 1988).

15. Dickson, *The New Politics of Science*, especially chapters 4–7; Langdon Winner, *The Whale and the Reactor* (Chicago: University of Chicago Press, 1984); Dhirendra Sharma, *India's Nuclear Estate* (Delhi: Lancers, 1983); Shiv Visvanathan, 'Atomic Physics: The career of an imagination', and 'On the Annals of the Laboratory State', both in Ashis Nandy, ed., *Science, Hegemony, and Violence* (Delhi: Oxford University Press, 1988).

16. There is one important similarity: renunciation in all these cases can be seen to be linked to the removal of less than legitimate regimes, whether military in Latin America or apartheid in South Africa. For more details on the Latin American cases see my 'Stepping Back from the Threshold? Latin America and South Asia', Occasional Paper Series No. 15, Henry Stimson Center, Washington, DC, 1993. I do not discuss the removal of nuclear arms from the non-Russian republics of the former Soviet Union, as they did not emerge as a result of independent nuclear programmes.

17. By identifying 'national development' as a particular moment in the history of economic change and North–South relations, I do not suggest that it still exists in its pure form. The new ideological common sense of 'economic liberalisation' is similarly time- and place-specific.

18. See for instance, Hans Singer, 'The Mechanics of Economic Development', *Indian Economic Review*, August 1952 and the critique in Hollis Chenery et al., *Redistribution with Growth* (Oxford: Oxford University Press, 1974).

19. See Jacob Viner, 'The Economics of Development', in A.N. Agarwala and S.P. Singh, eds., *The Economics of Underdevelopment* (New York: Oxford University Press, 1963), especially p. 31; and Albert O. Hirschman, *The Strategy of Economic Development* (New Haven: Yale University Press, [1958], 1961), especially chapter 11.

20. Most egregious is probably W.W. Rostow, 'The Takeoff into Sustained Growth', *Economic Journal* Vol. 66 (March 1956), pp. 25–48. See also S. Kuznets, 'Underdeveloped countries and the pre-industrial phase in the advanced countries', in Agarwala and Singh, pp. 135–153.

21. See Lucien Pye, *Aspects of Political Development* (Boston: Little, Brown, 1966).

22. This is termed 'economic nationalism' by Robert Gilpin in *The Political Economy of International Relations* (Princeton: Princeton University Press, 1987).

23. This follows from the well-known definition used by Walter Lippman. See *US Foreign Policy: Shield of the Republic* (Boston: Little, Brown, 1943).

24. Noam Chomsky, *Deterring Democracy* (London: Verso, 1992).

25. David Campbell, *Writing Security: United States Foreign Policy and the Politics of Identity* (Minneapolis: University of Minnesota Press, 1992); Bradley Klein, *Strategic Studies and World Order: The Global Politics of Deterrence* (Cambridge: Cambridge University Press, 1994).

26. Michael Shapiro, 'Warring Bodies and Bodies Politic: Tribal Warriors vs. State Soldiers', in Michael J. Shapiro and Hayward R. Alker, eds., *Challenging Boundaries* (Minneapolis: University of Minnesota Press, 1996).

27. John Broughton, 'The Bomb's Eye View: Smart weapons and military TV', in Stanley Aronowitz, Barbara Martinsons and Michael Menser, eds., *Technoscience and Cyberculture* (New York: Routledge, 1996), pp. 139–66; Paul Virilio, *Speed and Politics* (New York: Semiotext(e), 1986).

28. Cf. R.B.J. Walker, *Inside/Outside: International Relations as Political Theory* (Cambridge: Cambridge University Press, 1993).

29. The Ur-text of neo-realism remains Kenneth Waltz, *Theory of International Relations* (Reading, Mass.: Addison-Wesley, 1979).

30. For a discussion of political language see Murray Edelman, *Political Language: Words that Succeed, Policies that Fail* (Orlando, Fla.: Academic Press, 1977).

31. For a clear statement of the logic of proliferation built into IR theory see Scott Sagan, 'Why do states build nuclear weapons: Three models in search of a bomb', *International Security* (Winter 1996–97), pp. 57–9.

32. Sagan, 'Why do states build nuclear weapons', p. 56.

33. For a useful summary of the possible factors leading to the PNE and a chronology of decision making based mostly on newspaper reports, see Bhabani Sen Gupta, *Nuclear Weapons: Policy Options for India* (Center for Policy Research/ New Delhi: Sage, 1983), pp. 1–9. Ultimately there is no hard evidence for the various scenarios regarding causes or timing of the explosion.

34. See chapter 3 below.

35. There is a huge literature on this subject which is impossible to summarise here. The present state of the debate appears to be concerned with establishing that a condition akin to nuclear deterrence between the US and USSR does exist in South Asia. See Devin Hagerty, 'Nuclear Deterrence in South Asia: The 1990 Indo–Pakistani Crisis' *International Security*, 20, 3, (Winter 1995–96), pp. 79–114.

36. Raja Ramanna, *Years of Pilgrimage* (Delhi: Viking, 1994).

37. Most well-known are Arif Dirlik, 'The postcolonial aura: Third world criticism in the age of global capitalism', *Cultural Critique* (Winter 1992); and Aijaz Ahmed, *In Theory: Classes, Nations, Literatures* (London: Verso, 1992). There is a wonderful response to these and other critics by Stuart Hall, 'When was the "postcolonial": Thinking at the limit', in Iain Chambers and Lidia Curti, eds, *The Postcolonial Question: Common Skies, Divided Horizons* (London: Routledge, 1996).

38. David Harvey, *The Condition of Postmodernity* (Oxford: Blackwell, 1989), p. 68.

39. The idea of modularity is drawn from Benedict Anderson, *Imagined Communities: Reflections on the Origin and Spread of Nationalism*, expanded edition (London: Verso, 1991), especially pp. 113–40.

40. For a similar argument see Sankaran Krishna, *Postcolonial Insecurities: India,*

Sri Lanka and the Question of Eelam (Minneapolis: University of Minnesota Press, forthcoming).

41. In 'Politics as a Vocation', *From Max Weber: Essays in Sociology*, trans. and edited by H.H. Gerth and C. Wright Mills (New York: Oxford University Press, 1958), p. 121.

42. R.B. J. Walker, *Inside/Outside: International Relations as Political Theory* (Cambridge: Cambridge University Press, 1993).

43. William Pietz, 'Fetishism and Materialism', in Emily Apter and William Pietz, eds., *Fetishism as Cultural Discourse* (Ithaca: Cornell University Press, 1993), p. 147.

44. Bob Jessop, *State Theory: Putting Capitalist States in Their Place* (University Park: Penn State Press, 1990), pp. 117–18. Jessop works with explicit derivation from N. Poulantzas, *Political Power and Social Classes* (London: New Left Books, 1973) and *State, Power, Socialism* (London: New Left Books, 1978).

45. Claude Lefort, *The Political Forms of Modern Society: Bureaucracy, Democracy, Totalitarianism*, translated by John B. Thompson (Cambridge, Mass.: MIT Press, 1986), p. 189.

46. Pranab Bardhan, *The Political Economy of Development in India* (Delhi: Oxford University Press, 1984), p. 34.

47. Achin Vanaik, *The Painful Transition: Bourgeois Democracy in India* (London: Verso, 1990), p. 18. Emphasis added.

48. See the superb analysis by Sudipta Kaviraj, 'Indira Gandhi and Indian Politics', *Economic and Political Weekly*, XXI, 38–39, September 20–27, 1986, pp. 1697–1708.

49. Ritu Menon and Kamla Bhasin, 'Recovery, Rupture, Resistance: Indian state and abduction of women during Partition', *Economic and Political Weekly*, Annual Review of Women Studies, 24 April, 1993, pp. WS2–11.

50. The contrast between the Indian establishment response to the Indian National Army (INA) trials and the Royal Indian Navy mutiny is fascinating. To the best of my knowledge, a careful study has never been done, especially to draw out the implications for future civil–military relations.

51. David C. Potter, *India's Political Administrators: From ICS to IAS* (Delhi: Oxford University Press, 1996), especially pp. 150–66.

52. Francine Frankel, *India's Political Economy, 1947–1977* (Princeton: Princeton University Press, 1978), pp. 88–90.

53. Partha Chatterjee, *The Nation and Its Fragments: Colonial and Postcolonial Histories* (Princeton: Princeton University Press, 1993), p. 205.

54. Cited in Gyan Prakash, 'In the beginning was Hindu Science', paper presented at the conference 'Nationalizing the Past', Goa, 1993. A more recent version of the paper can be found in *Critical Inquiry* (Spring 1997).

55. There were others: I have chosen to focus only on a vision of science that was compatible with the postcolonial position, though differing from Nehru's in certain critical respects. For another view see Ashis Nandy, *Alternative Science* (Delhi: Allied, 1978).

56. *Science and Culture*, vol. 1, no. 1 (June 1935), p. 1.

57. Constituent Assembly of India (Legislative) Debates, second session, vol. 5 (1948), p. 3320. Hereafter CAI Debates.

58. CAI Debates, p. 3334. Emphasis added.

2

CREATING THE INDIAN
ATOMIC ENERGY COMMISSION

This chapter is about the formation of the Indian Atomic Energy Commission, the state institution that came to monopolise the production of atomic energy in India. The first two sections analyse the practice and institutions of science in the West and India in order to understand, first, under what conditions the physicist Homi Jehangir Bhabha returned to India from England in 1939, and, second, how science as experimental practice was inserted into the discourse of the postcolonial state. The third section shows that science and national security as state practices were closely related even before independence. The fourth section of the chapter, an analysis of the Indian constituent assembly debates on atomic energy (1948), further develops this theme. It demonstrates that atomic energy was understood, from the outset, to be intimately related to the state's national security interests: an understanding which generated both support and concern among the assembly delegates. The final section argues that, notwithstanding the close association of science and national security, atomic energy was inserted into the state apparatus through a series of conjunctural events. The conclusion modifies a model of scientific action proposed by Bruno Latour to understand the processes through which atomic energy became enshrined as the epitome of science for the Indian state.

'COLONIAL' SCIENCE

As the introduction shows, locating science in colonial India is all too often tied to the search for native practices arguably scientific in form that existed independent of dominant European institutions of science. If it could be established that these practices preceded European colonisation, so much the better. In the end, we are faced with a project of nationalist representation that seeks to create the categories of 'Western' and 'Indian' as opposing systems as an end in itself, with science as a residual factor that falls by the wayside. This is clearly unsatisfactory: certainly for its treatment of science, but also for its implicit spatial model. We find that, for different reasons, turning to science studies proper does not ease our problem.

The term 'colonial science' is deeply imbricated in the developmentalist schema set up by George Basalla.[1] Basalla's so-called 'diffusionist' model suggests that the growth of 'Western' science in different national settings was characterised by three phases, each marked by the degree of autonomy reached by local scientific institutions. The model argues that from its origins in the West, science spread over the world as a by-product of Western expansion and imperialism. The final stage of development is termed national science, when national institutions acquire sovereignty over local scientific practices, academies and journals. 'Colonial science' was the intermediate phase: a period when although some scientific activity took place in the colonies, it was still dependent on metropolitan institutions and scientists. This is not the place to engage with Basalla's typology for the sake of critique; others have managed that successfully.[2] Yet his view should not be dismissed out of hand. Basalla's typology has helped reinforce the idea that the science practised in most non-Western settings is derivative, inferior, and has yet to reach acceptable – read Western – levels of quality.

By not scrutinising the category of science except to note the existence of distinct locational practices, Basalla helps produce the idea that the same thing – science – can exist in different places. But in different places the thing called science, he says, looks different. Simply put, in the metropolis they 'do theory' and in the colony they gather data. This reinforces the existence of difference, a difference between colony and metropolis; yet we know that science, by its own self-representation, is a unified field of knowledge. Overcoming this contradiction is possible only when we realise first that Basalla's model helps to create the categories of 'colony' and 'metropolis' as places where different rules apply to the same object, science. We then realise that if the same thing, science, is practised in both places and yet science looks different in the colony and metropolis, it can only be due to the scientists themselves. Through his argument, Basalla falls back on and reinforces the impression of colonial scientists as derivative practitioners, not quite up to the standards of their metropolitan colleagues, valued more for the data they provide than the possibility of theoretical breakthroughs. In other words, once scientists enter the frame, 'colonial' becomes a euphemism for inferior.

The stability of this model hinges on the direction of flows: raw facts and data move from the colony to the metropolis, while accomplished scientists and developed scientific institutions flow from the metropolis to the colony. These boundaries must remain inviolate in order to retain the definitional purity of the model. Even as the model acknowledges change over time in a particular place – colonial science eventually becomes national science – it cannot sustain the idea of border-crossing during the existence of a hierarchy of scientific spaces. Yet, as we know, these borders were crossed often, especially from the colony to the metropolis. In particular, colonial scientists moved from the colony to the metropolis and did not always go back. Once they were there, what did they do? Can colonial science be performed in the metropolis? How do we know it is still the metropolis if there are colonial scientists present? This chapter begins by turning the category 'colonial science' on its head.

METROPOLITAN SCIENCE AND COLONIAL SCIENTISTS

A young Indian student from Bombay went to Cambridge University in the mid-1920s to study engineering. He had wanted to study physics, but his law-yer father, concerned about the long-term prospects of his son's career in a colonial setting, insisted the boy study a practical subject instead. Eventually the father won over the lawyer: he relented and agreed that if the young man managed to get a first-class degree in engineering he could continue his studies in physics. Homi Jehangir Bhabha passed his engineering tripos with a First in June 1930. He could now turn to his real love, physics. This was an exciting time for a physicist to be at Cambridge. The Cavendish and Mond Laboratories were leading centres of physics in the world. Under the leadership of Ernest Rutherford, a New Zealander who had moved to England, the Cavendish was churning out remarkable results in the new atomic physics. For example, in the early 1930s, Chadwick discovered the neutron, Walton and Cockcroft caused light elements to transmute by bombarding them with high-speed protons, Blackett and Occhialini demonstrated electron pairs and showers through their remarkable photographs, taken in a cloud chamber developed by H.H. Wilson, another Cavendish scientist. It was, as I have noted, an exciting time to be in Cambridge – particularly if you were an experimental scientist.

The passage above is deliberately written in the breathless style associated with hagiographies of Homi J. Bhabha.[3] Bhabha's life and career are so overdetermined in Indian narratives of modernity and development that it is difficult to see him as a colonial scientist; he appears in most domestic narratives already fully formed. In the many books, articles and pamphlets on Bhabha, the period of satisfying his father's wishes flows into his scholarly life at Cambridge and then, at the end of the 1930s, incipient patriotism mounting, we hear of his return to India, initially for a holiday but eventually a lifetime. The mention of names like Rutherford, Chadwick, and Blackett in discussing this period work to acknowledge that Bhabha was on close terms with the world's leading physicists; he was their equal by association. Depending on the source, some mention may also be made of the theoretical work he was engaged in at the time. It is usually taken for granted that here was a world-class scientist.

But read against this grain, traces of another story may be seen inscribed in the interstices of this modern fairy tale. Bhabha did in fact make an impact on his peers, but it was not always the one expected of a scientist. Even as Bhabha rarely, if ever, shows up in the primary scientific histories of the period – an extraordinarily well studied period – he appears in a number of autobiographies in cameo roles.[4] But it is not merely a story about Bhabha that is inscribed intertextually. Bhabha as a person is incidental to the figure brought to life by scattered textual fragments: the figure of the colonial scientist who brings to the fore the anxieties and ambivalences of metropolitan Western science.

For all the remarkable work being done in Cambridge, especially in the early 1930s, it was not a place well known for contributions to theoretical physics. Niels Bohr in Copenhagen, Werner Heisenberg in Germany, Max Planck in Switzerland – these were among the names that conjured up the same thrill for the theoretically inclined as Rutherford, Chadwick, and Blackett did for young experimentalists. In general, there were very few scientists who could do both theoretical and experimental physics at a world level. The brilliant Italian, Enrico Fermi, who would build the first atomic 'pile' in Chicago in 1942, was the only acknowledged exception.

In the early 1930s, the only internationally renowned theorists at Cambridge were Paul Dirac and Ralph Fowler. Dirac, who was then still a lecturer, disliked taking on students and tried to spend as much time as he could with his peers in Europe and the United States where he was held in high regard.[5] Fowler was a mathematician who had drifted into quantum mechanics and worked largely on questions in astrophysics. Bhabha, who wanted to do work in theoretical physics at Cambridge, was thus immediately made marginal by his choice of field. In the absence of anyone else, Fowler agreed to be his supervisor but, as we shall see, the two did not get on very well. After moving from engineering Bhabha received a number of fellowships from the university to continue his studies. He first received a Salomons studentship in engineering, and then, in 1932–33, a Rouse Ball travelling studentship in mathematics.[6] Bhabha used this fellowship to go to Europe and spend time studying with various senior scholars, notably Wolfgang Pauli in Zurich, Enrico Fermi in Rome, and Niels Bohr in Copenhagen.

Everyone in Europe was curious about Bhabha. Unlike his Indian contemporary, astrophysicist S. Chandrasekhar, who was self-effacing to the point of invisibility, Bhabha was not shy about engagement with Europeans. While Chandra, as he was known, would stand outside the closed door of his supervisor's office for hours waiting to be invited in, Bhabha would strike up conversations with strangers in trains about the books they were reading.[7] Bhabha is repeatedly described as 'handsome', 'cultured', 'wealthy', 'proud' – in a word, sexy. Much to the envy of his colleagues, 'very pretty' women threw themselves at him. As one of his colleagues put it, 'He was ... so handsome and with such a fine figure that women were mad about him. I myself saw how a beautiful Canadian model lost her mind at his appearance.'[8] With the combination of his good looks, easy manner and obvious wealth, it comes as little surprise that one colleague's wife 'liked to refer to [Bhabha] as the fairy tale prince'.[9]

This curiosity was tempered by confusion. Questions and doubts particularly surrounded his origins. One scientist remembers the first time he saw Bhabha: 'I remember travelling north in the train from Berlin, opposite to a dark-skinned man whom I took to be an Italian.'[10] Another recalls the way 'he skilfully evaded questions about his background'.[11] Confusion about his origins took other forms as well. Bhabha, in one instance, is described as introducing a German scientist to Beethoven's late string quartets. In a number of other places authors draw attention to his proclivity for painting very modern-looking art. One scientist says, for example, 'had [Bhabha] wanted to, he could undoubtedly have become a professional painter; his talents seemed substantial enough'.[12] The paintings themselves are commented on by a number of writers. They are described as uniformly dark and gloomy. 'The pictures he showed me were all characterised by an extraordinarily sombre mood such as I had never seen before; they were dominated by the darkest colours and especially by black. I could not fathom the psychological background of the universally sombre mood but it was profoundly impressive.'[13]

Bhabha's alterity grows with every additional comment. He is markedly different from his peers, so much so that they must all comment on it in various ways. Even as so many of the comments above seem to be generally positive in tone, it is striking that there is nearly always a hostile modifier added later in the text, as if to expose the real Bhabha, to put him in his place. Otto Frisch, who mistook him for an Italian, mentions that Bhabha saw him reading an Edgar Wallace book before they had introduced themselves. Bhabha then asked, 'you are a physicist?' Frisch replied in the affirmative, and in a double-edged comment tells us, 'a really good scientist knows how to draw correct conclusions from wrong assumptions'. Later, Frisch, the one who was introduced to Beethoven's late quartets by Bhabha, mentions that he would irritate his host 'by complaining that his gramophone ran fast and played [the quartets] in the wrong key'.[14] In other words, he implies that Bhabha was a charlatan: Bhabha could not tell that the quartets on which he was holding forth so impressively were being reproduced incorrectly. Walter Elsasser, who was so impressed with Bhabha's painting, immediately adds, in the very next sentence, 'I was less taken with Bhabha's efforts in theoretical physics.'[15] Elsasser suggests that perhaps Bhabha should have become a professional painter rather than waste his time in the exclusive pursuit of physics.

But there is more than jealousy or personal dislike in this encounter. Hendrik Casimir, whose wife had called Bhabha a 'fairy tale prince' recounts how when Bhabha came to Zurich to work with Wolfgang Pauli, he brought a letter of reference from his guide in Cambridge, Ralph Fowler. Fowler's letter, which Pauli showed to Casimir, was not the usual confidential letter of recommendation and support. Fowler used the occasion to express deep annoyance with Bhabha. He was too 'opinionated and unruly', Fowler wrote, and needed a 'strong hand'. Fowler ended the letter saying, 'you can be as brutal as you like'.[16] Casimir tells us this story ostensibly in order to inform us about Pauli's personality. He reports that Pauli was so amused by Fowler's comments that Bhabha was immediately in Pauli's good books.

But our introduction to Bhabha through the device of Fowler's letter is less simple. His 'opinionated and unruly' characteristics could, in other contexts, be taken to be the hallmarks of a brilliant mind chafing at the limits of physical theory and relentlessly questioning assumptions in order to move scholarship forward. But these characteristics are hardly valorised. The letter makes clear that the subject is like a spoiled child who has not been reared properly. Bhabha, it implies, does not know his place and speaks out of turn. He needs to be disciplined by a paternal figure; Pauli's institute in Zurich is thus likened to a boarding school where the British send their unruly boys to be taught – brutally – how to behave in normal society. But this is the international community of physicists we are talking of, not little boys. The trope of childhood continues elsewhere as well.

Bhabha doing science in Europe had clearly crossed more than a few boundaries: he was, unlike most scientists then or now, wealthy, cultured, a man of the world, as well as being, for some, a 'first rate' theoretical physicist.[17] A Renaissance figure, he drew the attention and admiration of all those that he met, a condition that only added to the anxiety of how to understand this figure – was he a colonial scientist or wasn't he? – and hence how to understand themselves. Bhabha's class position was awkward but it was explained away by describing him as 'the offspring of a very old, wealthy, and powerful family of Mysore', by gently evoking the image of the oriental despot with untold wealth of uncertain provenance.[18] His physical attractiveness to white women was a problem, but perhaps it could be folded into the question of his exotic wealth. Ultimately, of course, race is the issue, but this was difficult for the European scientists to acknowledge explicitly. The norm of modern science is that it is a universal practice: anyone can take part, we are told, as long they are good enough.[19]

But these norms had presupposed firm boundaries between metropolis and colony. They had not expected to find colonial scientists in Western laboratories who could not be distinguished from Western scientists. There were no rules on how to deal with this hybrid form: these scientists sought to see Bhabha as a colonial body but his mind – fully expressive of Western culture and the arts as well as the upper reaches of physics – would not let them. Bhabha's figure, both body and mind, turned on its head the category of 'colonial scientist'.

The ambivalence expressed through the figure of Bhabha is most vivid in an anecdote told by Hendrik Casimir, who describes himself in his autobiography as a 'good friend' of Bhabha's.[20] In an oral history interview with Charles Weiner for the History of Quantum Physics project, he describes Bhabha as a source of considerable confusion.[21] When he first met Bhabha, Casimir recounted, Bhabha had not yet learnt much quantum physics due to the lack of guidance in Cambridge. His main guide to the field was Paul Dirac's seminal book, *The Principles of Quantum Mechanics*, first published in 1930. Having read little else, he sounded just like Dirac, mimicking his views and opinions, seemingly unaware that some of the formulations in the book were controversial and contested. In retrospect, Casimir tells his interviewer, Bhabha reminded him of nothing more than the figure of the savage in Aldous Huxley's *Brave New World* (1946). In the well-known novel, Huxley's savage, a man out of time and place, learns English from reading a set of Shakespeare's collected plays he finds lying in the premodern reservation that is his home. As a result, the savage speaks an archaic form of English only barely understandable to the hyper-modern figures gaping at him. This was how the scientist Casimir retrospectively remembers the first encounter with his 'friend' Homi Bhabha, recalling explicitly Huxley, but

also perhaps Prospero and Caliban. This was how Bhabha was represented in the West – almost speaking physics but not quite, physically
present but betraying his unscientific origins, a child of the world who
had yet to come to full maturity.

By the time of the interview and his autobiography, Casimir had
tried to come to terms with the ambivalence generated by Bhabha's
figure. He could not allow himself to have any doubts regarding Bhabha's
'true' origins, yet he cannot but recall the original doubt engendered by
the colonial scientist in his laboratory. What Bhabha cast into doubt was
the very difference between colony and metropolis that is built into the
institutions of science. Casimir needed to shore up the crumbling wall
between reason and race – the boundary that separated the metropolis
from the colony – in order to ensure that he was the civilised one. That
was why Casimir could admire Bhabha's given qualities – his looks, his
charm, and his wealth – as a way of reminding us that Bhabha's mind
was 'unruly', as befitted the idiot savant he really was. Thus, if Bhabha
could speak to him, it was in a garbled tongue, not fully comprehensible.
The figure of Bhabha had to be split and his physical body foregrounded
in order to reassert his racial difference and thus to come to terms with
him.

This horrifying anecdote expresses a deep ambivalence toward the
figure of the colonial scientist, an ambivalence that we have seen over
and over again as Western scientists recount their encounters with him,
an ambivalence that speaks from the heart of the doubt that in fact there
were any firm boundaries around the metropolis – or Western science.
As Frantz Fanon puts it, 'The white man's eyes break up the black man's
body and in that act of epistemic violence its own frame of reference is
transgressed, its field of vision disturbed.'[22] The act of violence inscribed
by Casimir is double-edged: in the moment that it resolves for him
Bhabha's inferiority by reminding us of his colonial origins, it also proves
to him that the *différance* of Western science lies outside the field of
science. 'Western' science cannot be known unambiguously by location
or personality; it depends on an act of power in order to know that it is
dominant.

It should now come as no surprise that the ambivalence surrounding
Bhabha's figure had an impact on the course of his career. Even as he
was an active member of the English physics community and getting
better known internationally, he did not have a permanent position at
Cambridge. Just before his departure to India and on the eve of the
Second World War, Bhabha applied for a Reader's position at Liverpool,
where James Chadwick, formerly of the Cavendish Laboratory, was
setting up a new department of physics. Bhabha was turned down.[23]

Chadwick explains that he felt that someone of Bhabha's calibre would be wasted in a place like Liverpool, so it was not for any apparent scientific deficiency that Bhabha was rejected. However, we get an insight into the constraints underlying the decision when Chadwick goes on to explain that he was also forced to reject, for the same position, the application of the expatriate German physicist Heitler.[24] As he put it, Liverpudlians would not understand why they were being taught physics by a German during the Second World War. The figure of the colonial scientist could have been no less confusing for the young students of Liverpool. How could they be taught physics by a colonial subject? Simply put, if Bhabha was good enough to teach them physics, couldn't the Indians be good enough to run their own country? Nevertheless, Bhabha left England in the summer of 1939 and found himself stuck in India as the war broke out.

We know that as early as 1941 Bhabha was thinking about staying in India and building a new school of physics, if for no other reason, as he confesses in a letter to his friend and mentor P.M.S. Blackett, than to reduce his extreme isolation from the practice of 'Western' science. However, having a group of young physicists around him was obviously not going to be enough. Bhabha ends the letter saying 'I look forward eagerly to being able to return to England.'[25] But Bhabha had no position waiting for him abroad, as he repeatedly claimed in India.[26] It may well have been that there would be no problem getting a job in a Western university, but what Bhabha did not seem fully to recognise at this time was that the world of science had changed fundamentally as a result of the war. In contrast to the halcyon days of the 1930s and before, when physicists from all over Europe moved easily back and forth between each other's laboratories and countries, the 1940s marked the end of what we might call 'continental' physics in favour of a 'nationalised' physics. The wholesale incorporation of physicists into the war efforts of all the principal belligerents made it clear to scientists and politicians alike that science in the service of the state could be of significant mutual benefit. The upshot of this was that the nationality of scientists now acquired a meaning that could not be divorced from politics, and political leaders would never be quite as sanguine about the free flow of information across national borders as they had once been.[27]

Back in India, it had been made clear to Bhabha by the colonial authorities that he could not participate in the Allied war effort.[28] Bhabha appears to have had no doubt that had he been in England, contributing toward the war would have been possible; presumably he felt that the British government would not have been so harsh in England, with so many of his Cambridge colleagues already working for the military and ready to vouch for him. Nevertheless this rejection by the colonial state clearly focused on his racial origins rather than his scientific abilities. Even though Bhabha was part of a wealthy, Westernised, respected élite in India, he was not able to crack the colonial edifice in the way he wanted. Bhabha was being faced again, in a different way, with the contradiction between the powerful consensual myth of the universality of science in theory and its parochiality in practice that he had faced before. Even as he offered himself to science again and again, his national, colonial origins emerged unerringly and denied him the access that he felt he had in every other way – intellectually, culturally, and experientially.

In any event, however, Bhabha did decide to settle down in India, an event which has always been read by his hagiographers as a mark of patriotism emerging from his first real contact with the motherland.[29] From here on Bhabha's incipient nationalism – a lofty idealism – is over-determined in the historical narrative; hagiographers tend not to see the pragmatism we can read in his official correspondence. As he put it in a famous letter written to the chairman of the Sir Dorabji Tata trust, the family foundation which had created a research position for him in Bangalore to carry out his cosmic ray research, 'I have come more and more to the view that *provided proper appreciation and financial support are forthcoming*, it is one's duty to stay in one's own country and build up schools comparable to those that other countries are fortunate in possessing.'[30] This approach paid off handsomely. By 1944 Bhabha had used his family contacts and leverage with the government of Bombay to provide him with the funds to set up a 'big school of research in the fundamental problems of physics', an institution which would eventually become known as the Tata Institute of Fundamental Research (TIFR).[31]

For the early part of the war, actively courted by departments of physics in Allahabad, Bombay, and Calcutta, Bhabha dressed 'as if for the opera' and listened longingly to Mozart recordings on the gramophone in the Mysore State guest house.[32] While we could read this as a doubly imagined nostalgia, for a mode of being rapidly disappearing, and for a specific locational practice, the 'break' that hagiographers find emergent from his new location we see in his scientific work.

COLONIAL SCIENCE AND THE NATIONAL QUESTION

Once in Bangalore, Bhabha continued to do research in a number of areas, including studies of cosmic rays, the area where he had first made his mark in physics.[33] He had also begun to expand his scientific horizons beyond theoretical work and engage directly in experimental physics. Using jerry-rigged Geiger counters he had designed and initiating the use of nuclear emulsions in India, Bhabha began a series of experiments designed to study the penetrating effects of cosmic radiation, initially with the help of American air force planes stationed in Bangalore, and later with high altitude rubber and plastic balloons. These experiments relied at least in part on the work of the US physicist and Nobel Laureate Robert Millikan, who had come to India to study the latitude effect on cosmic rays in 1939, and had delivered a series of lectures at the Institute of Science in Bangalore.[34]

The onset of these experiments suggests a number of shifts. First, the experimental move marked a significant divergence from the work Bhabha was known for. As noted, he had always been one of the outsiders in yet another way in Cambridge, a theoretical physicist where there was a pride of experimentalists. Now Bhabha was engaging directly in experimental work, expanding his repertoire of experience and expertise, and working toward providing the experimental proofs of his own theoretical work: closing a scientific circle, so to speak. Second, the experimental instruments for measuring cosmic rays – the Geiger counter instruments, the nuclear emulsions, and the high altitude balloons – were cobbled together using a variety of instruments and objects lying close to hand. While the apparatus was by no means successful at first, the lack of resources had led to the need for skilful and innovative design based on the first principles of physics. The apparatus worked and provided scientifically acceptable data with repeated trials, even though it looked completely unlike more commonly used equipment and thus betrayed its hybrid origins.

Third, the experiments were predicated on a particular location. High altitude balloon experiments were best carried out close to the magnetic equator, where low energy particles were screened off by the earth's magnetic field and high energy cosmic rays could be observed with less background interference.[35] 'The special advantages that India offered for cosmic ray work [were] the availability of a wide range of latitudes from magnetic equator in the south to 25 degree north magnetic latitude in Kashmir, [all] within the boundaries of a single country.'[36] In fact, this was why Millikan had come to Bangalore in the first place. In the days before it was feasible to build large particle accelerators, observing the natural formation of high energy cosmic ray showers proved a cheap and effective way of understanding the behaviour and establishing the existence of new nuclear and sub-nuclear particles.[37]

This foregrounding of India's 'natural' characteristics as a stimulus to scientific ingenuity in the presence of resource constraints would continue to characterise Indian 'big science' in years to come.[38] In the early 1950s, a series of experiments designed to detect, among other things, the interaction of cosmic ray neutrinos, were conducted in a mine shaft at the Kolar Gold Fields near Bangalore. The mine shaft is described as one of the longest in the world (more than two miles deep), and while it no longer contains any gold, its depth became the reason to carry out these experiments there, as at such depths it is possible to detect the natural presence of neutrinos without the distorting effects of atmospheric radiation. Similarly, a large steerable radio telescope was set up in South India, near Ooty (now Udhagamandlam), which was 'mounted on a hill slope such that its axis of rotation [was] parallel to the rotation axis of the earth.... After an intensive search an appropriate hill was located.'[39] Here the advantage of adopting this design is that it 'allows a celestial object to be tracked from horizon to horizon by a simple mechanical rotation of the antenna from left to right'.[40] The obvious attraction of the manipulation of nature to provide a solution to major scientific problems took on a distinctly nationalist hue in India. It was assumed that Indian scientists could not compete with their Western counterparts for funds to build large experimental facilities. Hence, conducting big science experiments through this 'reading' of the Indian landscape was represented as an especially creative nationalist response to the lack of resources compared to the West.

Bernard Peters,[41] a colleague of Bhabha's, later pointed out that '[this research helped] to instil in young Indian scientists the confidence that in spite of innumerable obstacles such as financial stringency, lack of technical experience and lack of traditions in experimental sciences, they could by means of hard work and devotion and by means of their own ingenuity achieve scientific results of the very first order, in no way inferior to those obtained elsewhere'.[42] In other words, as the idea of internationally credible, self-reliant experimental science slowly became a conceptual possibility for the young physicists and mathematicians working with the renowned Homi Bhabha, their practices coincidentally provided a convenient and consistent point of entry into political debates around the need for self-reliant national development.[43]

In other words, the line between the laboratory and the world was being reformulated in a completely new way. The impact of the first cosmic ray experiments in Bangalore is not as important in scientific or personal terms as the interpretation given to the activities conducted there. What became possible was for the scientists at the Indian Institute of Science to construct an image of their own work that mapped perfectly on to a dominant image of nationalist thought. Laboratory practice in the scientific world was being given tangible expression in political terms – it could be seen as self-reliant, autonomous, and Indian, operating under harsh conditions of 'financial stringency' and 'lack of traditions', and, finally, it was successful according to an objective (international) standard. So successful was this mapping that it may be legitimately asked, who seduced whom? The laboratory in colonial India was now producing the concrete expression of the scientific state that was yet to be. The metonymic move from the laboratory to the state produced a state that could work like a laboratory – it appeared to give hard proof to the idea that all that was needed for a strong, independent postcolonial state was, adopting Nehru's evocative phrase, to 'make friends with science'.

The possibility referred to in the introduction, that Nehru's inscription of the discourse of science and nation would lose its national origins by being located in international space and world time seems to have been finessed. Bhabha's cosmic ray experiments, firmly rooted in the Indian landscape, appear to be the epitome of an independent, national science, thus actively denying that possibility. Yet perhaps not completely. The irony of this powerful move from laboratory to state is that in their foregrounding of India's physical resources and geographic location as the stimulus to their ingenuity, the Bangalore scientists could be described as doing 'colonial science'! If for Basalla, the value of the colony (India) can be read through its representation as a fecund and static entity available for scientific inquiry, was it any different for Bhabha and his group? While writing a very different script for their work, both Bhabha's and the colonial scientists' scientific raw material was of the same qualitative essence: their common question, 'what could "India" do for science?'

JAWAHARLAL NEHRU AND SCIENCE

These constant references to science did not mean that the ambiguities of its meaning had been clarified by the nationalist élite. In his presidential address to the Indian Science Congress in 1947, Nehru spoke of the relationship of science to development, and of atomic energy to war, using the term 'science' in two very different ways but consistent with the larger objectives of the postcolonial project. In relation to development, science was valued both for its instrumental value ('transformative' science) and, as a practice, as a model for human societies. On the one hand, Nehru challenged the scientists in his audience to think not merely of their 'individual search for truth', but to put their energies at the disposal of the community. 'So science must think in terms of the 400 million people in India.' On the other hand, he said, 'I firmly believe that it is through the method and spirit of science that we can ultimately solve our problems. All the world over it is because we forget the scientific approach that many of our troubles arise.' Again we see the reference to an idealised scientific practice as the preferred mode through which the new Indian subject is created, living in a world that has been transformed by the systematic imposition of science.

Even as Nehru hoped to harness the power of science for national development, the association of war and science was never far from his mind. 'I know how difficult it is for a line to be drawn between scientific work for peace and for war. This great force – atomic energy – that has suddenly come about through scientific research may be used for war or may be used for peace. We cannot neglect it because it may be used for war ... we shall develop it, I hope, in co-operation with the rest of the world and for peaceful purposes.' This bifurcation in science was fundamental, Nehru believed. 'Science has two faces like Janus: science has its destructive side and a constructive, creative side. Both have gone on side by side and both still go on. [...] Hiroshima became a symbol of this conflict.'

Science is thus seen as inherently neutral, even if ambivalent, which brings to the fore the individuals responsible for its production – scientists. But scientists too can be misled, according to Nehru. 'I think it is desirable and necessary that men and women of science should think also about the way they have been misused and exploited for base ends and should make it clear that they do not want to be so exploited.' Even as science is presented as the necessary instrument for national power, we find the institution of science and its agents made less credible. As Nehru explains himself, we realise that the locus of power and responsibility that determines the final use of science has shifted, from science to scientists, and finally to himself. 'A person like me who is not exactly a man of politics has to take an intimate part in political activity. I have often asked myself why this is so. Why should I go into politics? It is so because it is not possible to progress in any field, more particularly in the field of science, until you remove the vast number of fetters which prevent people from functioning as they ought to.' The power of science, which was meant to remove the fetters of underdevelopment, is now seen to need a facilitator of its own. There is a strong sense of self-sacrifice in his words as Nehru goes on to explain, 'It is for this reason [to build a just political community] that a large number of us who might otherwise have functioned in other fields and who may even now function in other fields when the chance comes[,] have largely confined our interests intensively to the political field.'[44]

Through this exegesis, Nehru's understanding of his relation to Bhabha and the atomic energy establishment becomes clearer. Recognising both the ambivalent powers of science, which could be used for peace or for war, and the possibility of the subversion of scientists, these dangers could be resolved only by super-patriots like Nehru himself acting on their own best instincts and using their political authority. It should be noted that once this decision had been made, based on the larger interests of the state, opposition to these plans acquired a distinctive danger. Not only was opposition an illegitimate attack on the judgement of those who made these plans, but it weakened the state by opening up the possibility of the emergence of the 'other', dangerous, face of science, and the gullibility of the men and women of science.

Hence, quite independently of the personal relationship between the two men,[45] implicit confidence in the Nehru–Bhabha project came from the combination of the 'objective' analysis of history that Nehru out-lined in his Constituent Assembly speech announcing atomic energy and through the laboratory demonstration of the possibility of a postcolonial science. This confidence demanded that opposition had to be prevented at all costs, and legitimised prevention in the larger interests of the state. Hence, it was the dialectic between a teleological historical understanding that foregrounded science and a laboratory practice that seemingly proved the possibility of independence that framed the figures of Nehru and Bhabha – of Politics and Science – in relation to each other and to the postcolonial state.

ATOMIC ENERGY AND NATIONAL SECURITY

We have traced the emergence of a new discourse of science and nation, as shaped by Jawaharlal Nehru. Owing to the historic conjuncture of independence and the violent end of the Second World War, atomic energy was poised to become the rhetorical epitome of the new science–nation nexus. Hence, by the time of the Constituent Assembly debates on atomic energy (1948), the public association of atomic energy and national defence was so strong that Nehru could not begin his introduc-tory speech but by noting that congruence. The atomic bombs that had forced Japan's surrender and ended the Second World War just a few years before had left a powerful impression on the minds of nationalist leaders, reinforcing the power of science for state ends, and India's own shortcomings in this regard. So powerful was this association that even as Nehru attempted to produce a rationale for India's atomic energy pro-gramme that delinked atomic energy and defence, the other delegates rejected this move firmly. At the end of the debate, and in response to a direct question, Nehru was reduced to saying despairingly, 'I do not know how you are to distinguish between the two [peaceful and military uses of atomic energy]', and 'Of course if we are compelled to use [atomic energy] for other purposes, possibly no pious sentiments of any of us will stop the nation from using it that way. But I do hope that our outlook in regard to this atomic energy is going to be a peaceful one ... and not one of war and hatred.'[46]

Two shifts are apparent by this time, the first that makes atomic energy the epitome of a modern scientific project, and the second that foregrounds national security as a core rationale for state behaviour. These moves are all visible in a note Nehru wrote to the Cabinet as early as 1946, where he stated, 'Modern defence as well as modern industry require scientific research both on a *broad* scale and in *highly specialised ways*. If India has not got highly qualified scientists and up-to-date scientific institutions in large numbers, it must remain a weak country incapable of playing a primary part in a war.'[47] Scientists and their institutions were now seen as crucial components of the national move to modernity, in matters of both war and peace. The note goes on to argue that the state should set up both a scientific manpower committee (the 'broad scale') and an Atomic Energy Commission ('highly specialised ways').

Yet Nehru's eloquent opening speech on the need for atomic energy for Indian development appears to have one glaring inconsistency. If in fact the Indian atomic energy programme was concerned solely with peaceful ends, as he claims, then what was the need for excessive secrecy? In fact his demands for secrecy go so far as not to permit any legislative oversight at all. The speeches that follow Nehru's ignore this consideration and almost uniformly applaud the government for beginning an atomic energy project.

Delegate Seth Govinddas, for example, says, 'It would have been a matter of surprise had this Bill not been presented to this free legislative Assembly [soon] after the dawn of freedom.'[48] K. Santhanam agrees: 'I welcome this Bill and I hope in the years to come we shall endow the Atomic Board or Commission with more and more powers.'[49] H.V. Kamath adds, 'This Bill has not come a day too soon.'[50] Was Nehru's influence and the consensus around atomic energy so powerful that delegates refrained from questioning the need for so much secrecy for a peaceful project?

Thus, it is almost with a sense of relief that we read the intervention from S.V. Krishnamurthy Rao, delegate from Mysore, who puts his finger precisely on this contradiction: 'The [stated] object of this Bill is the development and control of atomic energy. I am afraid, Sir, it deals only with controls.'[51] He goes on,

I certainly agree with the Hon. the Prime Minister that we should have all control [of atomic energy] as far as military purposes are concerned. But why should we have control for peace[ful] purposes? In fact, I have compared this Bill with the English and the American Acts ... I want to know therefore, from our Prime Minister, why when England and America – who are practically at the peak as far as atomic research is concerned – have not got such restrictions, why we in India should have such restrictions on atomic energy so far as peace purposes are concerned.[52]

Krishnamurthy Rao, who stands alone in disagreeing with Nehru outright, is primarily concerned with the illiberal nature of the Bill. He asks why the public, industrialists, and the scientific community at large cannot be consulted, as in England, and why the provisions of the Bill cannot be toned down to simply ban the export of strategic minerals – the only stated rationale for the need for secrecy.[53] Having identified this inconsistency in Nehru's argument, Krishnamurthy Rao does not press the larger case. Rao would be satisfied if the Bill appeared to give the state fewer powers, and if more people were consulted in its framing. In that sense, he appears to be actually seeking to build a negotiated consensus on atomic energy, not reject the Bill altogether.

But Nehru's reaction is quick and hostile. He proceeds to try and discredit Krishnamurthy Rao and suggests that the latter is unaware of the larger context in which these matters of state are being discussed. We find that Nehru is particularly concerned to prevent pubic opinion being gauged, ostensibly because there is no time to be lost: 'I should like this House to appreciate that time is an important element. I will go further and say that it is a vital element.... In a short while later it may become impossible for us even to deal in such matters with other countries.... If we do not take advantage of an opportunity when it comes our way, we may not have that opportunity for some time.'[54] In noting that this un-explained 'opportunity' might be lost, Nehru returns again to his power-ful argument that links India's subjugation under colonialism with historic opportunities missed. But this time the tactic is less successful. Faced with the rejection of his compromise, Krishnamurthy Rao has a short, heated exchange with Nehru that exposes even more clearly the in-consistencies in Nehru's position:

RAO: May I know if secrecy is insisted upon even for research for peaceful purposes?

NEHRU: Not theoretical research. Secrecy comes in when you think in terms of the production or use of atomic energy. That is the central effort to produce atomic energy.

RAO: In the Bill passed in the United Kingdom secrecy is restricted only for defence purposes.

NEHRU: I do not know how to distinguish between the two [peaceful and defence purposes].[55]

Nehru has been forced to admit that the secrecy he is asking for cannot be separated from the defence-related ends of the atomic energy project. Trying to displace the difference between theoretical and experimental research onto the difference between peaceful and defence-related ends of atomic energy research, he admits in the end that he cannot sustain this dichotomy. He cannot deny, in effect, that the Indian atomic energy programme has a military component from this moment of inception.

Reading the account of this debate nearly 50 years later, what is striking is the way that the tenor of the discussion changes at this point, after this admission has been made. Almost as if with cynical relief that the necessary rhetoric of international peace and goodwill has been dispensed with, we hear a new set of voices speak out, voices that lay out a very different idea of the purpose of India's atomic energy programme. These are voices that appreciate the need for state power in the international system and see atomic energy as the logical means to achieving that power.

Shibban Lal Saksena argues that a country can only be a credible force for peace if it has the force to back it up. Reflecting perfectly the convoluted logic of what would eventually be called 'realism' in international relations theory, he says,

> Unless we are in point of military strength [sic] a very big nation and unless we can have a say in world affairs, I do not think we can make the world pacific. Our national genius being pacific I would then like to tell the world that we must ban the use of atomic energy for warfare and even outlaw war. But we cannot do it by preaching and good wishes alone. *Unless we have the capacity to use atomic energy for destructive warfare, it will have no meaning for us to say that we shall not use atomic energy for destructive purposes.*[56]

Until this point, the discussion has centred around the uses to which atomic energy can be put. The primary question appears to be whether peaceful or military ends will dominate the Indian programme. Put another way, this discussion has traced only the discursive breakdown of Nehru's original position – which sought to deny belligerent ends to India's atomic energy programme by arguing that atomic energy was the historically appropriate response to India's development needs. It would be easy to assume that notwithstanding the different ends to which the political élite saw atomic energy being put, the object itself, atomic energy, was not under question. This is not true.

Turning to a closer examination of the delegates who had initially hailed the state's efforts in developing atomic energy, we can see, in their variety of justifications for the Bill, a variety of doubts about the project of state science and atomic energy. For K. Santhanam, the issue was all about who would control atomic energy. He is sure that the state is the most appropriate owner of something as dangerous and mysterious as atomic energy: '[I]t is essential that in this field at least, the whole thing, from beginning to end, should be exclusively a state monopoly. We cannot afford to let private interest meddle with an energy of such explosive nature and such vast possibility as atomic energy. *I would rather have it that atomic energy not be exploited at all in this country than it should get into unregulated, private, reactionary hands.*'[57]

So the real enemy here is private capital. In fact, so central is Santhanam's concern about private capital that it overwhelms his doubts about the efficacy of atomic energy. As he puts it, 'At present it is still rather uncertain as to how far atomic energy will be useful for industrial purposes [...] It is only because I think that for the good of the country and of humanity it should not be allowed to be tampered with by extraneous hands − *and not so much that there is a great possibility of our exploiting that power for industrial purpose in the near future* − that I welcome this Bill.'[58] In short, this supporter of the Bill does not believe that atomic energy can have any peaceful, industrial uses. But he wants to ensure that private interests will not get it.

Not all the delegates share these doubts about the utility of atomic energy. Dr Sitaramayya of Madras, a chemist by training, takes precisely the opposite tack. He argues that atomic energy will clearly work, the problem with the Bill is the state's monopoly. Sitaramayya invokes the authority of science to argue that the measures being taken by the state to control atomic energy are unnecessary and overcautious. He states that, in the years to follow, as atomic energy becomes a 'matter of daily occurrence ... we shall be laughing up our sleeves that our elders were so nervous about [atomic energy] that they had to pass a law ... making it a monopoly of the state'.[59] Unquestioning of the utility of atomic energy and the ability of scientists to produce socially valuable goods, Dr Sitaramayya is none the less concerned about the implications of the state's control of atomic energy. According to him, the result of a state monopoly is likely to be much greater insecurity.

> Perhaps if it had been left open to anybody to make research in this new domain it would have served to diminish the chances of war in the world much more than when it is kept a monopoly and a secret. As things stand, each nation believes that it has a potent weapon in its hands which is far more destructive than the weapons known to its neighbours, and therefore I doubt very much whether, after all, this monopoly and this element of secrecy ... is not destined to promote the war-spirit and the preparations for war, more than of peace.[60]

Dr Sitaramayya seems sure that atomic energy will be used to produce weapons of war. But he suggests that it is the very instruments of
monopoly and secrecy that will be the eventual cause of the proliferation
and use of these weapons. Being a scientist, Sitaramayya has no doubt of
the potential of peaceful uses for atomic energy; his subversive critique
rests on the structural concern that state monopolies might bring about
a situation where weapons are the natural outcome of atomic energy
programmes. Far better in his view is to let all scientists do research on
atomic energy in the open, which will ensure benevolent, progressive
outcomes.

However, not all the delegates believe the same myths as, and of,
scientists. Both H.V. Kamath and Seth Govinddas cast doubt on the
ability of scientists to manage this resource effectively. Govinddas says,
toward the end of his speech, 'We have given many famous scientists to
the world of science. But ... we have never been unanimous in our
views. Our differences have never permitted us to take the maximum
advantage of these great men.' The fault, it appears, lies with Indian
élites – had they only been able to agree, Indian scientists would already
have carried out various national development projects. But Govinddas
then goes on to say, in a remarkable statement, 'Scientists differ all over the
world and they are not an exception in India. We hope the scientists who are
set on this task ... will be unanimous. The difference of scientists can
strangle this work in its inception.'[61]

The significance of this statement lies at two levels. First, and most
directly, Govinddas has moved the burden of the historic disjuncture
between science and politics on to the scientist; this is no more than
passing the political buck. Much more important, however, is his suggestion that scientists, not just in underdeveloped India but worldwide,
need not agree. But can scientists disagree about science? Seth Govinddas'
suggestion goes to the heart of the scientific project. One source of the
authority of science has always been the dual ability of scientists to
regulate themselves and to come to conclusive, unambiguous and in-
ternally logical conclusions about their nature of their work, scientific
controversies, and their meaning. It is precisely this self-regulating
function that is being directly questioned. Recall that Govinddas is not
an opponent of the atomic energy project, rather, he is a firm ally. If
even he cannot restrain his doubts in public, it appears to point to the
fragility of the state-scientific project as a national project, even as atomic
energy was becoming firmly, legally and financially, situated in the
apparatus of the state.

What we have traced in this section are various contestations embedded in the official debate around atomic energy, contestations that reflect

political battles being fought on other registers, and in other domains. For instance, one contestation was the issue of public versus private property, another was the issue of government monopoly: these were the existing socialist and liberal agendas, so to speak. These discourses intersected across the domain of atomic energy, and, notwithstanding the outcome of the debate, remain imbricated in the larger discourse of the state and science today. Delegates supported atomic energy for a variety of different reasons, reasons that were often at loggerheads with each other, yet the outcome was favourable to the nuclear scientists. In other words, it was precisely the multiplicity of meanings that could be expressed through the sign of atomic energy that forged an apparent consensus and permitted the legal passage of the Atomic Energy Bill.

But we cannot forget that the discourse spilled over the limits defined by Nehru at the moment that he could not deny, faced with Krishnamurthy Rao's pointed questions, that the atomic energy programme had a military component. We realise that the association of atomic energy with national defence served to support the provisions of the Bill, not undermine them, and made Krishnamurthy Rao's concerns with secrecy redundant. Since it had been admitted, or rather could not credibly be denied, that the atomic energy programme would aid India's defence, the need for secrecy and other restrictions was made obvious.

THE INDIAN STATE AND SCIENCE

It is worth remembering that from the First World War onwards, the colonial state had in fact been closely involved in the relation of science and national security. Prior to that time the state had followed a *laissez-faire* policy when it came to industry in general, a policy which in large part continued for non-strategic industry. In spite of the many calls that had been made for the promotion of science in colonial India for the improvement of both agriculture and industry, going back to the 19th century, the colonial government had been less than willing listeners. Editorials even in the pro-establishment Calcutta newspaper, *The Statesman*, in 1877 pointed out that 'there is not a man today in any one of the [state Ministries] that even professes to have the smallest acquaintance with agriculture as a practical art or as a science'.[62]

Taking an openly nationalist line, articles in the popular science magazine, *Science and Culture*, called for scientific research in national planning from 1940 onward and pointed out repeatedly that only state support would enable industrial development to occur in India.[63] The justification for state intervention was explicit: on the basis of the recent historical experiences of Russia and Germany, it was argued that scientific research was crucial if the state was not to be vulnerable but was to grow and become powerful.[64] For instance, 'The philosopher's Germany of 1860 was converted, as a result of systematic planning, in course of a few years, into a highly industrialised modern state that could throw gauntlet [*sic*] to all the other powers combined for world-supremacy.' This desirable outcome, according to one article, was the direct result of the creation of scientific institutes in Germany, such as the Kaiser Wilhelm Societies.[65]

With the First World War and the danger of 'India's all important industries being exposed to risk of stoppage, her consumers to great hardship, and her armed forces to the gravest possible danger', the colonial state finally responded with the creation of the Indian Industrial Commission (1916) and the Munitions Board (1917).[66] The commission, with its majority of Indian members, strongly urged the creation of all-India scientific services and a chain of specialised national laboratories. Driven by strategic concerns, especially the 'gravest possible danger' of the diminution of the armed forces, the state was finally willing to intervene in the economy and concede that science could be harnessed to state ends. This led to the creation of a number of ordnance factories to produce defence goods; more defence production factories followed the reports of the later Chatfield and Rogers Missions.[67]

By the time of the formation of the new state, the idea of science as an instrument of national security was explicitly defined within the state apparatus. This relationship is most starkly demonstrated in three internal reports written in the period just before and after Indian independence. These reports, the first written by A.V. Hill, Secretary of the Royal Society and a noted biologist, who visited India in 1943–44, the second, the Wansbrough Jones Report (1946), and the third, the Blackett Report of 1948, all position science and defence in inextricable relation to each other through the common goal of 'self-reliance'.

Hill toured the country's scientific establishments extensively at the request of the government of India, and provided a series of recommendations to the colonial state suggesting a centralised system of scientific administration, expansion of the funds dedicated to scientific activities, some reorganisation of the existing state scientific establishments and the formation of institutes of technology on the model of the Massachusetts Institute of Technology. A significant part of his report, *Scientific Research in India* (1944), which is apparently about developing science in India, is devoted to the needs of the defence establishment and of the security of the state. With respect to defence, and presumably with the pressures of the ongoing world war weighing heavily on him, Hill stressed the need for self-reliance in the design and manufacture of war materials in India, and for 'devising the technological methods of her defence' through growth in the institutions of science.[68]

Hill's stress on self-reliance in defence through science is underscored heavily just four years later in the report submitted by P.M.S. Blackett to the Defence Ministry of independent India.[69] The Blackett report, which laid out in explicit form the relation between indigenous defence production and national development, was fundamental in setting the preferred course of defence policy in India for the next few decades. Blackett had been invited to India on the basis of a recommendation by Bhabha and a chance meeting with Nehru on a plane. His report, submitted to the government of independent India, was a long-term plan for the defence of the state and was crucially dependent on the growth of an independent scientific branch. Blackett, who had been a colleague of Bhabha's at Cambridge and was closely identified with the invention of operations research techniques for wartime logistics and planning, represents the epitome of the figure of the scientist allied to the state for common purpose. He would return to India often in the next decade as an informal adviser to the Indian government.

Underlying Blackett's report is 'the understanding that it is the intention to make India as nearly as possible a self-supporting defence entity as may be at the earliest possible date'.[70] The similarity to Hill's objectives is remarkable. Yet, this 'understanding' was neither invented by Blackett nor did it come from Hill. Blackett took the quotation on self-reliance verbatim from the 'Report on Defence Science' (1946) written by Dr O.H. Wansbrough Jones, a British defence scientist advising the colonial Indian government. This overt intertextuality points not only to the continuity between these reports and their authors and the defence policies of the colonial and the postcolonial state, but above all to the consensus on the preferred relation between state, defence, and science in India – the objective of self-reliance. It should be mentioned that the goal of 'self-reliance', commonly thought of as a constant factor explaining the course of Indian development until the 1980s, was not explicitly described as an objective of the state planning mechanism until the early 1960s and the Third Five-Year Plan.

The discussion so far contextualises the relation of science to development and to national security: in particular, we have shown that science and defence were closely linked at the material, institutional level and in the self-understandings of nationalist élites, and also that atomic energy was positioned to become the epitome of the science–state relationship. Yet the discussion has only identified what social scientists call 'tendencies,' which still leaves open a variety of material outcomes. The conjunctural event that came along to force atomic energy into defining the relation between science, defence and development was a classic moment of the postcolonial state: the event brought together the insecurities of the new state over control of its territory, natural resources, and an ambiguous external threat.

TERRITORY, RESOURCES, AND THE ATOMIC ENERGY COMMISSION

Prior to the discovery of uranium ores in Bihar, it was assumed that the primary fissile resources in India were the thorium-containing monazite sands in Travancore, a principality on the south-west coast of India. From the early part of the century, the economic value of the sands was known, and four firms, the largest a British firm, Hopkins and Williams Ltd, had been awarded concessions for their extraction. Sales until 1939 had been made primarily to the US, UK, France and Germany, mostly for use in the lamplight and gas mantle industry. From the start of the Second World War, however, the War Trade Intelligence Department of the British colonial state had kept a careful eye on the processing of the sands and the final users, fearing that German agents might attempt to get access to the thorium.[71] In other words, with the start of the war the strategic value of these minerals had became paramount in the minds of the British.

This insecurity was exploited by the Dewan of the princely state of Travancore, C.P. Ramaswamy Iyer, who was trying as hard as he could to extract larger payments from the British concessionaires and to get them to set up processing factories. In 1945, Ramaswamy Iyer permitted Andrew Corry, minerals attaché of the US Embassy, to make a complete survey of the area, hoping to attract other, particularly US, firms to bid for concessions and thereby increase his own leverage.[72] The explosion of two nuclear devices in Japan in August 1945 only confirmed the Travancore government's impression of the value of the thorium sands to foreign buyers. At the end of August, Ramaswamy Iyer informed Corry he would be embargoing all shipments of monazite 'except those essential for war needs'.[73] The war being for practical purposes over at this point, this statement meant that all exports would cease. The extracting companies began an extended series of negotiations with the Dewan hoping to change his mind, to little avail. When, in early April 1946, the newly created Council of Scientific and Industrial Research (CSIR) in Delhi announced that they would begin a survey of Travancore searching for atomic minerals, the Dewan immediately responded, announcing that he would refuse to let any outside agency, the colonial government included, get access to the sands.[74] A week later he backed away from this position, agreeing to discuss the issue further with the Indian government. Something must have come of the discussion, for when the CSIR's Board of Atomic Energy Research met in Bombay the next month, a press release noted that the Board 'appreciated the measures' being taken in Travancore to preserve the nation's natural resources.[75]

From the middle of 1946, the pace of change heated up. While an embargo on exports of the sands had now been in place for a while, it was rumoured that the Travancore government was negotiating a new agreement with British Titan Products and du Pont to construct a titanium plant, and was making other arrangements to sell monazite sands to various foreign agencies.[76] Once made aware of these negotiations, Nehru and Bhabha were determined to prevent this happening. Their efforts were widely supported, both by those who favoured state monopoly over sub-ground resources and those who wished to keep the hundreds of nominally sovereign principalities in India well under the national state's control.[77]

The importance of the monazite sands loomed particularly large as it was still thought that these were the only currency India had for exchange in the economy of atomic materials. Atomic energy had not yet been commodified, and the understanding was that if India lost its only unit of barter, the monazite sands, the country's progress in the development of an atomic energy industry would be distinctly set back. Nehru's sense of urgency in this matter led to the rapid issue of a series of notes to the Cabinet and other state agencies, first aimed at preventing the export of the materials and, second, nominating Bhabha as scientific adviser to the government. This decision officially acknowledged Bhabha as the national expert on atomic energy.[78]

Bhabha was now within the interstices of the state system. His status was still far from fixed or clear and his authority even less. But this would not stay so for long. Even before formal independence from Britain, as noted earlier, the Council for Science and Industrial Research had created a Board of Atomic Energy Research, with Bhabha as chair. This ensured that Bhabha's official position was more permanent and that his fledgling atomic energy establishment would begin to receive a greater proportion of its funds from the state.[79] Bhabha was careful to keep his research institute, the Tata Institute of Fundamental Research, organisationally separate from the atomic energy establishment, but, in the early years especially, there was little difference between them. He soon began to consolidate his political position through the Atomic Energy Board, to advise Nehru more closely, and began the process of delinking the Atomic Energy Board from the CSIR and creating an autonomous agency for atomic energy.

In the confusion and aftermath of the partition of the British colony of India and the communal riots that both preceded and followed the formation of India and Pakistan, Bhabha remained unscathed and focused on his larger goal. Now an official part of the state, albeit a somewhat marginal part, he began to look abroad for resources, materials and expertise on atomic energy. His first approach was to the UK, Canada, and France. The rapidity with which this process took place seemed to leave even Nehru a little nonplussed. When Bhabha asked Nehru, barely half a year after the formation of the Atomic Energy Board, for an open-ended statement confirming his position as an official representative of the Indian government for his forthcoming foreign trip, Nehru hedged. 'It is rather difficult to write in the air and I do not wish to make what might be called official approach at this stage to governments', he wrote, even as he did give Bhabha a guarded letter of reference.[80]

Bhabha's foreign visit was none the less successful in a number of ways, ineluctably proving his value to Nehru and to the development of atomic energy in India. Notwithstanding his lack of fully official status, or perhaps not being fully aware of it, the Canadians offered to give India a ton of uranium oxide, while the French agreed to set up arrangements for the exchange and training of scientists and to share scientific information. International arrangements of this kind would soon pay off as the British AEC would soon become closely involved with Indian atomic energy development and the French would help build a factory for the extraction of fissile materials in Travancore. Further, Bhabha obtained a good sense of the state of progress in atomic research in these countries and concluded that the Indian effort was not far behind.

On his return to India, Bhabha wrote a long report to Nehru, and had discussions with Defence Minister Baldev Singh. As the atomic energy establishment began to take shape, the implications for defence were never far from the minds of all concerned. As Nehru wrote to Baldev Singh, not only did the 'future belong to those who produce atomic energy', but 'Defence [was] intimately connected with this.'[81] Bhabha's return to India and his report to Nehru seemed to galvanise the two of them into action. In short order, Nehru agreed to present Bhabha's recommendations on atomic energy to the Cabinet and, pointing again to the intertwined relation of atomic energy and defence, asked the Defence Minister to consider setting up a scientific advisory committee, with Bhabha as one of the members.[82] A month later, an Atomic Energy Bill was introduced in the Constituent Assembly which moved all activities relating to atomic energy under one agency and which provided for strict sanctions against any breach of its many provisions. The speed at which the Bill was drafted and pushed through the Assembly is indicative of the pace of events behind the scenes, suggesting that the Bill was necessary to formalise negotiations and actions that had already been set in motion.

The day after the debates in the Assembly, at a meeting of the CSIR's Board of Research on Atomic Energy, the following resolutions were passed. The government was pressed, as soon as possible, to set up an atomic pile (the old term for a nuclear reactor) and allocate Rs. 80 lakhs for research and capital equipment.[83] The Board also resolved that the government should try and set up heavy water capabilities as soon as possible. Finally, 'in view of the desirability of keeping secret', the results of the ongoing surveys for atomic minerals, all survey units would be centralised under the Board.[84]

A few weeks later, Bhabha sent a long memorandum to Nehru, literally a blueprint for the organisational structure of the atomic energy establishment, foregrounding the need for secrecy. In order to keep activities secret, he argued, a small, 'high powered', centralised body controlling atomic energy research had to be set up rapidly (the Atomic Energy Commission), reporting only to the Prime Minister. Among other recommendations, the note argued that the CSIR's Board of Atomic Research be closed down, the Atomic Energy Commission have its own secretariat, and that close to Rs. 100 lakhs be made available to the Commission for the next four years. Bhabha asked for Nehru's permission to continue negotiations with Britain, France and Norway under conditions of complete secrecy. He also went on to request that he be allowed to prepare each bilateral agreement in its entirety, which would only then be submitted to the Indian government for its approval.[85]

Three weeks later, Nehru sent a note to the Cabinet to authorise the funds Bhabha had asked for. The opening line indicated that he had completely accepted the logic of the demands Bhabha had laid out earlier: 'Any consideration of this matter [atomic energy] involves a discussion of highly technical processes many of which are secret.' Explaining that atomic research had considerable social and industrial value as well, and that present needs included co-operation with foreign countries, he asked for Rs. 100 lakhs to be disbursed over a period of four years. His note then suggested setting up a heavy water plant and recommended that the Atomic Energy Commission would be constituted as a 'small, high powered body' and report directly to his office.[86]

On 15 August 1948, the first anniversary of Indian independence, a three person Atomic Energy Commission was created, with Bhabha as chairman. The other members were also scientists: K.S. Krishnan, soon to be appointed the first director of the National Physics Laboratory, and

S.S. Bhatnagar, director-general of CSIR. Just a month before, on 16 July, this same troika had also been appointed to the newly created Scientific Advisory Committee to the Ministry of Defence, later called the Defence Science Advisory Board.[87]

In a few short months, operating on two fronts, at the level of the Constituent Assembly and within the departments of the state, Nehru and Bhabha issued a series of rulings to monopolise and control atomic energy under their joint command. Bhabha was given full official permission to negotiate in the name of the state while Nehru took on the responsibility to manage and oversee, at Cabinet level, the atomic energy establishment. The end product of their activities was to delink the Atomic Energy Board from oversight by scientific or other committees within and without the state structure, to set up a heavy water plant, to begin surveys for atomic minerals, and to ensure massive funding for unspecified scientific activities for the next four years. By the end of this process, Bhabha and Nehru were able to insulate completely the atomic energy establishment from the eyes of the public and its elected representatives through official secrecy and legal punishment.

MONOPOLISING SCIENCE

The process we have described could be read simply as the creation of a state institution through the use of overt political power. But the AEC was a scientific institution as well. What other issues does this aspect raise? Why was it necessary for the AEC to have the kind of monopoly it sought, from a scientific point of view? We turn to the work of Bruno Latour to help us refine our understanding of what was at stake in the formation of the AEC as a monopolising public scientific institution.[88] Crucial to the mission of the public scientist, Latour argues, are processes he calls *translation* and *displacement,* culminating in the objective to 'make the outside world come through the laboratory' to solve their problems. The immunologist Louis Pasteur's problem, to paraphrase Latour's famous study, was to make the various *audiences* of farmers, veterinarians, state health policy makers and others recognise first the relevance of his work for their interests (translation), second, metaphorically to expand the walls of the laboratory to encompass the outside world (displacement), which makes fluid the conventional meaning of the term *inside/outside,* and, third, to specify his scientific solution as the only credible solution to their problem.[89]

It is sometimes easy to forget that Latour's original model, based on a wealth of details and thick description, is none the less located in the 19th century and within a very specific context. The richness of his case materials and the persuasiveness of his rhetoric allow Latour to slide over a crucial dimension, without which his story is surely incomplete. This dimension is power.[90] After all, what Latour is pointing out is that the discourse of expertise, of the professional efficacy of science as the universal solution to modern social problems, is in the process of being reified. This absence is made most clearly visible if we think of the work of another French theorist, namely Michel Foucault. Reading Foucault on the prison or the clinic against Latour on the laboratory makes the absences in Latour's work startling, for Foucault is concerned with showing precisely how the discourses of knowledge are shaped by power and powerfully create the institutions that produce what we now call scientific expertise.[91] Inserting Foucault into a reading of Latour is necessary before we turn to the case under consideration, namely the Indian atomic energy establishment, for while Latour's insights about the mechanisms by which the laboratory represents the outside world are crucial, we equally need to be aware of the power of the discourse of science in India. Most important, given that there already exists a discourse that legitimises science and valorises it enormously, the problem that Latour frames for Pasteur is very differently situated in twentieth-century postcolonial India, even as his terms of reference like *audiences* and *inside/outside* remain useful dimensions of analysis.

For the nuclear scientist Homi J. Bhabha, building a political apparatus and technological system around atomic energy in the India of the 1940s, the problems of translation and displacement were quite different from Pasteur's. First, he did not need to interest people in his laboratory, for people were already interested. Second, he did not have to convince (outside) audiences that within his laboratory lay the solutions to their problems, for they already believed that. What Bhabha did have to do was to convince people that the specific scientific solutions he had to offer were precisely what the country needed, and that no one else could provide those solutions. In other words, while outside audiences were already convinced that science contained the solution to India's dual problem of economic underdevelopment and political subjugation, they had to be shown both that atomic power was the specific answer to these problems and that only Bhabha could split the atom for India.

To understand Bhabha's framing of the inside/outside problem in this context, we have to realise that for him the point of greatest vulnerability came from the possibility that some other Indian scientific laboratory would produce a competing product. The efficacy of these alternative designs notwithstanding, the availability of two (or more) potential solutions to India's problems – desirable as it might have been for the country – would clearly blow the lid off the presumed objectivity of science and its assumed ability to make unambiguous decisions about the superiority of one set of practices over another. I am not suggesting that Bhabha had any doubts about his ability to deliver a suitable and efficient scientific solution. Rather, he did not want to have to prove the superiority of his product in a scientific competition: he implicitly understood Latour's argument that the moment alternative scientific solutions have to compete, it is rarely possible to contain the contest solely within the laboratory. The contest was most likely to expose the social bases of scientific knowledge, undermining the objectivist logic propping up the discourse of science.

In order not to have to expose his scientific practices to the judgement of either other scientists or the public, Bhabha determined to resolve this scientific difficulty politically. Starting in the late 1940s, he began a political process to ensure that no one else, no other laboratory, could provide the scientific commodity – atomic energy – that had come to be defined as the pre-eminent solution to India's problems. His drive to capture state power can be understood, hence, as a pre-emptive move to monopolise the production of atomic energy in his own laboratory. Unlike the Pasteurian solution, the boundaries between 'inside' and 'outside' had to be made even more impermeable for the scientist to make visible the solution to the problem. Bhabha's political monopolisation of atomic energy was decisive in strengthening the already existing conjuncture of science and state in India.

NOTES

1. George Basalla, 'The spread of Western Science', *Science*, 156 (May 1967), pp. 612–19.

2. For a summary of the critiques of Basalla see Kumar, *Science and the Raj, 1857–1905* (Delhi: Oxford University Press, 1995).

3. To take just one instance, 'In August 1943, a brilliant young scientist who had returned to India in 1939 in the middle of an outstanding academic career at the Cambridge University to become a Reader and then a Professor at the Indian Institute of Science, Bangalore and on whom the coveted fellowship of the Royal Society of London had been conferred at the age of 32 ...' B. V. Sreekantan, *Tata Institute of Fundamental Research, 1945–1970* (Bombay: TIFR, n.d.), p. xi.

4. This is not to imply that Bhabha should not have appeared in those histories. He should have: it is precisely the absence of Bhabha's figure from 'official' narratives that begins this exercise.

5. There is an apocryphal story about Dirac being asked by his wife whether he had any students. His reply, 'I had one, but he died.' Quoted in Rudolf Peierls, *Bird of Passage: Recollections of a physicist* (Princeton: Princeton University Press, 1985), p. 122.

6. 'Homi Jehangir Bhabha, 1909–1966', *Biographical Memoirs of Fellows of the*

Royal Society (by Lord Penney), vol. 13 (London: The Royal Society, 1967), p. 39.

7. For a description of Chandrasekhar in Cambridge see Kameshwar S. Wali, *Chandra: A biography of S. Chandrasekhar* (New Delhi: Penguin, 1991), especially p. 83.

8. Leopold Infield, *Why I left Canada: Reflections on Science and Politics* (Montreal: McGill–Queen's University Press, 1978), p. 161. Hendrik Casimir says 'he had the knack of becoming befriended by interesting people (and also with very pretty girls)', *Haphazard Reality: Half a century of science* (New York: Harper and Row, 1983), p. 139.

9. Casimir, *Haphazard Reality*, p. 139.

10. Otto R. Frisch, *What Little I Remember* (Cambridge: Cambridge University Press, 1979), pp. 53–4.

11. Walter M. Elsasser, *Memoirs of a Physicist in the Atomic Age* (New York: Science History Publications, 1978), p. 162.

12. Elsasser, *Memoirs*, p. 161.

13. Elsasser, *Memoirs*, pp. 161–2.

14. Frisch, *What Little I Remember*, p. 54.

15. Elsasser, *Memoirs*, p. 162.

16. Casimir, *Haphazard Reality*, p. 139.

17. 'First rate' is Otto Frisch's term in *What Little I Remember*, p. 55; Rudolf Peierls calls him 'a bright young theoretician' in *Bird of Passage*, p. 122.

18. Elsasser, *Memoirs*, p. 162.

19. See also the section 'Who gets to do Science' in Sandra Harding, ed., *The 'Racial' Economy of Science: Toward a democratic future* (Bloomington: Indiana University Press, 1993), especially pp. 197–200.

20. My understanding of ambivalence is drawn largely from Homi K. Bhabha. See his 'Interrogating Identity: The Postcolonial Prerogative', in David Goldberg, ed., *Anatomy of Racism* (Minneapolis: University of Minnesota Press, 1990), and 'The Commitment to Theory', in Jim Pines and Paul Willemen, eds., *Questions of Third Cinema* (London: BFI Publishers, 1989).

21. H. K. Casimir, interview with Charles Weiner, Center for History of Physics (New York: American Institute of Physics), mimeo.

22. Cited in H. K. Bhabha, 'Interrogating Identity', p. 185.

23. James Chadwick, interview with Charles Weiner, Center for History of Physics, (New York: American Institute of Physics), mimeo, p. 89.

24. This was a time when German expatriate scientists were being given any kind of position in order to allow them to stay in the United States and United Kingdom, as it was well understood that some of them would be in grave danger if they returned to Germany. Chadwick would have been following in illustrious footsteps if he had hired Heitler, who eventually found a position in (postcolonial) Dublin.

25. Bhabha to Blackett, File G.33, Blackett Papers, Royal Society of Great Britain, London.

26. For instance, 'For some time after [returning to India in 1939] I had the idea that after the war I would accept a job in a good university in Europe or America...' Bhabha to Sir Sorab Saklatvala, 12 March 1944, Appendix B, TIFR File, Tata Archives, Bombay.

27. Cf. Daniel Kevles, *The Physicists: The history of a scientific community in modern*

America, 2nd ed., (Cambridge, Mass.: Harvard University Press, 1987).

28. Bhabha to Blackett, File G.33, Blackett Papers, Royal Society. He notes in the letter, 'One wishes one could take more share in helping on the cause in which one believes. I would certainly do whatever I could if I were in England. But in India this is unfortunately not possible as the attitude of the Government is as die hard as ever. The mis-rule would astonish you.'

29. For instance, 'The five year period Bhabha spent in Bangalore (1940–45) was the crucial stage during which he re-established an identity between him and his country and became aware of the role that he could play in the development of India, then on the threshold of independence. He discovered his mission in life ...' B. M. Udgaonkar, '"Growing Science" – from Bhabha's writings', *Science Today*, Bombay, October 1984, p. 76.

30. Bhabha to Sir Sorab Saklatvala, Appendix B, TIFR file, Tata Archive, 12 March 1944, p. 6. Original emphasis.

31. Bhabha to Sir Sorab Saklatvala, Appendix B, TIFR file, Tata Archive, 12 March 1944, p. 1. This is a particularly abbreviated version of the founding of the TIFR. The full story deserves a monograph of its own.

32. Interview with Raja Ramanna by Bikash Sinha, *The Telegraph* (Calcutta), 26 June 1987.

33. Possibly Bhabha's most significant contribution to theoretical high-energy physics was the early work he did with W. Heitler on the 'cascade' theory of cosmic ray showers and his later article on the behaviour of the emergent particles. The latter hypothesis has since been modified as the penetrating particles which Bhabha thought would be 'π' mesons turn out to be 'μ' mesons. Cf. (with W. Heitler) 'The passage of fast electrons and the theory of cosmic ray showers', *Proceedings of the Royal Society*, 159A (1937), 432; and 'On the penetrating component of cosmic radiation', *Proceedings of the Royal Society* 164A (1938), 501. See also B.V. Sreekantan, 'H.J. Bhabha: His contributions to cosmic ray physics', and Virendra Singh, 'H.J. Bhabha: His contribution to theoretical physics', in B.V. Sreekantan, Virendra Singh, and B.M. Udgaonkar, eds., *Homi Jehangir Bhabha: Collected Scientific Papers* (Bombay: Tata Institute of Fundamental Research, 1985), especially pp. xiv–xv, xxviii–xxix.

34. 'Visit of Dr R.A. Millikan to India', *Science and Culture*, vol. 5, no. 7 (January 1940), p. 413.

35. Bernard Peters, 'The Primary Cosmic Radiation', Presidential Address of the Physics Section, Indian Science Congress, Agra, 1956. Reprinted in *Science and Culture*, vol. 21, 10 (April 1956), pp. 576–89, especially p. 581.

36. B.V. Sreekantan, 'H. J. Bhabha', p. xvi.

37. Peters, 'The Primary Cosmic Radiation', p. 576.

38. I do not develop the discussion of Indian 'big science' here. Bigness, in this case, is meant largely in economic terms. For a useful general discussion see Peter Galison and Bruce Hevly, eds., *Big Science: The growth of large scale research* (Stanford: Stanford University Press, 1992), especially the introduction and conclusion.

39. 'Radio Astronomy and Theoretical Astrophysics', *Tata Institute of Fundamental Research, 1945–1970* (Bombay: Tata Institute of Fundamental Research, n. d.), p. 293.

40. 'Radio Astronomy', p. 293.

41. Peters was an émigré German–American physicist from the University of

Rochester who had left the United States after being denounced by Robert Oppenheimer before the US House of Representatives Committee on Un-American Activities. Bhabha had given him a position at TIFR. For Peters's unsuccessful attempts to clear his name, see the correspondence between Peters and his former adviser Ernest Lawrence (11 June 1949 and 20 February 1950), in the E. O. Lawrence Papers, Box 26, Bancroft Library, University of California, Berkeley. Oppenheimer, in turn, was invited by Nehru to move to India when his security clearance was removed due to allegations that he was a Communist sympathiser.

42. Bernard Peters, 'Bhabha and Cosmic Rays', *Science Reporter* (New Delhi), vol. 3, no. 10 (October 1966), pp. 455–7.

43. Experimental vs. theoretical science, an issue I have not discussed, is another trope that marks 'colonial science', as the following quotation suggests. 'As I have seen many times, those who come from cultures far from the circle of modern Western rationalism seem to be impelled to plunge directly into the most profound problems of the Universe, of Matter, or of Life, never bothering about lesser, more accessible and more practical problems.' Elsasser, *Memoirs*, p. 162.

44. All quotations from J. Nehru, 'Science at the service of the community', Presidential Address, 34th Indian Science Congress, Delhi, 3 January 1947, in *Selected Works*, vol. 1, pp. 369–75.

45. '[Bhabha] had ties with Nehru through family and science, having tea or dinner with Nehru almost every two weeks. These men shared the same patrician background with proximity to wealth and political influence; both had been to Cambridge, both lived like bachelors and considered themselves connoisseurs of art, music, food, etc. Their mutual attraction enabled them to speak the same language.' Robert Anderson, 'Growing Science in India – 2: Homi J. Bhabha', *Science Today* (Bombay), November 1976, p. 50.

46. Constituent Assembly of India (Legislative) Debates, second session, vol. 5 (1948), pp. 3328, 3334. Hereafter CAI Debates.

47. Nehru, 'Defence Policy and National Development', note of 3 February 1947, in *Selected Works of Jawaharlal Nehru*, vol. 2, Second Series (Delhi: Jawaharlal Nehru Memorial Fund), p. 364. Hereafter *Selected Works*.

48. CAI Debates, p. 3319.

49. CAI Debates, p. 3319.

50. CAI Debates, p. 3322.

51. CAI Debates, p. 3325.

52. CAI Debates, pp. 3324–5.

53. 'I think it would be sufficient if we restrict the export of atomic minerals like uranium and thorium from India, that would suffice our needs for the present', CAI Debates, p. 3326.

54. CAI Debates, p. 3327.

55. CAI Debates, p. 3328.

56. CAI Debates, p. 3333. Emphasis added.

57. CAI Debates, p. 3319. Emphasis added.

58. CAI Debates, p. 3333. Emphasis added.

59. CAI Debates, p. 3323.

60. CAI Debates, p. 3323.

61. CAI Debates, p. 3319. Emphasis added.

62. Quoted in O. P. Jaggi, *History of Science, Technology, and Medicine in India,*

vol. 9, 'Science In Modern India', (Delhi: Atma Ram and Sons, 1984), pp. 40–41.

63. See, for instance, the May 1940 issue, with articles on the Board of Scientific and Industrial Research in Britain and India and the need for scientific research in national planning. *Science and Culture*, vol. 5, no. 11.

64. *Science and Culture*, vol. 5, no. 11 (1940), pp. 640–41.

65. 'Germany's Organization for Research: The Kaiser Wilhelm Society', *Science and Culture*, vol. 1, no. 4 (September 1935), p. 162.

66. *Report* of the Indian Industrial Commission, 1916–18 (Calcutta: Superintendent of Government Printing, 1918), p. 56.

67. A. L. Venkateshwaran, *Defence Organisation in India* (New Delhi: Publications Division, Government of India, 1967), pp. 291–2.

68. Hill, *Scientific Research in India*, Tracts/695, Royal Society, 1944, p. 32. See also Ward Morehouse, *Science in India*, Administrative Staff College of India (ASCI) Occasional Papers, Hyderabad, 1971, pp. 23–4.

69. P. M. S. Blackett, 'Scientific Problems of Defence in relation to the needs of the Indian Armed Forces' (1948), [also titled 'Report on Defence Science for India's Armed Forces']. File G.4, Blackett Papers, Royal Society.

70. Blackett, 'Scientific Problems', p. 1.

71. Files L/P&S/13/1294 and L/P&S/18/D220, India Office Library, London.

72. See File L/P&S/13/1286, 17 (AB), India Office Library, London.

73. Memo from Wendel to Marks, 'Travancore Monazite Exports', Attachment 2. 14 November 1946, Washington, D.C. S/AE Files, US National Archives, p. 1.

74. Wendel to Marks, 'Travancore Monazite Exports', p. 2. The CSIR was created in 1942.

75. 'Govt. Must Encourage Thorium Research', *Morning Standard* (Bombay), 21 May 1946.

76. The British did reach an agreement with the Travancore government to supply them with monazite sands for a three-year period, starting 1 January 1947, but apart from a single shipment this contract was never filled. Cf. memo for Ambassador-designate Loy Henderson, 17 September 1948, *Foreign Relations of the United States*, vol. 1, 1948, pp. 758–66.

77. Ramaswamy Iyer's motive in continuing to politicise this issue was related to ambitions larger than monazite. By making representatives of foreign companies and states deal with him directly, he made a case for the sovereignty of Travancore, which he hoped would translate into leverage when the question of accession to the new Indian state came about.

78. Nehru, Note to the Cabinet, *Selected Works*, vol. 4, pp. 554–5.

79. In 1946, the CSIR gave TIFR only Rs. 75,000. CSIR to Sir Sorab Saklatvala, Appendix E, TIFR File, Tata Archive (Bombay).

80. Nehru to Bhabha, *Selected Works*, vol. 4, pp. 554–5.

81. Nehru to Baldev Singh, *Selected Works*, vol. 5, p. 420.

82. Nehru to Baldev Singh, *Selected Works*, vol. 5, p. 420.

83. Approximately US$2.4 million in 1948 dollars.

84. Appendix 1 of 'Note on the organisation of atomic research in India', dated 9–10 April 1948, in 'The Architects of Nuclear India', special issue of *Nuclear India*, vol. 26 (October 1989), pp. 5–6.

85. 'Note on organisation of atomic energy', 26 April 1948, *Nuclear India*, vol. 26 (October 1989), pp. 3–5.

86. Nehru, Note to Cabinet, 22 May 1948, *Selected Works*, vol. 6, pp. 349–50.

87. A. L. Ventakeshwaran, *Defence Organisation*, pp. 283–4.

88. Bruno Latour, 'Give me a laboratory and I will raise the world', in Karin D. Knorr-Cetina and M. J. Milkay, eds., *Science Observed: Perspectives on the social study of science* (London: Sage, 1983); and *Science in Action: How to follow scientists and engineers through society* (Cambridge: Harvard University Press, 1987).

89. Latour, 'Give me a laboratory', pp. 144–53. This third aspect, which might be termed 'authority', or the consolidation of a certain conjuncture of power/ knowledge, is the least developed component of his model. What would have been particularly useful here are comparisons with cases of failure. 'Translation' and 'displacement' are perhaps necessary but by no means sufficient for a 'scientific' solution to a social problem.

90. For the most startling example of this calculated blindness see 'Centers of Calculation', in *Science in Action* and compare with 'Census, Map, Museum', in Benedict Anderson's *Imagined Communities*, expanded edition, (London: Verso, 1991).

91. Michel Foucault, *Discipline and Punish: Birth of the Prison*, trans. Alan Sheridan (New York: Vintage, 1979).

3

POSTCOLONIAL MODERNITY:
BUILDING ATOMIC REACTORS
IN INDIA

This chapter follows the development of the civilian atomic energy programme through its first decade and after, examining especially the Atomic Energy Commission's obsessive desire to build atomic reactors. The story told so far has been in large part a domestic narrative: the argument being that the multiple discourses of modernity and legitimacy recounted above were crucial in helping to constitute and imagine the possibility of a postcolonial state. I ended the last chapter by showing how the institutional foundations of the Indian atomic energy programme lay in monopolising atomic energy and making tangible the barriers between them, domestic society and the state – actions enshrined in the Atomic Energy Act of 1948. We find that secrecy appears, in contradictory fashion, to be the most characteristic feature of the peaceful Indian nuclear programme.

The secrecy that shrouded the atomic energy programme now reached deep into domestic society. Survey expeditions led by jeeps equipped with Geiger counters were searching for atomic minerals in the far reaches of the country; scientists and engineers in universities were discouraged from carrying out research in nuclear physics; large sums of money that could have been spent on any number of other purposes were dedicated to the furtherance of this closeted programme.[1] But even as I mention these features of the relationship of atomic energy to civil society, it is important to emphasise also that these restrictions were, by and large, not widely objected to, nor seen as particularly onerous, especially from the viewpoint of political élites. Atomic energy was invested with a great deal of legitimacy and popular support. There seemed little doubt in the public's mind that the atomic scientists would come up with the goods. Not only this, it was also understood that progress in this field would come slowly. Atomic energy was an object of the future and to control it would surely take time. But the wait would be worth it, for the outcome was promised to be a truly postcolonial product – an indigenous, independent, Indian atomic energy programme.

If the previous chapter was about how secrecy was woven into the structure of the atomic energy programme from the outset, this chapter examines how patterns internal to the functioning of the atomic programme emerge in relation to a foreshortened horizon of time within which to take action – what I call 'urgency'. This sense of urgency was not merely latent. As we shall see, the foreshortened horizon of time was noticed by the atomic scientists and constituted itself reflexively as well as being an external, analytic condition basic to their objective of building an atomic reactor. I argue that urgency is produced and experienced as a result of the following material conditions: challenges to the atomic complex from civil society, the initial strategy chosen by the atomic establishment to acquire expertise, the later rush to acquire a foreign reactor from competing external agencies, and the systemic need to enter the national development system. Through the deployment of the thematic trope of urgency, we identify one of the key parameters of postcolonial modernity. By the same token, however, what we are also mapping is a field of action which is immediately larger than the national. Scientific discoveries taking place in other countries, geopolitical imperatives that configured India as an international player, the transnational scientific community: all these and more produce a field that crosses and intersects with the stated institutional goal of producing an atomic reactor.

This chapter unpacks the problems that the still-forming atomic energy complex had to face and overcome in the 1950s, to prevent coalitions forming against it, to engage different audiences for its reproduction in other domains and forms, to keep a step ahead of new meanings attributed to atomic energy and to mobilise them as in the past. The contradictory answer to the dilemmas of the Indian atomic energy establishment is found in the realisation that while building a nuclear reactor was, on the one hand, the objective of the atomic scientists, on the other hand, the price for doing this successfully was the loss of their autonomy as atomic scientists.

URGENCY: FENDING OFF DOMESTIC CONFLICT

Even before the formation of the Atomic Energy Commission in 1948, the CSIR's Board of Atomic Energy Research had commissioned the noted Himalayan geologist D.N. Wadia to conduct a survey of the Travancore sands and then to continue to search other parts of the country for materials such as beryl and uranium.[2] Wadia's search proved successful, and by 1952 Bhabha could announce that India had discovered 'large deposits' of uranium ores in Bihar suitable for industrial extraction.[3] In the years following independence, a monazite processing factory had been set up in Travancore (Kerala) and the TIFR nuclear physics section was slowly beginning to take shape. But these and other developments were apparently not enough for some within the atomic energy establishment. As one scientist was to put it many years later, 'as the years passed, despite many achievements in the field, a mood of discontent began to grow in the atomic energy community. *Compared with countries the world over*, India's rate of progress was thought poor, keeping in view the fact that with the setting up of the AEC, the financial constraints were supposedly removed in order to organise research for *peaceful purposes*.'[4]

This juxtaposition of positive international achievements and the implied failure of India's indigenous development of atomic energy for 'peaceful purposes' is puzzling. The most significant international achievements in atomic energy in the early 1950s had been almost completely in the military field. The Soviet Union had tested its first atomic device in 1949, which had been followed by US thermonuclear (hydrogen) bomb tests a year later. The Soviets had then developed their own thermonuclear bomb by 1953. The British had tested an atomic weapon in 1952. It was only in 1954 that the world's first working electric power producing reactor was commissioned in the Soviet Union. The one potentially significant non-military development in those years was the United Nations Atomic Energy Commission, which had been set up in 1946 in a valiant attempt to control the spread of atomic energy. This organisation folded two years later with little to show by way of accomplishment. Various plans to control atomic energy globally, whether initiated by scientists or state policy makers, had led nowhere.[5] India too had nothing to show for these years, especially in the military field, but surely this was not surprising as it was supposed to be engaged in peaceful research.

One way of understanding this sense of discomfiture is to look to the site of officially sanctioned atomic energy research – the Tata Institute of Fundamental Research. While the institute was growing in size in these years and its staff producing internationally acceptable science, especially in mathematics, theoretical and cosmic ray physics, the nuclear physics section lagged behind in terms of tangible accomplishments.[6] This was partly due to the lack of necessary equipment and the small number of qualified scientists, but the outcome was an atomic energy project that was not meeting expectations commensurate with its self-image, public statements, and resource base. Given that this project still had a high degree of popular legitimacy, whose expectations in particular were the AEC not meeting?

The excessive attention and funding given to the state's atomic energy programme had raised the ire of Indian scientists excluded from this cash cow, some of whom were well known and powerful enough potentially to cast serious doubt on the whole enterprise. Most vocal and prominent among these dissenting scientists was the Palit Professor of Physics at Calcutta University, Meghnad Saha. Saha's hostility is easy to understand. After all, if not for the vagaries of class ties and old boy networks, he, not Homi Bhabha, could easily have been the creator of the Indian atomic energy programme.[7]

As early as 1939, Saha had seen the potential of atomic energy for development and had written about it in his popular science magazine, *Science and Culture*.[8] In the late 1930s, when the Indian National Congress created a National Planning Committee, the forerunner of the post-independence Planning Commission, Saha had been one of its members. The chairman of the Congress' planning committee was Jawaharlal Nehru. In other words, Saha's connections to Nehru predated Indian independence by a decade – considerably more time than Nehru had known Homi J. Bhabha, the eventual founder of the atomic energy programme.

Nehru and Saha were in close concert ideologically, as socialists and as unmitigated votaries of large-scale industrialisation.[9] Nehru was also in complete agreement with Saha's scathing critique of Gandhian ideas of national development.[10] To take just one instance of Saha's vitriolic editorial pen (writing in 1940): 'Nor should we forget that the [colonial] Government of India has had a strange ally … in some of our leaders of public opinion who have been so impressed by the evils of the modern capitalistic world that they have not hesitated to declare that the introduction into India of the scientific and technical methods of the West should be resisted.'[11] Saha's editorials, from this period on, had been consistently and stridently arguing the need for industrialisation and for the role of science in national development – a position that we usually associate with Nehru. Saha argued that scientists should take the lead in national development efforts, that the state take on a more active role in promoting industry, and, in general, forcefully made the case for a scientific approach to India's development problems.[12]

After Homi Bhabha's return to India during the Second World War, and the consolidation of close ties between Bhabha and Nehru, Meghnad Saha's influence in national science policy making declined precipitously. Robert Anderson suggests that by this time the Indian physics community had split into two factions: the 'Calcutta–Allahabad axis' dominated by Saha and his students, and the Bangalore group, preserve of Nobel Laureate C. V. Raman, once a leading Calcutta scientist himself, but who had since broken all ties with Saha.[13] Saha's dislike of Raman would soon extend to Bhabha. Deeply resentful of the latter's close rapport with Nehru, Saha had become the most vocal critic of the AEC's activities as soon as he realised that he would be excluded from the country's atomic energy institution.[14] It is easy to understand Saha's bitterness at being ejected from this powerful coalition just at the moment when the orientation he had been fighting for became dominant. [15]

Saha's marginality from the centre of state power after independence meant that he had little influence on the general direction of scientific policy. But this would change. In the country's first general election, in 1952, to the surprise of his scientific colleagues, Saha ran for the lower house of Parliament from the Calcutta Northwest constituency as an independent candidate (with the support of the Left parties) and won. Once in the Lok Sabha, Saha used his position as an elected MP to become an influential and widely regarded critic of the government's views on a number of issues, most notably atomic energy policy.[16] He forced public debate on atomic matters on a number of occasions, paying particular attention to the difference between what the AEC had promised and what it had done. What stung the AEC and their parliamentary supporters most was Saha's repeated charge of incompetence: 'India has got an Atomic Energy Commission and five years ago [1948] it had announced that we were going to set up a nuclear reactor within five years. This is 1954 and nuclear reactor has not been set up.... I do not know how long it will take us to make good this proposal. It may take us years to set up a nuclear reactor.'[17]

However, even as Saha raised the issue of the incompetence of the AEC, he was not casting any doubt on atomic energy – either as a form of energy or a means of development. Rather, Saha was opposed first to the strategy being adopted for the development of atomic energy in India and, second, to the special status given to Bhabha's clique of scientists. As he said in a speech to the Lok Sabha:

[T]he Atomic Energy Commission, which you have got now, has to be scrapped and we must start our work on a broad basis. First of all, there should be no secrecy. If you read our Atomic Energy Act you find that it does not tell us what to do, but it simply tells us what is not to be done. We shall not export neptunium, we shall not do this, we shall not do that and so on. [Second] ... There is a common prejudice that atomic scientists are in a special class by themselves. It is a great fallacy; it is an illusion. There [were] no atomic scientists to start with. The atomic scientists have been ordinary chemists, ordinary physicists, biologists and others. When this great discovery came they turned their minds to the discovery and tried to find out how to utilise that for the different purposes. So the atomic energy scientist is not a new race that has come into existence.[18]

The AEC was defended furiously by Nehru on this occasion, but Saha was not deterred.

Saha's concern that atomic energy would soon be completely beyond informed public scrutiny was heightened by two developments. In mid-1954, a new entity, the Department of Atomic Energy (DAE), had been created as a free-standing state agency reporting only to the Prime Minister in order to formalise further the state's monopoly on atomic energy research. This followed on the heels of the creation of the Atomic Energy Establishment (AEE) in Trombay, a suburb of Bombay. The newly created atomic energy facility was designated as the primary site for atomic energy research and production in the country, officially marginalising Saha's own institute, the Institute for Nuclear Physics, in Calcutta. Bhabha's position was going to be even more invulnerable if these developments were allowed to stand unchallenged.

Returning from a study trip abroad in September 1954, Saha insisted on and succeeded in convening a special meeting of leading politicians and other members of the political élite to discuss his proposals regarding the future of atomic energy in India. The meeting was held at Teen Murti House, the prime minister's residence. Saha began with an impassioned speech for the immediate and full-scale development of atomic energy as a national priority. After a long introduction discussing the inevitable need for atomic power in the country's development, he made a number of concrete suggestions: first, that the French model was the most appropriate for India to follow as it sought complete self-reliance yet disavowed secrecy,[19] and, second, that the system of administration of atomic energy in India be changed completely and a new atomic energy act be brought into effect. Under his plan advisory boards of scientists and politicians would help the Prime Minister to decide the broad contours of nuclear policy, and, in a direct attack on Bhabha's multiple administrative and executive roles, the administrators of the atomic energy programme would be appointed as full time employees who did nothing else: 'under no circumstances should they be allowed to have any other job'.[20] The political leadership was hearing, probably for the first time, a sustained attack on one of Nehru's vanguard projects from a source whose nationalist and scientific credentials were impeccable.

The stage was set for a direct confrontation between the scientific critics of atomic energy and the AEC. Faced with this mounting pressure, Nehru agreed to hold a special conference inviting scientists from all over the country to assess the progress and future of the Indian atomic energy programme. The conference was held at the National Physical Laboratory (NPL) in Delhi on 26 and 27 November 1954.[21] This choice of location suggests that Saha had already lost part of the battle. The director of NPL was K. S. Krishnan, a well-known physicist who had been C. V. Raman's scientific assistant and collaborator and hardly an impartial adjudicator, given the chilly state of relations between the 'Bangalore scientists' and Saha's group in Calcutta. Krishnan had served as an atomic energy commissioner from its inception and was a close friend of Bhabha. According to one eye witness, Krishnan stepped in at crucial moments during the discussion to 'ease the tension-rid atmosphere' and would eventually 'save the day for [the AEC]'.[22] Krishnan would also sum up the proceedings of the conference in an interpretation that clearly favoured the AEC's rate of progress.

Choosing the NPL as the site for the first semi-public discussion of the AEC and atomic energy policy was thus to affect the outcome of the conference from the outset. This bias, structured toward avoiding criticism of the AEC at all costs, is apparent in the way the conference agenda was set up. Rather than seeking to address directly the appropriateness of the AEC's strategy in developing atomic energy, the conference became a means to share information about atomic energy and to inform the scientific public about what had been achieved thus far. Nehru's opening remarks defined the parameters of discussion. As he saw it, the issue of atomic energy had two components: a scientific one and a technological one. The former could be the domain of the universities, but the latter was restricted to the state alone – not for its national security implications, as India was uninterested in military applications of nuclear power – but 'due to the cost involved'. On this disingenuous note the conference proceeded. The first presentation was by Bhabha who gave an overview of atomic energy development in India. The rest of the agenda was divided into three sessions structured to prevent options other than those already chosen by the AEC from being discussed. The bulk of speakers were drawn from the Tata Institute of Fundamental Research (TIFR) and the nascent atomic energy establishment at Trombay. By and large, the texts of conference papers avoided specific details about the Indian programme whenever possible, choosing instead to speak in vague generalities about the value and importance of atomic energy for development. Saha did manage to give one of the papers on the second day of the conference on 'Considerations in the Choice and Design of Reactors', but this very marginality indicates the limited impact of his intervention.

The success of the AEC in defusing the most public challenge to its monopoly of atomic energy activities speaks volumes for its relative influence and power. The significance of Saha's frustrated attack derives from the fact that he represented the most respected component of the Indian scientific community. Saha, and those around him such as the famous physicist S.N. Bose (of Bose–Einstein statistics fame), could not be dismissed either as anti-national or as uninformed public, which made this challenge extremely serious. Yet, even with Saha's investment of all his scientific authority and parliamentary privilege, he was unable to shift appreciably the boundaries of atomic energy, either as an institution or in strategic terms. There would never again be any serious public discussion of changing the institutional framework of the AEC or of exposing their activities to any significant degree of outside scrutiny. Hence, rather than see this encounter as a meeting where the atomic energy establishment won out over heavy opposition, it is perhaps more useful to see this conference as confirmation of the atomic scientists' dominance over other domestic scientific communities and state agencies.[23] The most tangible challenge the critics were able to lay down was to suggest that the AEC, as currently constituted, would not be able to build a working nuclear reactor for many years to come.

As an observer sympathetic to Saha put it delicately,

> It is apparent that there are two schools of thought among the leading scientists in the country regarding the possibility of atomic energy in India. One of these, represented mainly by the members of the Atomic Energy Commission and the Scientific Departments of the government holds that India will be able to construct in a period of five years a full scale production plant for atomic energy. The other school, consisting mostly of scientists outside the official sphere, however, do not subscribe to such optimistic views.[24]

While the AEC had won this round, the sense of urgency now had a specific referent. Their challenge was to build a reactor as soon as possible in order to forestall any further public criticism of the AEC.

We can see that the atomic energy complex had acquired a considerable degree of domestic power and influence in the mid-1950s. They had managed to weather their first major public attack with relative ease, even as they had to accept that the challenge of building a reactor would now have to be their first priority. But success in this effort would come at considerable cost to their scientific pride. In order to acquire a reactor, the Indian atomic energy programme had no choice but to expose itself to the gaze of the international scientific community. To request foreign assistance was to acknowledge how little had been achieved domestically and to admit how hollow was the goal of Indian self-reliance. The conditions of secrecy that cloaked this enterprise would never be so valuable as now – in order to hide from *domestic* eyes the limitations of the state scientists working for national development.

URGENCY:
SEARCHING FOR A REACTOR

Creating the conditions for an Indian atomic energy establishment through formal legal protection, massive funding, and bureaucratic insulation had only been an initial step towards institutionalising this complex. It allowed the atomic energy complex to be separated from both the state and civil society and gave the atomic scientists the freedom to experiment without the constant scrutiny of the public. The next step was the creation of the technological and scientific infrastructure for producing atomic energy. The most obvious artefact to be created, made more urgent by the challenge laid down by Saha, was an atomic reactor.[25] How was this to be done?

Given the close association of atomic energy with military ends internationally, and the centrality of atomic energy to the making of the postcolonial project in India, building a reactor would appear to have to be a local project. Hence, it comes as no surprise that statements appear in the press arguing for a policy of fostering local knowledge and training in atomic energy matters because, 'in the present international situation [India was] unlikely to obtain the information from the countries which are the most advanced in the field'.[26] Yet, as we shall see, at the same time as these public statements were being made, the Indian AEC was deeply involved in secret negotiations with the United States, Britain, Canada, and France for information and expertise related to atomic energy.

If the goal was to produce an atomic reactor solely through the application of indigenous resources and expertise, one basic problem had to be addressed. Even though the theory of atomic fission was no secret and some experiments in nuclear physics had already been carried out in India, producing an indigenous reactor *in the near future* was beyond the immediate capacity of the Indian nuclear establishment, given its small size and lack of practical experience in reactor fabrication. It would probably take a number of years, perhaps even more than two decades, before a working reactor and its component parts – fuel rods, control systems, engineering fabrication – could be assembled using only domestic resources and technology. If one took a pragmatic view of this situation, however, creating this artefact purely indigenously seemed unnecessary. After all, a handful of countries had considerable nuclear expertise that they might be willing to share with India under the right circumstances. Yet, for obvious reasons, this calculated approach was not one that sat easily with the rhetoric deployed by both governmental and scientific élites, particularly the primacy of independence and self-reliance in the postcolonial project. The utility of the pragmatic strategy, developing relationships with countries with tested knowledge in the nuclear field, seemed self-evident to the Indian atomic establishment. These pragmatists could argue that once the initial conditions were in place, regardless of national origin, independent Indian development of an atomic energy programme would proceed. The strategy of association with foreign countries was presented as nothing more than a 'latecomer' strategy: jump-starting the process by not wasting time reinventing the atomic wheel. A necessary condition for this policy to succeed, therefore, was that it be done without the public's knowledge, a condition easily obtained due to the considerable secrecy surrounding atomic energy.

Thus, the first strategy adopted for the development of an Indian atomic energy establishment was as follows.[27] India's large reserves of rare earths such as thorium, and strategic minerals such as beryllium and manganese, would be offered to select foreign countries in exchange for expertise, funds, and materials that could directly benefit the atomic energy programme. The ease with which these transactions could be made was linked to a number of institutional practices that were already in place. First, the 1948 Atomic Energy Act: this legislation monopolised all aspects of the field of atomic energy for the state and included in its broad definition of controlled substances uranium, thorium, plutonium, neptunium and beryllium, as well as 'any other substance which the Central Government may … prescribe, being a substance which in its opinion is or may be used for the production or use of atomic energy'.[28]

Second, the AEC, although it reported directly to the Prime Minister, was formally a part of the Ministry of Natural Resources and Scientific Research. This ministry was responsible for the extraction and utilisation of state-owned raw materials and underground minerals. The chief secretary of this ministry, its highest-ranking civil servant, was Dr Shanti Swarup Bhatnagar, a well-known industrial chemist and close colleague of Bhabha. Bhatnagar, who as the first Indian director of the Indian Council of Scientific and Industrial Research had given grants to Bhabha's institute, was also one of the three members of the Atomic Energy Commission (the other two being K.S. Krishnan and Bhabha). Bhatnagar made sure there would be no interference with the AEC's plans from the bureaucrats under his control. Little wonder then that foreign governments would treat statements from these two individuals, Bhabha and

Bhatnagar, as tantamount to official state policy. But there was little time to waste. The Indian AEC had to strike the best possible bargains with foreign agencies as soon as possible to ensure first that the momentum built up domestically behind atomic energy did not dissipate; also because the longer they waited, other international sources of raw materials might emerge or new technical processes be developed that made their barter commodities unnecessary.[29]

It should be noted that this sense of urgency was somewhat ameliorated by international conditions in the 1950s. Even though knowledge and information about atomic energy was carefully controlled and monitored, especially by the United States, this information was by no means an American monopoly. Further, the superpowers' Cold War approach to international relations, which saw the countries of the third world in zero-sum terms, also helped pragmatic Indian negotiators. The strengths and limits of the barter strategy are best seen in one of the early Indian interactions with the United States government. A 1952 letter written by Bhabha in his capacity as chairman of the Indian AEC to his US counterpart, Gordon Dean, asks outright for 'all de-classified information on reactor theory, design and technology'. The letter continues, 'in particular, we should be glad to have the detailed designs of such reactors that have been completely de-classified, together with all operational data that may have been obtained concerning them'. This direct and even crude request is immediately followed by a statement that contextualises the Indian request in Cold War bargaining terms: 'We have been given to understand that the big graphite reactor at Harwell [UK] has been more or less completely de-classified and that the large heavy water reactor at Chalk River, Canada, has been largely de-classified.'[30] The letter also asks for ten tons of heavy water over the next two years and 'in return, [the Government of India] is prepared to make available for your Commission during the same period certain quantities of thorium in the form of a suitable compound, or uranium ore or some compound of uranium'.[31] As a sweetener, the letter ends with the suggestion that as Indian beryllium production had increased recently, there might be a possibility of providing the US with more beryl than had been originally agreed upon in the joint Indo–US agreement.[32]

All the elements of the Indian strategy can be seen here: the backdrop of a request for specialised nuclear information and the mention of international competitors juxtaposed against the offer of new and larger supplies of rare earths and atomic minerals. But this letter could only be a starting point.

Some factors worked against a close US–India relationship. American diplomatic annoyance at India's non-aligned foreign policy stance never freed itself from the suspicion that here was a subtle form of, if not international communism, certainly anti-American behaviour. US private corporations that used rare earths and strategic minerals for commercial purposes mobilised their contacts in the US Congress to protest against government stockpiling, arguing that this practice affected their interests adversely by driving up the price of raw materials. Other sources of raw materials appeared: in the case of monazite, Brazil and South Africa – countries that, at least in the latter case, appeared willing to supply large quantities of thorium to the United States on a strictly cash basis.[33] Negotiations with the United States constantly foundered on the Indian desire to set up processing plants within the country rather than simply entering into contracts to sell unprocessed raw materials. Finally, US stockpiles for some of these materials were also close to capacity, making the need to ensure a long-term supply superfluous. Thus we have, after much internal debate, the US government Interagency Committee on Beryl and Monazite rejecting the Indian proposals 'in their present form ... without prejudice'. Likewise the US Atomic Energy Commission reported to the National Security Council that the AEC was not interested in continuing discussions on the possibility of acquiring Indian minerals due to the existence of a new supplier – the apartheid regime of South Africa.

But a few conditions were in India's favour. The American strategic desire to stockpile minerals in the event of another prolonged international conflict meant that there was nearly always a demand for some of the raw materials India was offering in trade, especially thorium, beryllium, kyanite, and mica. Further, the ties that appeared to be developing between India and the Soviet Union were always an issue of concern. For example, considerable efforts were made by US agencies to track Bhatnagar's travels in the USSR, to identify who he met and talked to, and, in general, to monitor the growth of Communist influence in India.[34] Developing close ties with India acquired new importance for the US after the victory of the Chinese Communists over the pro-US Nationalist (Kuomintang) government in 1949.

The barter strategy was also partly effective in working with the US government due to its complex bureaucratic structure. Even if the AEC and the interagency committee were not in favour of acquiring Indian supplies, the Department of Defence was interested in obtaining some Indian rare earths and was not averse to helping India to build a processing plant – they even allocated US$1. 4 million from contingency funds for such a purpose. The State Department too believed in helping India in whatever way it could: for them it was an issue of promoting relations with a potential ally in the fight against the growth of international

Communism.[35] When the United States government did decide to acquire some of these barter materials, they took considerable pains to make it clear to the Indian government that requests to trade came with no strings attached. When William Pawley (later to become president of CBS television) led a mission to India in June 1951 seeking an end to the Indian embargo of monazite, he was given permission by his superiors to agree to help Indian efforts in setting up a monazite processing factory.[36] Pawley's meeting with Indian Cabinet Secretary N.R. Pillai began with a lengthy statement affirming that he and colleagues in the State department had lobbied successfully to separate these negotiations from the Indian Food Aid Bill then being presented to Congress. Faced with this understanding of their sensitivities, the Indian government acceded gracefully and Pawley returned to the United States with a firm but one-time sale of 500 tons of monazite.

Recounting these instances of interaction between various branches of the United States government and the Indian atomic energy programme should not give the impression that the US was actively interested in helping the Indians to develop an atomic energy programme. There is little question that, in the last instance, the American attitude is best summed up by the concluding line in a Defense Department memorandum to negotiator Pawley: 'You should obtain from the Indian Government a commitment to prevent ores and compounds of uranium and thorium from reaching Iron Curtain countries.'[37] It is most likely that no one in the US government even considered it possible that India would be in a position to develop an independent atomic energy project – military or civil – for many decades to come. Certainly US government documents of the period betray no fear of Indian activities in the atomic arena, even though one of their representatives in Delhi repeatedly pointed out the considerable interest, even among the lay public, in atomic energy in India.[38] From the point of view of the United States, the interaction between them and the Indian AEC was driven by larger strategic concerns, concerns in which the United States' interest was paramount.

But if the US might have been unexpectedly thoughtful when it came to dealing with India directly, it was less concerned with the impact on India as a result of its relations with other countries. The constant efforts of the United States to control the nuclear activities of its allies after the war led to considerable bitterness among many, especially in Britain and France. Both countries felt that scientific accomplishments in their countries before the war, and the work of their nationals during it, had had a lot to do with the American ability to build the Nagasaki and Hiroshima atomic bombs. The French, after all, had even taken out patents on atomic fission methods as early as 1940.[39] After the war, however, as Margaret Gowing puts it, 'in the absence of American willingness to cooperate [on nuclear issues], Britain was committed to an essentially independent atomic project'.[40] Bertrand Goldschmidt, a French nuclear scientist who had worked in the United States and Canada contributing toward the allied war effort, is even more explicit about US attitudes towards its allies – now in his words 'atomic rivals' – and accuses them of a form of racism.[41] The Soviets were in any event not going to heed US calls for atomic restraint: they were well on their way to developing nuclear energy for military ends and eventually for civilian purposes as well.[42] Similarly, the Canadians, who had a head start over most other countries due to the Anglo-Canadian wartime project, were completely unwilling to halt their programme despite much US pressure.[43]

The US policy seeking to monopolise and control international atomic energy production had an interesting side-effect. As a result of the lack of international co-operation in this field in its early years, each nuclear state set upon a distinct strategy to develop atomic energy, a strategy that was concretised in unique national reactor designs.[44] The French developed gas-cooled natural uranium reactors and would eventually become world leaders in fast-breeder technology; the Canadians built a family of heavy water moderated natural uranium reactors, the so-called CANDU reactors; while the US and the USSR specialised in enriched uranium light water reactors, driven in some part by the needs of their nuclear submarine programmes. Not surprisingly, this led to a situation where building a fully fledged atomic power system based on foreign purchases was made extremely complex. Different reactor systems were not necessarily compatible with each other owing to considerable conceptual, design, and component variation, nor was experience gained in one system necessarily transferable to another. In other words, when India and other latecomer countries were trying to decide which kind of reactor would most suit them, making a particular choice of reactor usually also implied getting into a long-term bilateral relationship with the supplier country involved. Latecomers' leverage against the sellers – that is, setting them off against each other – would typically end with their first purchase.

URGENCY ASSUAGED:
THE BRITISH CONNECTION

Bhabha first approached his old friends and scientific colleagues in the United Kingdom, India's most obvious international partner for historic reasons, in 1948.[45] Although the British were interested in acquiring supplies of monazite, they were less willing to test the limits of US disapproval, and turned down his first request for scientific assistance.[46] Following discussions with Frédéric Joliot-Curie, then head of the French atomic energy commission, who had approached India with the suggestion of a joint project in atomic energy, Bhabha again approached the UK Atomic Energy Authority suggesting formal scientific and technological collaboration some months later. Harry Tizzard, scientific adviser to the British government, was sympathetic to the idea of scientific collaboration, but noted obliquely 'there are serious difficulties in the present state of the world' as he turned down the possibility of a formal agreement.[47] Bhabha's patience began to wear thin. A later communication to the British states quite bluntly that 'if [co-operation is not possible] then we shall clearly have to follow other roads which we know are open to us, leading to the same objectives'.[48]

This hard-line approach seemed to make the British more encouraging. They had been keeping a careful eye on the state of India's negotiations with both the French and the US and were loath to be driven away from opportunities in their former colony. From the early 1950s, Britain found itself drifting into a closer relationship with India on atomic energy. This drift was not altogether unconscious. Bhabha was dealing with former Cambridge mentors and colleagues, especially Sir John Cockcroft, whom he had got to know during his time at the Cavendish Laboratory, and who was now in charge of the UK Atomic Energy Authority's main facility at Harwell. Cockcroft, Lord Tizzard, and Edwin Plowden, the most senior scientific advisers to the post-war British government, were all in favour of helping Bhabha and the Indian atomic energy project.[49]

The French had not progressed very far in atomic reactor research at this time and were considered by the Indian AEC to lag behind the British, the Canadians, and the US; this impression was in spite of the fact that their first research reactor went critical in 1948 and the French Atomic Energy Commission (CEA) settled on the formal details of their first power reactor in 1951.[50] The lack of political stability in the early years of the Fourth Republic, institutional tensions between the atomic energy agency and the state electric power company, and the dismissal of Joliot-Curie as head of the CEA for political reasons helped to give the impression that the French atomic energy effort was struggling. Nevertheless, following new CEA head Francis Perrin's visit to India in December 1950, the French agreed to collaborate with India in the development of a monazite processing factory and to help train Indian engineers and scientists. We get a sense of the impact of the global atomic energy restrictions applied by the US when we realise that the Franco-Indian agreement was the first bilateral international nuclear project after the Second World War. The Soviet Union did not seem to figure at all in India's plans during this period.

Even before the formation of the Indian AEC, Canada had agreed to supply India with a ton of uranium oxide with an eye to obtaining thorium from India in return, following Bhabha's visit in 1947.[51] In the years immediately after Indian independence, the Canadians were not an important focus of Indian atomic energy plans relative to other areas of collaboration. The two countries worked closely on some important international issues, in particular, the formation of the specialised agencies of the United Nations Organisation, in setting up the Colombo Plan which would provide aid and assistance within the British Commonwealth, and during the armistice negotiations after the Korean war. This 'special relationship' was soon to spread to the nuclear arena as well but, as we will show, it would also end there.[52]

By the mid-1950s, driven by the challenge from Saha, Bhabha's requests for technical assistance and collaboration had a more precise focus. He needed British help to build a nuclear reactor as soon as possible to counter his domestic opposition and to fulfil the atomic energy commission's stated objectives. Bhabha and Bhatnagar had a series of meetings with British officials through the spring and summer of 1954 requesting help for building a reactor and converting uranium ores into metal for fabrication. In June 1954, Bhabha asked Cockcroft to supply him with five tons of heavy water. The British demurred, noting that their heavy water stock was fully committed to their own needs, and suggested that Bhabha approach instead another former Cambridge colleague, W. Bennett Lewis, now vice-president of Atomic Energy of Canada Limited (AECL).[53]

Later that year Cockcroft wrote to Bhabha offering him a practical solution to his problem. In his letter, dated 23 September 1954, he asked, 'Have you considered the possibility of building a research reactor of the "swimming pool" type? These have been described fairly exhaustively in *Nucleonics* and other publications. They require, of course, enriched uranium but it is possible that this could be made available to you from the UK.'[54] Bhabha jumped at this possibility. He replied at once: 'We would gladly consider this possibility…. I would like to know how much enriched uranium it would be possible to make available, and the terms and conditions including time schedules under which it could be made available. The time element is very important, since we would like to undertake such a reactor if it could be set up in a very short time, so we have something to work with while our other plans mature.'[55] The details were negotiated over the next few months. Bhabha was able to get not only six kilograms of enriched uranium fuel rods from the UK, but also detailed engineering drawings and other technical data. All the British got in return was a promise that the AEC would look very favourably at the purchase of a British reactor in the near future. Bhabha wrote, 'I understand that one might be in a position to discuss seriously an atomic power station for India by the middle of 1956 and if things develop as expected, it might be possible to have such a power station in operation in India by 1962.'[56]

The AEC engineers swung into action and began work on the swimming-pool reactor around the clock. Apart from the excitement at finally being able to begin work on a reactor, they had another reason not to waste time. Homi Bhabha had made a bet with John Cockcroft that the Indian reactor would be ready in one year. Bhabha's optimism led him to write to Cockcroft in December 1955 that he was close to winning. Six months later the two exchanged notes deciding the texts of the official letters of congratulation and reply. The one megawatt (1MW) swimming-pool reactor, later called *Apsara*, finally went 'critical' on 4 August 1956, after a number of slowdowns and difficulties in the final stages. Bhabha had lost the bet by a few days and offered to take Cockcroft out to dinner in Paris, unless he preferred it 'paid in London'.[57]

Notwithstanding the lost bet, the AEC had now built a working atomic reactor. It was, as one Indian scientist put it, their 'first taste of success', and the atomic scientists were jubilant. Finally, in their own eyes, they were a 'force to reckon with'. The first person to know of their accomplishment was the Prime Minister; even at this moment of scientific achievement the AEC could not but see this event in political terms. They could now be sure that domestic critics (Saha was no longer alive) would have to cease their carping about the state of progress in the Indian atomic energy programme. The predominantly political interpretation of this event continued as news of the reactor's criticality became public. This was, it was repeatedly pointed out, 'the first atomic reactor to go critical in Asia (other than the Soviet Union)'.[58] Clearly the message was India had stolen a march over China, the only other Asian country that was remotely in a position to develop a nuclear programme. Finally, it is impossible not to note how, all through the representation of this event, the reactor is presented as a purely indigenous affair. Even though it was admitted that the fuel rods, and essential 'electronic valves [and] some associated components' – a lot less than plans, drawings, and the all-important fuel rods – had been imported, these details were lost in the shuffle of national pride. *Apsara* was represented in the domestic media as an Indian reactor built with local ingenuity and expertise.[59] The first hurdle had been crossed, but, given the way it had come about, the AEC was not much closer to developing indigenous capacity for building a nuclear power reactor.

OTHER INTERNATIONAL SUPPLIERS

Having resolved their initial need to build an atomic reactor in order to assuage domestic concerns did not mean that the AEC's task was over. The *Apsara* reactor was a small research reactor, which would be useful for conducting minor scientific experiments and for gaining expertise in reactor maintenance, but it was a long away from providing the base on which a nuclear power industry could be based. For that the AEC would need to build, or obtain, a nuclear power reactor, a system many times larger than a research reactor and far more complex to maintain and run efficiently. At this point, the Indian atomic community did not have the experience or expertise to produce such a reactor indigenously, but, owing to a particular conjunction of international events, it would turn out that they would not need to.

The Atoms for Peace programme, announced in the United Nations by US President Dwight D. Eisenhower in 1953, rested on a premise that sought to control atomic weapons proliferation simultaneously with the development of an international civilian nuclear power industry. The change in US policy represented by this announcement had come to pass with the belated realisation that the short-lived American monopoly in atomic energy was irretrievably lost. The next best alternative, from the US point of view, was to control access to atomic energy among those nations that had not yet taken steps toward building nuclear programmes. Exports of atomic energy would constitute a source of continuing influence in those countries and, if of US origin, also improve the US balance of trade. In other words, even as the bulk of US efforts in the nuclear field continued to be directed towards the military uses of nuclear power at home and abroad, there was now, as indicated by the title of the new programme, an emphasis on the peaceful potential of atomic power – the other, supposedly benign face of this object.

These sentiments are well captured in memos written in 1954 by US Assistant Secretary of Defense Robert LeBaron to Admiral Richard Strauss of the US AEC and President Eisenhower:

> We are engaged in a life and death struggle against the communist movement in which our principal hope lies in the early exploitation of peacetime [nuclear] power ... This remarkable outpouring of new scientific accomplishment [by US scientists] within the last five years has been substantially equalled by the Russians, ... and will, in my opinion, presently be equalled by similar accomplishment in the laboratories of British scientists ... *The deterioration of our military*

posture can only be overcome by recognizing the appreciation of our peacetime prosperity which is inherent in the utilization of these newly discovered atomic phenomena for peace. The real risk in the world today is not in the health hazards from reactors out of control but in fear in people's minds of the horrors of atomic war.[60]

One of the most important outcomes of this new attitude towards atomic energy was the suggestion to hold an international conference on its peaceful uses. This seemed a suitable way of vividly and publicly demonstrating that one of the promises associated with this substance might soon bear fruit. Even though atomic energy had so far been associated only with destruction, this conference was meant to represent one of the first steps towards convincing the international community that atomic energy also had the potential to transform the human condition in positive ways. But it is important not to make too much of the rhetoric of that moment. Even as the international community made these tentative steps toward ameliorating the destructive potential of atomic energy in favour of its peaceful uses, existing and potential nuclear-capable countries were engaged in negotiations towards the creation of the International Atomic Energy Agency, the institutional centre of an international regime to control nuclear materials, thereby implicitly legitimising nuclear weapons as instruments of foreign policy.[61]

In order to make clear that parochial interests did not drive this international conference, it was proposed that it be held under the auspices of the United Nations Organisation. This suggestion was eagerly accepted by Dag Hammarskjöld, UN Secretary General, who promptly constituted an international Scientific Advisory Committee (SAC) to organise the event. The SAC was composed of scientists drawn from Brazil, Canada, France, India, the Soviet Union, the United Kingdom and the United States. While it might have been hoped, initially, that this conference would lead to new patterns of international association, the meetings of the Scientific Advisory Committee reflected perfectly the relative power quotients within the prevailing international order.[62] The terms of the Cold War entered the discussion from the outset, with careful and elaborate balances being struck at every turn to ensure that none of the arrangements smacked of any alteration in the global status quo.[63] To take just one typical example, 'Red' China could not be invited to the conference, in spite of having a nuclear physics community, as it was not a member of the United Nations at the time; further, its inclusion would undermine Taiwan's control of the Chinese seat in the UN, as well as attract more attention to the achievements of the Communist bloc than was desired by the US and its NATO allies.[64]

Cold War obsessions took other forms as well. While the Soviet Union had been invited to the conference and had a representative on the advisory committee, they saw the conference as primarily a Western initiative. In order to keep face and hew to the official line that the USSR was a genuine force for world peace, the Soviet Union could not boycott the meeting. They had to act in some way, but without undermining the UN conference directly. Thus, with the official excuse that they wanted to ensure that all the Soviet contributions to the atomic energy field be made public – something that would not be possible under the restrictive conditions of the United Nations conference – the USSR Academy of Science held its own international atomic energy conference in Moscow just before the UN conference, in the first week of July 1955.[65] An Indian attendee reported dryly that 'countries receiving the Marshall aid were conspicuous by their absence'.[66]

Everything to do with the UN conference had to be discussed and approved with geopolitical considerations in mind, hence the Western delegations took steps well before the first SAC meetings to hammer out a joint front, especially on symbolic issues. Even before the announcement of United Nations sponsorship of the conference, I.I. Rabi, a Columbia University physicist and Nobel laureate, who would represent the United States on the SAC, visited various British, Canadian, and French scientists. Their wide-ranging discussions tried to decide not only which international agency should sponsor the conference and where and when it should be held, but also which countries should be included on the advisory committee.[67] Not all issues could be decided in advance, and eventually a small group of US, British, French and Canadian diplomats meeting at the United Nations finalised the organisational details of the conference. It was agreed to hold the conference in Geneva, rather than Rome, Brussels, Cambridge, New York, or Montreal, for the usual reason: neutral Switzerland was the place least likely to provoke objections from other countries.

An issue of considerable symbolic importance was the choice of conference president. The United States initially wanted a Swiss national to be the president, but it was eventually agreed that it would be in the best spirit of the conference (or, more accurately, since all the other delegates were unacceptable to someone) that an avowedly non-partisan figure be appointed president. The least politically objectionable possibility turned out to be the Indian delegate to the advisory committee, Homi Bhabha, who had the strong backing of the British delegation.[68] This carefully crafted outcome was of course not the interpretation that emerged in India, where news of Bhabha's appointment was greeted with great jubilation. If there had ever been any doubts about the quality of the Indian AEC, this announcement put them to rest. Clearly Indian scientists, or at least some of them, were in the first rank internationally, as proven by the choice of Bhabha to be the nominal leader of this prestigious international conference.

Notwithstanding these inauspicious beginnings, the conference proved to be a grand success. It soon became clear to the scientists gathered in Geneva (and their political leaders) that in spite of the distinct national styles of development, basic research was proceeding along very similar lines and had reached approximately the same point in a number of different countries. In other words, the weight of official secrecy that had been placed on the field of atomic energy research by various states had neither the desired effect of acquiring results that no one else had, nor the absolute superiority of one country over all others. The once cosmopolitan scientific community, which had been 'nationalised' since the Second World War, was back in effect by default, finding that they had duplicated plans and projects across national boundaries without re-alising it. What also became clear from the many presentations was that no country had made much progress toward the active utilisation of atomic energy for civilian energy production.

In an event quite unforeseen by the planners of atomic energy and development in India, Canada used the occasion of the UN conference to enter the field of international atomic exchange. The Canadians had, like the British, suffered the privations of close alignment with US strategic desires in the past, and sought to make their difference with the United States more apparent. 'The Canadians were not only embarking on a project, they were fulfilling a vision of Canada's place in the new world order.'[69] Some months before the conference, the Canadians de-cided that the most appropriate gesture to make this international event meaningful beyond rhetoric and scientific exchange – and to ensure that their initial foray into this arena would have a high chance of success – would be to offer India one of their NRX research reactors. Not only did Canada and India have a 'special relationship', but India was the developing country most advanced in atomic energy capabilities at the time. The Canadian foreign ministry felt the publicity attendant with making this gesture at the Geneva conference would also help to create an international market for atomic energy, a market which Canada would then be well positioned to exploit.

The idea of giving India a reactor seems to have originated either with Nik Cavell, the Canadian administrator of the Colombo Plan, or W. J. Bennett, head of Atomic Energy of Canada Limited (AECL), the state corporation in charge of atomic energy production.[70] Whatever its origins, the idea of offering India assistance for its atomic energy pro-gramme soon found allies across the agencies of the Canadian govern-ment. Not only would this gesture give Canada a chance to show off its hard won atomic technology abroad and thereby set the stage for further possible commercial ventures in this field, it would also formalise the difference between US and Canadian approaches to both atomic energy and North–South relations.[71]

Whether in the Canadian atomic energy establishment or in the External Affairs Ministry, hardly a dissenting voice spoke up. In fact, the intensity with which the idea caught on soon transmuted into enormous leverage attributed to the recipient. When Jules Leger, under-secretary of the Canadian foreign ministry, raised the question of what would happen to the plutonium produced by the reactor, he swiftly added that, 'this [problem] presumably could be surmounted especially if we assume that one way or another a country like India will acquire a reactor from some source (friendly or otherwise) and will be producing this material'.[72] The existence of 'other sources (friendly or otherwise)' which might help India would prove an important spur to Canadian decision makers. When the Canadian team of Stoner and Cavell visited Delhi early in 1955, they found to their horror that not only were United States embassy personnel discussing nuclear co-operation with India but that the Soviet Union might be doing the same.[73]

In the third week of March 1955, a series of high-level meetings were held in Ottawa bringing together the atomic energy establishment and senior bureaucrats from the ministries of Finance, Trade and Commerce, and External Affairs to discuss and formalise the Canadian offer to India. Their deliberations were brief and cabinet approval came just as quickly. By the end of March 1955, the Canadians were ready to go. On 5 April, W.B. Lewis, vice-president of Atomic Energy Canada Limited, wrote to Bhabha informally letting him know of Canadian interest in helping the Indian atomic energy programme. The choice of Lewis as official correspondent was calculated. Not only had he been at Cambridge University's Gonville and Caius College in the 1930s, as had Bhabha, but both had studied physics, become members of the select discussion group, the Kapitza Club, and eventually would serve together as members of the UN's Scientific Advisory Committee on atomic energy. An informal approach from a close scientific colleague was to take any impression of seamy politics out of the offer.

The Indians received the Canadian suggestion with caution, in marked contrast to the enthusiasm that underlay the Canadian gesture. Their first response was to ask whether accepting this offer meant that Canadian aid for development would be reduced proportionately. Their second response was equally cautious. Bhabha's reply to Lewis suggested that he was more interested in a British reactor of 'more advanced design' than the Canadian NRX.[74] For the next few months, the Canadians waited to hear the official Indian response. In June, Bhabha reported that he still preferred a British reactor but was also considering a US-built swimming-pool reactor.[75] In desperation, and seeing the deal slipping away from them, the Canadians agreed to supply extra funds for the reactor under the framework of the Colombo Plan, thereby ensuring that India would not be deprived of its normal quota of development aid. In July, Bhabha passed a message on through Nehru that he would rather have the more advanced NRU reactor, but the Canadians rejected this option out of hand. Finally, Lewis managed to convince Bhabha at the UN conference that the present Canadian offer was the best under the circumstances, and that the 40MW NRX was quite suitable for India's purposes. India eventually signed an agreement with Canada to build the eponymous Canada-India reactor in September 1955. Success again at little cost, but a 40MW research reactor, while better than a 1MW research reactor, is not a power reactor.

POWER REACTORS AND NATIONAL DEVELOPMENT

The AEC now turned to the task of obtaining a nuclear power reactor. Before examining their options more closely, it is useful to take a brief detour through an atomic reactor.[76] There are two ways of producing energy from atoms, through fission (energy from splitting atoms apart) and fusion (energy from forcing atoms to combine). Commercial technology to produce fusion reactors does not yet exist. With respect to uranium-fuelled fission reactors, a number of choices must be made. The fuel can be either 'natural' or 'enriched'. Enriched uranium differs from natural uranium by the number of fissile (U-233 or U-235) atoms per unit. By 'enriching' – increasing the fissile complement of natural uranium – nuclear (fission) reactions are made more likely. Both the Soviet Union and the United States use 'enriched' uranium reactors for electricity production, while the French and the Canadians use natural uranium. The technology necessary to enrich uranium was and is extremely expensive.[77]

Other choices to be made include the kind of moderator and the coolant. The moderator, which helps to increase the chance of fissile reactions within the fuel 'core' of a reactor, is a substance that needs to be able to slow down mobile neutrons sufficiently for them to be absorbed by the uranium fuel core. For this reason, it is important that the moderator not absorb too many neutrons itself. Moderators in common use include heavy water (French, Canadian), graphite (British), and light water (US and USSR). Cooling systems – their function self-evident – include gases like carbon dioxide and (heavy or light) water.

By the mid-1950s, India had discovered quantities of uranium sufficient to power a number of natural uranium reactors. Apart from the fact that the technology for and the expense of enriching uranium was beyond Indian means at this time, there were other reasons to choose a natural uranium reactor system. While the AEC had discovered some uranium, its most extensive atomic fuel resource was thorium. This suggested that any self-sustaining long-term strategy had to be thorium based. But thorium cannot be used directly as a fuel. It can, however, be combined with plutonium in a special reactor to produce electricity and U-233 (a fissile material). Thus the first step to utilising thorium is to produce sufficient quantities of plutonium. Plutonium, which is produced in a reactor as an end-product of fuel burnup (regardless of whether the fuel is enriched or natural uranium), can be used to 'blanket' thorium in a second-stage reactor, allowing it to become fertile, and thus to produce the highly fissile isotope of uranium, U-233. The U-233 produced in this way can be used as fuel in a third stage 'breeder' reactor. The planned culmination of the Indian strategy was a family of breeder reactors fuelled by U-233 which, because of the physics of these elements in the core, would produce as much new fuel as was being used up. Hence, for a self-sustaining long-term atomic programme to be feasible, the AEC needed to ensure that it had access to the plutonium that was produced in their first-stage reactor: they needed an 'unsafeguarded' reactor.[78]

Plutonium is best known for reasons that have little to do with converting thorium to uranium 233. It is the primary fissile material used in the first generation of military nuclear weapons, so-called 'atom bombs' of the kind exploded over Nagasaki. As a result, control over plutonium became (and continues to be) a key node in the attempt to control the spread of nuclear weapons material worldwide. Monitors over the plutonium produced in the normal course of reactor functioning is one of the elements of 'safeguarding' nuclear facilities. For the Indian strategy to work, they would need unimpeded access to plutonium, that is, they would need to obtain an unsafeguarded reactor, but not for the usual reasons. They needed this plutonium to make their breeder strategy work. Finally, we should also note that at the time of embarking upon this strategy, the technology for breeder reactors did not exist. The Indian AEC's long-term strategy was based on scientific principles – the physics and chemistry of atoms and its knowledge of the domestic resource base – not on the knowledge of existing technology.[79]

By the end of the 1950s, reflecting the altered international context and in some contrast to their attitude a decade before, the US atomic energy establishment was now keen to get involved in India. Pro-India groups within the State Department in particular had long been encouraging other branches of government to develop a closer relationship with India, but had not made much headway. Until 1959, the most significant bilateral interaction between the US and Indian atomic energy commissions had been the sale to India of 21 tons of heavy water for use in the Canada–India NRX reactor. When, in late 1959, Bhabha first approached the US atomic energy commission with his proposal to set up nuclear power plants of 250MW capacity in India, there was considerable enthusiasm for this plan, yet it was tempered with caution. The question of costs and finances were at the forefront of US concerns: there was doubt regarding the basic Indian assertion that nuclear power was competitive with conventional power at selected locations. Early US estimates, which were included in the joint India–US memorandum following Bhabha's visit, stated clearly that capital set-up costs for nuclear plants were US$335 per kilowatt compared to US$180 per kilowatt for conventional power plants. In other words, nuclear power would cost nearly twice as much as conventional power. This sobering statistic was moderated by an optimistic but unconvincing and unsupported assessment assuring readers that 'estimated unit power costs from nuclear plants … are expected to be almost equal and ultimately less than those from conventional plants'.[80]

The US AEC's considerable interest in developing ties with India can be seen from an internal report produced after a visit to India in early 1960.[81] The report is quite comprehensive about the state of Indian expertise, infrastructure, and capabilities related to atomic energy. A number of cautions are expressed repeatedly throughout the report, for instance the high capital costs of reactor construction, the need for large amounts of foreign exchange, the limited degree of sub-contracting that would be possible, the need to import most of the heavy equipment, the lack of qualified middle managers, and so on. Given these serious handicaps, the report's summary ends on an unlikely positive note: 'the momentum which has been created through the recent exchanges with India make it particularly desirable to proceed promptly with the development of such arrangements'.[82] We are being told that decisions would not be made on the basis of a technical, cost-benefit analysis, but that political considerations were to dominate.

In case the message was not clear, and in a remarkable parallel with the Canadian decision to make further concessions to India a few years earlier, the report also states that Indian plans to develop nuclear power would continue regardless of US assistance. The US was being offered an opportunity to get into the act early; if it didn't somebody else would.

This was not an idle threat. A global tender for applications to build India's first large power reactor was submitted in 1960. The front runner was the Canadian CANDU reactor: a heavy-water natural uranium reactor that fitted India's strategy and resource profile closely. Other contenders were the British and French gas-cooled graphite-moderated natural uranium reactors which also fitted the overall criteria of the global tender. But at the last minute, an American light-water enriched uranium reactor was also included, after 'representatives of General Electric Company and Westinghouse met [AEC scientists] and explained to [them] that their reactor systems using enriched uranium were much more economic to build and operate'.[83] In the end the AEC contracted with both the Canadians and the US to build atomic reactors. An agreement was signed with the US to build twin 200MW enriched uranium reactors at Tarapur near Bombay, and with the Canadians to build similarly sized natural uranium reactors in Rajasthan. A few months later India received an US$80-million loan from the United States for the construction of the Tarapur reactors.[84]

Negotiating with the Canadians for one of their natural-uranium-fuelled heavy-water-moderated reactors is easy to understand. Its profile fitted the Indian resource base and was consistent with its long-term strategy. But Bhabha's focus on the United States during these many visits is particularly puzzling. It seems to make a mockery of the focus on self-reliance that was a central tenet of the Indian atomic energy effort. Of all the countries engaged in the atomic energy business, the US was the most concerned with proprietary norms and commercial returns, and the least likely to think that they should share information about nuclear technology with anyone else. This attitude was partly a reflex of the national security mindset that defined so much of US international activities during these years, but it was also a structural constraint: unlike the nationalised programmes everywhere else in the world, which controlled all aspects of atomic power, the US state atomic establishment was not in the business of building reactors. Private corporations, multinationals like General Electric and Westinghouse, were responsible for the production of commercial atomic energy and were unlikely to agree to share this privileged information with a client. Further, and most important, the US atomic industry used enriched uranium in their reactors, a condition that was incompatible with the AEC's long-term strategy of relying on domestic resources and technology. Producing enriched uranium was extremely expensive and involved sophisticated technologies, so much so that Bhabha had earlier stated categorically that India had no intention of constructing a plant to enrich uranium.[85]

Contracting with the US to build an enriched uranium reactor in India implied a permanent relationship with the United States, the only ones who could supply fuel for the reactor. To make matters worse, this fuel would have to be paid for in foreign exchange. This may not have been outright dependence, but it certainly fell far short of any kind of independence, and, as hindsight shows, the question of fuel supply would be subject to all the vicissitudes of the bilateral relationship between the two countries.[86] Further, the US would undoubtedly insist on intrusive safeguards for the materials used, the end-products (other than electricity), and probably the reactor equipment as well.[87] But a safeguarded US reactor would deny Indian scientists access to the plutonium they needed for their long-term self-reliance strategy to work.[88]

The Indian AEC was well aware of US sentiments on safeguards as this issue had been at the heart of Indian opposition to the US position in the negotiations on the creation of the International Atomic Energy Agency (IAEA) a few years earlier.[89] The Indian position at the multi-lateral negotiations leading up to the formation of the IAEA had always been to preclude the use of intrusive safeguards by insisting on a hard definition of sovereignty; in bilateral negotiations with the US, however, this position would be more difficult to sustain.

What this implies is that while the Indian atomic effort had been rhetorically marked from its inception as the epitome of the country's efforts at self-reliance, the meaning of that concept had been steadily diluted over the years. The only Indian demonstrations of expertise in atomic energy had depended upon assistance from other countries, notably the UK (fuel rods, designs, etc. for the swimming-pool reactor) and Canada (the NRX reactor). However, it could still be claimed (and was) that notwithstanding this assistance, these were pragmatic steps toward 'full' self-sufficiency, and would only help put the Indian effort on a more solid footing in the long run. Unlike the CANDU power reactors that would be built with Canadian assistance, however, a US light-water reactor could never be seen in this light. Not only was their design philosophy quite distinct from all Indian efforts up to this point, but it was a turnkey project. Indian engineers would learn little about how these reactors were built. Contracting for a US reactor would create a situation of dependence at least into the medium term and would increase foreign exchange outlays for fuel purchases. Finally, there was no guarantee that the plutonium that India needed for its long-term self-reliance strategy to succeed would be made available. The only way to understand this anomaly is to resort to the words of one of the atomic scientists: 'This [decision] was mainly to demonstrate to the Indian people that electricity could be generated from the atom economically.'[90] Was the Indian atomic energy programme now to be reduced only to a demonstration?

While the atomic complex was insulated from civil society through the provisions of the 1948 Atomic Energy Act and buffered from criticism from the excluded scientific community, it could not remain isolated in the context of the huge economic changes under way in the country. Atomic energy had always been presented as a vital technology in the country's economic development and now that it seemed to have come into its own (after the inauguration of the swimming-pool reactor, and the start of work on the NRX), it needed to be inserted formally into the country's economic development infrastructure, both conceptually and materially. This insertion would fulfil the original expectations of this resource, but was also vital for the atomic complex for one simple reason: to continue to sustain its expansion and to enter the next stage of growth, financing for its proposed chain of energy reactors would have to be drawn not from state science and technology budgets as before, but from national development funds.

In the late 1950s, the AEC had requested that a capacity of 1000MW of atomic energy be installed during the Third Five-Year Plan (1960/61– 1965/66). While the AEC did not expect to be able to produce anywhere near as much as 1000MW during this period, getting this proposition accepted by the Planning Commission was tantamount to an agreement that atomic power was a permanent response to Indian energy needs. The atomic scientists were well aware that atomic power stations take a long time – often a decade – to set up and get running. They seemed to be arguing that if they waited for domestic capabilities to reach the point when a purely Indian power reactor was possible – the self-reliance solution – at least ten years would have passed and the lustre of atomic power faded considerably.[91] The AEC had to act at once to get Planning Commission approval to set up plants which, once begun, would have to be completed. The cynical logic was that once the huge capital investments had been made, atomic energy would become a self-fulfilling reality.

As it turned out, the Planning Commission, in consultation with the Central Water and Power Commission, demurred from the scale of the AEC proposal; the planned contribution of atomic energy to national electrical capacity was reduced to 675MW. To reach even this amount of installed capacity would imply building at least four reactors over a five-year period. The AEC, it should be remembered, had not yet contributed anything to the country's electrical supply, and there was no domestic experience in operating a power reactor. The only means by which this grandiose plan would come anywhere near completion would be through massive aid and expertise from abroad.[92] But, in order to minimise domestic opposition to these plans, this specialised foreign assistance could not be seen to 'crowd out' funds already promised to India for its overall development. In order to prevent a Planning Commission veto of their plans on the basis of the high opportunity cost of atomic power stations, foreign assistance for atomic energy had to be given to India over and above the aid already promised in multilateral donor meetings.

Thus we find Bhabha repeatedly expressing two concerns at meetings with US agencies while discussing the purchase of an enriched uranium reactor. These concerns had nothing to do with atomic energy or science but were related to India's development programme. Bhabha's first concern, expressed in meetings with the US atomic energy commission in 1959, was that he be able to return to India with a statement indicating 'a favorable expression of interest' from the United States for building atomic power plants in India. The intended recipient of this endorsement was the Planning Commission, then in the process of finalising the country's Third Five-Year Plan. His other concern was that the funding for these reactors be drawn from new sources, in order not to reduce financial assistance already promised to India as development aid.[93]

It is in this context that we turn to two important institutional developments of the late 1950s and early 1960s. In 1958, the government issued a new constitution for the AEC which, among other things, reaffirmed the centrality of the chairman, who now had the 'power to overrule the other members of the Commission' (except the member for finance), expanded the commission's potential membership to seven and made the director of the atomic energy establishment in Trombay an *ex officio* member of the commission. These changes, according to the resolution, were driven by 'the newness of the field, the strategic nature of its activities, and its international and political significance'.[94] The expansion of the commission is surprising. A measure of AEC power had always been their ability to contain decision-making power to a very small number of people, all of whom were scientists. Now, even as the AEC centralised power further in the hands of the chairman, it was also opening itself up to elements of the state apparatus. Over the years new AEC members would be drawn from the upper echelons of the state bureaucracy, especially the prime minister's office. This was not a move that would in any way reduce the power of the institution, but it would bring a political voice directly into AEC deliberations. The interests of the AEC and the regime were beginning to meld.

A few years later (1962) the government introduced into Parliament a new Bill for atomic energy replacing the Act of 1948. Existing tendencies toward, on the one hand, the centralisation of power and, on the other, the proximity of the government and the AEC, first seen in the 1958 constitution, continued. The new Act expanded the powers of the state over atomic energy matters to an unprecedented extent, including overriding the provisions of any other law in the country (Clause 28) that might interfere with atomic energy; it expanded the scope of the state's potential appropriation of land, materials, and inventions relating to atomic energy; finally, the Act reduced the possibility of intervention by authorities like the Solicitor General in defining offences under the Bill even as it criminalised those offences further.[95] The draconian character of this Act seems difficult to understand. Just at the moment when the atomic energy complex was about to pass from its initial stage of growth and become fully integrated with the national development project, it sought to shield itself further from civil and political society through a series of rulings and legislation. The character of these laws seemed more suited to an organisation that had motives more sinister than merely providing electricity for development – even if the electricity would be more expensive than initially stated.

Was the Indian atomic energy effort so behind its planned schedule that such drastic measures were called for? In hindsight, it is possible to say that it was not. Much of the atomic energy complex was already in place or being built. The atomic scientists had fabricated a more or less domestically designed (if foreign fuelled) swimming-pool research reactor, 'the first in Asia'; sufficient quantities of uranium to power a small atomic power complex had been discovered, a uranium mill and metal plant built; separate plutonium and fuel element processing plants were being set up; the project to construct the CIRUS 40MW research reactor was well under way (the reactor would go critical in 1960); a steady stream of trainee scientists were graduating from the AEE's Trombay school; not only was a Scientific Policy Resolution proclaimed in the parliament in 1958, it was to Bhabha that Nehru turned to help write it. There is little reason to believe that the status of the atomic scientists was anything but high. It is difficult to conjure up reasonable domestic social and political pressures to explain the imposition of these legal shutters; it is in this context that we return to the discourse of urgency.

A CONCLUSION AND AN INTERPRETATION

Let us return to the scene of the Geneva UN conference on the peaceful uses of atomic energy in 1955. Conference president Homi Bhabha gave a memorable address on the first day of the conference, vitiating to some extent the knowledge that the Indian delegation had only seven papers to present to their international colleagues. Fully aware of the historic nature of the event and brimming with the confidence of his renewed international visibility, Bhabha gave a speech that was memorable for its lofty tone as well as for its visionary content. Apart from the unremitting optimism about the future repeatedly expressed, Bhabha's locution also bespoke a voice that came from a very different location.

While it was not the first time that anyone had spoken 'for' the entire world – after all, that orientation was implicit in every statement made by the leaders of the Soviet Union and the United States in their endless Cold War diatribes – his was a voice that evoked the universal in a distinctly new way. By adopting a politically non-parochial voice, a voice that was relatively unheard in the deeply divided international society of the time, Bhabha was able to make the political divisions that structured the prevailing international order appear petty and shallow. This move was vital to disturb the prevailing association of atomic energy with violence and international conflict and to overcome the implicit oxy-moron of a conference on 'peaceful uses' of atomic energy.

By explicitly adopting the persona of the ideal, apolitical scientist, Bhabha was able to situate himself as an observer not invested in the passions of this world, yet aligned within a Western tradition that the audience could not but identify with. This Archimidean stance allowed him, on the one hand, to claim that his discourse was beyond petty bloc interests, driven only by the logic of an endlessly progressing knowledge: the voice of the laboratory scientist who was only reporting what was. On the other hand, by employing a meta-historical argument, he was also able to represent all humanity within a single trajectory of progress that exposed the historicity of the present moment, and thus again made political boundaries meaningless. Bhabha's speech rejected, and thus made it possible to think beyond, the divisions that had structured the confer-ence itself; in so doing he articulated a claim that was both familiar and different, the voice of a scientist trained in the practices of the West, but also the voice of a world historian not beholden to Western events. It was a postcolonial voice and powerful in the difference it made audible.

Bhabha began his speech by noting that human history could be divided into three broad epochs: the river valley civilisations of the Middle East and South Asia, the industrial revolution of the seventeenth and eighteenth centuries, and the present atomic age. These epochs were distinguished by the character of their energy sources, a suggestion similar to the Marxian division of human history. In the earliest civilisations, Bhabha argued, all productive work was based on the use of the crudest form of energy, namely, muscle power, whether human or animal. Clearly not much could be done in these systems: 'it is important to note the severe limitations that this restricted supply of energy puts on the development of civilisation', he noted, and therefore it was not surprising that 'high levels of comfort and culture could only be enjoyed by a small minority of the population'.[96]

The next stage of human development occurred, according to Bhabha, in the seventeenth and eighteenth centuries when, as a result of 'scientific and technological developments', life was transformed by 'the increasing use of chemical energy, namely the use of fossil fuels like oil and coal'. No mention was made of *where* these developments had occurred, but this result was to lead to the 'industrialised pattern of society and civilisation'.[97] Bhabha's elision of location in his discussion of this stage effectively denied the West the authority typically attributed to it of ushering in the modern era. Bhabha's silence here stands in contrast with his specific attribution of the first stage of human history to the civilisations of Egypt, Mesopotamia, and India, and prefigured the discussion of the next stage, which adopted an explicitly global position, beyond national or regional location. He did not want to allow for the possibility of seeing these practices as anything but universal phenomena that could have emerged from anywhere. As a result, his speech consciously denied Western authority as the font of modern science and technology.

The next stage of human history was the present one: 'the acquisition by Man [sic] of the knowledge of how to release and use atomic energy must be recognised as the third great epoch of human history'.[98] But this third stage, which was just coming about, stood in uneasy relation to its predecessor. Unlike the transition from the first to the second stage, where the latter seemed to displace the former seamlessly, the second stage had not gone away. Oil, coal, gas, and hydropower, the primary sources of energy in the second stage, were still in use at the time when atomic energy appeared.

Why was it then historically necessary to move to the third stage? In order to explain this, Bhabha shifted from a discussion of the inevitability of technological progress to a different mode of argument: a mode made familiar some decades later by demographers and the reports of the Club of Rome. He pointed out that as chemical sources of energy came into widespread use the rate of use of these resources would go up enormously. He compared statistics of total energy use in the world ('since Christ' and since 1850) to make the point that as levels of economic development rose, the use of energy rose in parallel fashion. In other words, the degree of human 'civilisation' achieved and the rate of energy use were directly and causally linked.

But at the same time as this happened, he went on to say, the rate of population growth expanded enormously as well. From 1 CE, when there were a few hundred million people on the earth, 1,500 million people were alive by 1900, and 'experts' projected the world's population at century's end at between 3,500 and 5,000 million. To maintain these new individuals at the standard of living implied by industrial society would take an even greater proportion of energy than has been used thus far. And this was the problem. The energy sources that contemporary industrial civilisation depended on were finite: 'It is estimated that the known reserves of a number of metals used in industry will not last more than a few decades at their present rate of consumption.'[99]

This was the neo-Malthusian predicament presented by Bhabha: 'the absolute necessity of finding some new source of energy, if the light of our civilisation is not be extinguished, because we have burnt out our fuel reserves'. Faced with this grim scenario, however, there was no need to despair. 'It is in this context that we turn to atomic energy for a solution.'[100] According to this vision, the third stage of human history was not going to occur naturally but was a solution to an internal contradiction that had no other resolution. The stakes, as Bhabha pointed out, were enormous.

This was a message addressed to political leaders by an 'objective scientist'. In the same breath as he explained the energy problem as an immanent contradiction, Bhabha pointed out that, 'it is in this context that we turn to atomic energy for a solution'. After his explanation of the issue and the 'scientific' presentation of the problem, political leaders would to be left with no choice but to agree with Bhabha's solution. The third stage of development would not come about inevitably, as in the movement between stages one and two, but rather because there was no other available choice for rational man. Bhabha's speech did not avoid the association of atomic power with war completely but made it clear that for the third stage to emerge, international society would have to be constituted such that 'the major states have agreed to maintain peace'. This is because after the advent of an international nuclear power industry, fissile materials would be in the hands of so many nations. In order to prevent these materials from becoming a destabilising factor, world peace had to be ensured before the fact.[101]

There is a final statement embedded in the speech which prefigures a new order and is addressed to the world community of scientists. Bhabha pointed out that atomic energy had been made available to the people of the world through the efforts of 'scientists of many nations working in full and free collaboration'. The collaboration of a select class of people who stood above history and politics had been gravely hindered by the Second World War. The appeal to politicians to turn to atomic energy was also a call to let the scientists free. In this writing of history which explicitly draws on but rejects the logic of Marxism, Bhabha creates a new revolutionary subject, one that is not restrained by national boundaries or material relations of production. He addressed the scientists directly to remind them of their historic role: 'Those who have the good fortune to participate in this conference are privileged to be in the vanguard of the march of history.'[102]

But for the Indian AEC and its small coterie of atomic scientists, this presentation of the problem facing them was not comforting. By locating their national enterprise in world time and space, Bhabha's speech worked to produce an even more daunting enterprise than they had hitherto imagined. Already they felt themselves to be inadequate to the task before them; now they were being told that the 'light of civilisation' depended on them! And there was no time to waste. The pressure of population that was identified as the greatest constraint on the long-term development of human progress was nowhere more an issue than in India. The sense of urgency provoked by Bhabha's speech denied the atomic scientists the comfort of locating their enterprise safely within their domestic enclave. They were being told that, whether they liked it or not, they were part of a world-historical process. Through Bhabha's speech, Science – imagined as the agency of Man – was being located in direct confrontation with History – imagined as the agency of Nature – and Science had no choice but to win. The sense of anxiety and urgency produced by this historic confrontation was the most significant the Indian atomic scientists had to bear, both for the universal terms it was stated in, as well as for the audience, which was much larger than their professional colleagues and included the entire political class.

I have shown that the AEC and its state managers engaged in a series of political struggles with various social formations through the early 1960s. Seeking first to dominate the scientific field, then to insulate themselves from political conflict, the AEC shuttled between building nuclear reactors (or contracting to build them) and ensuring the legal means, through centralisation and the new Atomic Energy Act of 1962, to block public discussion of their activities. Their overall practices, I have argued from the outset, cannot be seen simply in economic or scientific terms. The AEC's work was the performance of the postcolonial: a loss of faith in atomic energy would lead to a deepening of the immanent legitimation crisis of the postcolonial state.

A paradox I have tried to point to is that even though public perception of the AEC was generally positive, and their bases of political support quite firm, at their moment of greatest strength, ever increasing degrees of political insulation – secrecy – came to shield the AEC from public scrutiny. Why? The simple answer to this question points to a deep ambivalence about the ability of atomic energy to deliver the ideological, let alone the strictly techno-economic, goods in the time frame expected of them. But to say this is to locate the answer outside the system I have been discussing, without reference to the terms of engagement of the AEC and science, without reference to the social relations of scientists and scientific practice. A more complete answer may be found when we examine the parallel economies of science and technology.

The AEC's efforts in its early years had primarily been to institutionalise scientific practices. The criteria governing these practices were located in the reception of this work in the transnational scientific community. The medium of this work was social: publishing scientific papers, making presentations at international conferences, corresponding with colleagues at home and abroad, sharing students and data. While this community's terms of reference had been developed over time through the deployment of tacit power and enforced social consensus, it was comfortingly circumscribed and closed.[103]

With the need to build nuclear reactors for electricity production, however, the AEC found itself in a different economy of production. The AEC's hard-won ability to produce effective scientific results was irrelevant when its principal objective was producing cheap electrical energy for national development. Under these conditions the atomic scientists' carefully insulated environment would be opened up, their mode of operation examined, and their audiences replaced. Most important, the criteria governing success would, first, be different and, second, no longer be under their control. The scale of what the scientists now had to accomplish had increased enormously. A power reactor would be many times larger than any atomic reactor they had worked with so far. It would be hooked up to an electrical grid which was permanently connected to hundreds of thousands of households and industries. The reactor's performance ratios had to be extremely high in order to service consumers adequately; mistakes or breakdowns in the supply of electricity would be immediately evident. If there were repeated failures, the public would soon realise that atomic energy was not the great panacea it had been given to understand. The criterion governing the activities of the atomic engineers was now something called 'efficiency', and evaluations of performance were made on the relative cost per atomic energy unit produced versus other sources of energy such as coal, oil, or hydropower. It is this last development that most vividly illustrates the enormity of the changes being introduced.

The atomic scientists were being ejected from a milieu where what they did was unique. There were no other laboratories competing with them, there were no other scientists disagreeing with their interpretations, nobody else doing what they did, as long as they worked in an environment protected by the strictures of the Indian Atomic Energy Act. They existed in a world where mechanical reproduction did not yet exist, where it was still possible to tell the difference between art and industry. But once they had left their protected enclave and begun to produce electricity for public consumption, the atomic scientists had to cede control of their private practices to other agents.

The success of the Indian atomic *engineers* now depended on events and non-events they had limited influence over. The first was the design and working conditions of a nuclear reactor conceptualised elsewhere under very different conditions: they had to hope that a foreign reactor would work perfectly and produce cheap electricity as promised. Second, the atomic engineers had to hope that the price of electricity did not drop further, that new reserves of coal would not be discovered, or that improved transmission techniques that reduced the loss of power over long distances were not invented. This would be a very different battle. At the moment when atomic energy would shift from being a demonstration of modernity to becoming integrated with and constituting the Indian modernist project, the viability of the project as originally designed breaks down for structural reasons. The initial conditions of secrecy that had allowed the atomic energy project, epitome of national self-reliance, to adopt a strategy that depended on international barter and goodwill were now, at this later date, inadequate to meet the conditions of domestic public visibility. At the moment when the atomic energy establishment was supposed to unveil its modern artefacts for public consumption (the condition of the fetish), when the peaceful ends of the programme would come into their own, it was realised that the indigeneity of the project would be challenged and the authenticity of its origins brought into question.

Until this moment, a great source of strength for the Indian atomic scientists had been the multiple valences of atomic energy. It had meant a source of cheap electrical energy to developmentalists, a means of overcoming neo-colonial domination to nationalists, a sign of masculinity and intellectual prowess to scientists, a resource for state power to socialists, and an instrument of foreign policy to realists and militarists.[104] The overdetermined meaning of the sign 'atomic energy' was precisely the source of its immense influence in postcolonial India. It was because so many unwitting constituents could find refuge within and through atomic power that it retained its significance. Under the new conditions of production, criteria of technical sufficiency would now become paramount. If in the past the fluidity of the meaning of atomic energy was its strength, decisions of how to produce atomic energy for commercial consumption implied also defining who would use it, or who it would be used for.[105] Hence, this 'technical' decision had immediate political implications, and, by the same token, meant the condensation of multiple symbolic meanings into a narrower and more rigid register accompanied, inevitably, by specific social users. Constituencies who would now be excluded as a result of this decision had to be told either to defer their expectations, or even that their visions for the use of atomic energy would never be fulfilled. In other words, the atomic scientists, via their institutional need to produce atomic energy, unwittingly cut themselves off from existing social alliances. This does not mean that alliances could not be remade or reshaped; that remains to be seen. To reduce the time necessary before old alliances could be remade, or to reassert the wider meaning of atomic energy before it was too late, the atomic scientists found themselves working against a clock of their own fabrication. A different condition of urgency thus emerges as the register of the atomic energy programme just when the atomic scientists appeared to have overcome their slow start and were in the process of fulfilling their historic mission.

The new restrictions regulating atomic energy, the 1958 constitution and the 1962 Atomic Energy Act, have to be read as a means of delaying wider social recognition of the fragility and inauthenticity of this enterprise. But that is not all. The enormous material and symbolic investment the state had made in atomic energy had to be considered. Deferring the recognition of this new position was not enough, atomic energy had now to be resuscitated in another form in order to keep the state's larger project of modernity alive. As we have seen from the constituent assembly debates, another orientation – national defence – had always been latent in the atomic energy project. Now, faced with the long gestation period of power reactors and the breakdown of self-reliance as a condition defining the postcolonial enterprise, there seems to have been little other choice. Building Canadian and US reactors in the hope that they would someday fulfil Indian ambitions of modernity was a tall order. The small likelihood of carrying out the development project combined with potential loss of what was distinctively Indian about the atomic energy programme could only be resolved by recombining the interests of the atomic complex and the state around the foundations of state identity: it meant an alliance with national security.

This functional reason – redefining atomic energy in order to save the postcolonial state – is framed slightly differently when seen from the point of view of the AEC. For the scientists, redefining the atomic energy project meant retaining their identity as scientists, rather than technologists, giving them a new lease of life while they grappled with a new scientific problem. But how would they do this? Their response, as we shall see in the next chapter, was to situate atomic energy within another realm of state activity, equally central to the state's ideological mission, equally justified in terms of *raison d'état*: they decided to build bombs. This option, it should be mentioned, was available to them only because of the peculiar condition of atomic energy, at one and the same time a potentially peaceful technique and a deliberate means of mass destruction. For the atomic energy agency and the state, the destructive ends of atomic energy had always been available as an option, stated explicitly by Nehru as early as 1946.[106] However, it is the conjuncture of state and science, and the internal structure of the modern state form – the immanence of national security – that allows this shift to come about and produce a new, equally postcolonial, atomic energy enterprise devoted to making bombs.

NOTES

1. Unlike in the case of China, the general population was not asked to join the state's search for atomic minerals. See John Lewis and Xue Litai, *China and the Bomb* (Stanford: Stanford University Press, 1988).

2. 'Government must encourage Thorium research', *The Morning Standard* (Bombay), 21 May 1946.

3. H.J. Bhabha, 'Science and the State: Atomic Commission's Work', *Times of India*, 20 March 1952, p. 1. See also front page of the *Statesman* (Delhi) of 21 January 1951 for the first statement of the discovery of 'uranium belts' – 'while the precise location of India's newly found uranium mines remains a well preserved secret, it can be stated that two uranium bearing belts have been discovered'. The location of the uranium belt was no secret to foreign agencies: only the Indian public remained in the dark about it.

4. Raja Ramanna, *Years of Pilgrimage: An Autobiography* (New Delhi: Viking, 1991), p. 61. Emphasis added.

5. Most notable of course was the Baruch Plan. See Barton J. Bernstein, 'The Quest for Security: American foreign policy and international control of atomic energy, 1942–1946', *Journal of American History*, 60 (March 1974).

6. Compare the list of scientific papers published in theoretical physics and mathematics against those published in nuclear physics in *Tata Institute of Fundamental Physics, 1945–1970* (Bombay: TIFR, n.d.).

7. This irony is at the heart of Robert Anderson's wonderful monograph, *Building Scientific Institutions in India: Bhabha and Saha* (Montreal: Center for Developing Area Studies, 1975).

8. See the reference in his obituary notice in *Science and Culture*, vol. 21, no. 9 (1956), p. 483.

9. For instance, in a letter to Nehru urging him to join the Planning Committee, Saha says, 'I am glad that the Congress has accepted our point of view that

in order to tackle some of the problems of poverty, unemployment, and national defence, the country must push ahead with schemes of large-scale industrialization.' dated 7 October 1938. Correspondence, Saha Papers, Nehru Memorial Museum and Library, New Delhi.

10. For Nehru's views on development, and especially how they differed from Gandhi's, see Partha Chatterjee, *Nationalist Thought and the Colonial World: A derivative discourse?* (London: Zed Books, 1987).

11. 'Scientific Research in National Planning', *Science and Culture*, vol. 5, no. 11 (1940), p. 641.

12. See the editorials in *Science and Culture*, especially vol. 5, nos. 9–11 (March–May 1940).

13. Anderson, *Building Scientific Institutions*. For more details from the Bangalore point of view, see G. Venkataraman, *Journey Into Light: Life and Science of C. V. Raman* (Delhi: Penguin, 1994), especially pp. 255–83.

14. Saha served on the CSIR Board for Atomic Energy Research, eventually resigning when he realised that Bhabha was trying as hard as he could to undermine him and keep him excluded from meaningful decision making. See the correspondence in the Saha Papers, NMML.

15. It is important to note that the two scientists were actually not far apart in most of their thinking about the role of science. Saha completely agreed with Bhabha and Nehru that the marriage of state and science was the appropriate means to usher in development in India, but they were engaged in a political battle to see who would be in charge. Politically, Bhabha, scion of wealth and powerful connections, and Saha, unremitting socialist that he was, were much further apart. I thank Sugata Bose for pointing this out to me.

16. For instance, see his letter to Nehru on 11 November 1953. Correspondence, Saha Papers, NMML, New Delhi.

17. Lok Sabha Debates, Sixth Session, vol. 5 (5 May 1954 to 21 May 1954). He was even more explicit in a letter to Nehru where he states that the only possible reason for the AEC's style of functioning and degree of secrecy was to build bombs. 23 May 1953, Correspondence, Saha Papers, NMML, New Delhi.

18. Lok Sabha Debates, Sixth Session, vol. 5.

19. The Indian Atomic Energy Act (1948) was closely patterned on the equivalent British Act.

20. The full text of Saha's speech is published in *Science and Culture*, vol. 20, no. 5 (November 1954), pp. 208–22. Quote from p. 219.

21. The full title of the conference was 'The development of atomic energy for peaceful purposes in India'.

22. Raja Ramanna, *Years of Pilgrimage* (Delhi: Viking, 1991), pp. 61–2.

23. See the discussion of this meeting in Ramanna, *Years of Pilgrimage*, pp. 61–2.

24. Priyadaranjan Ray, 'Development of Atomic Energy in India: An impression', *Science and Culture*, vol. 20, no. 8 (February 1955), pp. 363–4.

25. The challenge was to create an atomic reactor of any kind, not necessarily a power reactor.

26. H.J. Bhabha, 'Science and the State: Atomic Commission's Work', *Times of India*, 20 March 1952.

27. For the original statement see *Nuclear India*, Department of Atomic Energy,

vol. 26, October 1989, pp. 5–6.

28. Atomic Energy Bill, Constituent Assembly of India (Legislative), 16 April 1948, p. 1.

29. For a useful account of the US and UK efforts to monopolize the world's uranium and thorium supplies in the late 1940s and early 1950s, see Jonathan E. Helmreich, *Gathering Rare Ores: The diplomacy of uranium acquisition, 1943–1954* (Princeton: Princeton University Press, 1986).

30. Bhabha to Gordon Dean, Chairman, USAEC, 9 September 1952, Department of State Atomic Energy files (S/AE), US National Archives (NA), Washington, D.C.

31. Bhabha to Gordon Dean, Chairman, USAEC, 9 September 1952, Department of State Atomic Energy files (S/AE), US National Archives (NA), Washington, DC.

32. The British, who also had been offered beryl, expressed doubts whether India had as much beryl as they claimed. Memo dated 18 July 1951, File AB6/398, Public Records Office, UK.

33. Letter from R. Gordon Arneson to Chester Bowles, 8 May 1952, S/AE Files, NA, Washington, DC.

34. Letter from J. Bruce Hamilton to Andrew V. Corry, 14 January 1953, Department of State Atomic Energy files (S/AE), NA, Washington, D.C. See also 'Economic Aid to South Asia – MSP for FY 1953 – Summary of Facts for the Secretary', 17 March 1952, S/AE Files, NA, Washington, D.C.

35. R. Gordon Arneson, Memorandum for the Secretary: Continuance of Negotiations for Indian monazite, 16 April 1952, S/AE Files, NA, Washington, D.C.

36. Pawley was a good choice for these negotiations as he had acquired considerable experience in India during the Second World War building military airfields, and later was involved in commercial ventures in the country.

37. Memorandum for Mr Pawley, Department of Defense, 12 September 1952, S/AE Files, NA, Washington, DC.

38. See the telegrams, letters, and news clippings from Andrew Corry, Minerals Attaché in Delhi, from 1946 to 1952 in S/AE Files, NA, Washington, DC. When Bhabha wrote to Gordon Dean, Chair of the USAEC, in 1952 announcing that India had decided to build a 10MW nuclear reactor, Dean's reply ignores this rather significant detail completely.

39. Bertrand Goldschmidt, *Atomic Rivals* (New Brunswick: Rutgers University Press, 1990).

40. Margaret Gowing, *Independence and Deterrence: Britain and Atomic Energy, 1945–1952*, vol. 1, Policy Making (New York: St. Martin's Press, 1974), p. 159.

41. Bertrand Goldschmidt, *Atomic Rivals* (New Brunswick: Rutgers University Press, 1990).

42. See David Holloway, *Stalin and the Bomb: The Soviet Union and Atomic Energy, 1939–1956* (New Haven: Yale University Press, 1995).

43. See Robert Bothwell, *Nucleus: The History of Atomic Energy of Canada Limited* (Toronto: University of Toronto Press, 1988).

44. This outcome is a function of the condition that, except in the United States, each state monopolised atomic energy production through a state-owned corporation. The contrast here is with a typical capitalist industry where products

in competition often look more and more like each other over time as they begin to use common components, designs, and marketing strategies. The secrecy associated with each national nuclear industry, especially in the years following the war, prevented this kind of learning and cross-fertilisation from occurring. In other words, the global nuclear 'industry', if one can use that term, forms an extremely unusual case in theories of the firm, as rival producers of an identical product, nuclear reactors, do not make substitutes for each other. Rather the industry should be seen as being formed of multiple mini-monopolies, which is why pricing strategies vary so enormously.

45. The first approach from Bhabha to Cockcroft is dated 9 January 1948. The letter requests a meeting 'to discuss with you the possibility of cooperation in scientific research between England and India', File AB6/398, PRO.

46. C. J. Rowland of the London-based Board of Trade to Rowland Owen in the Embassy in Delhi, 6 September 1950, File AB16/515, PRO.

47. Tizzard to Cockcroft, 24 September 1948, File AB6/398, PRO.

48. Bhabha to Cockcroft, 10 December 1949, File AB6/398, PRO.

49. See the memoranda and desk notes in Files AB6/398, AB6/1250, PRO.

50. Bertrand Goldschmidt, *Atomic Rivals*, pp. 329–35, 338–48; and Gabrielle Hecht, 'Political Designs: Nuclear Reactors and National Policy in Postwar France', *Technology and Culture*, 35, 4 (1994), pp. 661–4.

51. Escott Reid, *Envoy to Nehru* (Delhi: Oxford University Press, 1981), p. 20.

52. The term 'special relationship' is drawn from the memoir of former Canadian High Commissioner to India, Escott Reid. See his *Envoy to Nehru*.

53. Letters dated 18 June, 27 June, 26 July, 15 September, 1954, between Bhabha, Cockcroft, and Plowden. File AB6/1250, PRO.

54. Letter, 23 September 1954. File AB6/1250, PRO.

55. Letter, 9 October 1954. File AB6/1250, PRO.

56. Bhabha to Cockcroft, 15 January 1955, AB6/1250, PRO.

57. Handwritten addendum to letter of 8 August 1956, AB6/1681, PRO.

58. All quotes from Raja Ramanna, *Years of Pilgrimage*, p. 63.

59. On hearing this, Cockcroft noted in an undated internal memo with some irritation, 'Did you see a press release from Delhi … this seems rather ungracious in view of the advice and help we have given and are asked to give. Presumably detailed plant designs and drawings do not constitute outside help!' File AB6/1250, PRO.

60. Robert LeBaron, extracts from draft memos to Admiral Strauss (AEC) and President Dwight Eisenhower, April and July 1954 respectively. Robert LeBaron papers, Box 3, Hoover Institution, Stanford, Calif. Emphasis added.

61. It should be mentioned that this event could be seen as an important event in the construction of a post-war international society. While the organizers hoped that holding a scientific conference on this scale would work to reduce the fear of global catastrophe, the expectation made vivid by the growing nuclear arsenals of the Soviet Union and the United States, it also reminded the world that atomic energy could be adequately represented only in global terms.

62. Thus we have the Soviet delegate insisting that each country could have no more than five of its citizens in important conference positions, 'not including the Presidents or Vice Presidents already chosen'. See the record of conversation of the conference advisory committee by Howard A. Robinson, 27 May 1955. I. I. Rabi

Papers, Box 55, Manuscripts Division, Library of Congress.

63. An instance of this care is the French insistence that individual scientists would be allowed to attend the conference only as members of their own country's official delegation. Their apparent concern was that the Soviets might invite Dr Frédéric Joliot-Curie, a French Communist who had once headed the CEA and who was now excluded from official French scientific circles. See the memo of conversation on organisation of the conference by William Hall, 7 January 1955, p. 2. I. I. Rabi Papers, Box 55, Mss. Division, LOC.

64. In fact, had the PRC been invited, it would have been clear how dependent on the USSR their scientific institutions were. This situation would change radically after 1955 and Mao's decision to acquire an independent nuclear capability. See Lewis and Xue, *China Builds the Bomb*.

65. See the inaugural address to the Moscow conference by Academician A. N. Nesmjanov, reproduced in translation in *Science and Culture*, vol. 21, no. 2 (August 1955), p. 77.

66. *Science and Culture*, vol. 21, no. 2 (August 1955), p. 76.

67. See the host of memos and letters dating to this period, especially the record of conversations between Rabi, Cockcroft, Chadwick, and others on 26 August 1954. I. I. Rabi Papers, Box 26, Mss. Division, LOC.

68. An editorial in *Science and Culture*, probably written by Saha, states that it was Bertrand Russell who suggested India's suitability as chairman as the only country 'truly friendly with both sides'. Cf. vol. 21, no. 3, p. 120. I have not been able to confirm this independently.

69. Iris Lonergun, 'The negotiations between Canada and India for the supply of the NRX nuclear research reactor, 1955–1956: A case study of participatory internationalism', unpublished MA thesis, Carleton University, Ottawa, August 1989, p. 48.

70. Iris Lonergun, 'The negotiations between Canada and India', p. 53.

71. Thus Jules Leger, under-secretary of external affairs would write to his superiors outlining the economic, political and scientific advantages of this proposal. Iris Lonergun, 'The negotiations between Canada and India', pp. 55–8.

72. Robert Bothwell, *Nucleus: The History of Atomic Energy of Canada Limited* (Toronto: University of Toronto Press, 1988), chapter 10 passim. The quotation is from p. 353.

73. Iris Lonergun, 'The negotiations between Canada and India', p. 55.

74. Iris Lonergun, 'The negotiations between Canada and India', p. 73, footnote 62.

75. Iris Lonergun, 'The negotiations between Canada and India', p. 73.

76. The following travelogue is largely drawn from David Hart, *Nuclear Power in India: A comparative analysis* (London: George Allen and Unwin, 1983), and W. Marshall, ed., *Nuclear Power Technology*, vol. 1, Reactor Technology (Oxford: Clarendon Press, 1983).

77. Enriched uranium can also be used in an atomic bomb, but must be enriched to a much higher level than that necessary for electricity production.

78. The term 'safeguarding' was not used in contemporary parlance but only became common a few years later, especially when the details of the IAEA's international monitoring role were being worked out. My thanks to M.V. Ramana for pointing this out.

79. For a description of the logic behind the thorium cycle and a description of Indian progress in the mid-1960s, see S.H. Ajwani, 'Thorium Cycle', *Nuclear India*, vol. 4, no. 8, April 1966, pp. 6, 8.

80. Atomic Energy Commission, Report of Discussion with Dr Bhabha, 10 November 1959, Appendix 'B'. Victor Gilinsky Papers, Box 211, Hoover Institution (HI).

81. Report of the Kratzer Mission from the US AEC to study the feasibility of nuclear power in India, mimeo, April 1960. Victor Gilinsky Papers, Box 211, HI.

82. Kratzer Mission, 1960, p. 6, Box 211, Victor Gilinsky Papers, HI.

83. M.R. Srinivasan, 'An Intermezzo', in *Selected Lectures of Dr M. R. Srinivasan* (Bombay: Department of Atomic Energy, n.d.), p. 7.

84. *Nuclear India*, vol. 8, 5–6 (January–February), 1970, pp. 8–9.

85. H.J. Bhabha, 'The role of atomic power in India and its immediate possibilities', paper submitted to the first international conference on the peaceful uses of atomic energy, August 1955. Reprinted in J.P. Jain, *Nuclear India*, vol. 2 (Delhi: Radiant Publishers, 1974), p. 17.

86. This was amply demonstrated after the Pokhran 'peaceful nuclear explosion', when the US Congress tried to prevent further shipments of nuclear fuel to India and passed the Nuclear Non-Proliferation Act (1978). The debate over shipments to India in 1978 split the US Nuclear Regulatory Commission with two commissioners seeking to abrogate the Carter administration's assurance to continue fuel exports. Cf. 'Commissioner Kennedy's views on issuance of XSNM-1060' and 'Separate views of Commissioners Bradford and Gilinsky', Victor Gilinsky Papers, Box 211, HI.

87. See the Tarapur 'Agreement for Cooperation' between the two states, especially Articles VI, VII, August 1963.

88. Indian scientists seemed under no doubt that they would not be given access to the plutonium from US-built reactors. They even tried to work out an arrangement that would reduce the net cost of the US reactor by including the buy-back price of plutonium in the overall estimates. Kratzer Mission, 1960, p.16, Box 211, Victor Gilinsky Papers, HI.

89. See the many statements made by Indian representatives and amendments submitted to the Conference on the IAEA Statute in J.P. Jain, ed., *Nuclear India*, vol. 2 (New Delhi: Radiant Publishers, 1974).

90. Raja Ramanna, *Years of Pilgrimage*, p. 69.

91. The standard line in the AEC today to describe the decision to build enriched uranium reactors takes the following form: 'it was decided to collaborate with the US for setting up a light water reactor (Boiling Water type) station in Tarapur in order to gain time and experience in the construction, operation, and maintenance of a nuclear power station, *as well as demonstrate the economic viability of nuclear power*', M.R. Srinivasan, *Selected Lectures*, p. 121. Emphasis added. Or, 'The first agenda of the nuclear plan consisted of putting up a power reactor of some kind whose reliability was to be decided on the basis of global tenders. *This was to demonstrate to the people of India that electricity could be generated from the atom economically.*' Ramanna, *Years of Pilgrimage*, p. 69. Emphasis added.

92. Up to two-thirds of the capital needed to build the reactor would have to be in the form of foreign exchange. Report of Kratzer mission, April 1960, p. 13. Victor Gilinsky Papers, Box 211, HI.

93. 'Report on discussions with Dr Bhabha', Director of Foreign Affairs, Atomic Energy Commission, 10 January 1959, Box 209, Victor Gilinsky Papers. The statement is attached as 'Appendix B'. Foreign aid as a percentage of Third Plan investment was sizable – 28%. Cf. Lloyd I. Rudolph and Susanne H. Rudolph, *In Pursuit of Lakshmi: The political economy of the Indian state* (Chicago: University of Chicago Press, 1987), p. 4.

94. Text of the DAE resolution in Dhirendra Sharma, *The Indian Atom: Power and Proliferation* (New Delhi: Philosophy and Social Action, 1986), pp. 1–2.

95. For the text of the Act see Dhirendra Sharma, *The Indian Atom: Power and Proliferation*, pp. 3–26.

96. From the text of Homi Bhabha's presidential address at the First International Conference on the Peaceful Uses of Atomic Energy, Geneva, 8 August 1955. Reprinted in *Science and Culture*, vol. 21, no. 3 (1956), p. 124.

97. Bhabha, Presidential Address, p. 124.

98. Bhabha, Presidential Address, p. 126.

99. Bhabha, Presidential Address, pp. 125–6.

100. Bhabha, Presidential Address, p. 126.

101. This is an argument that neo-realist theorists of international relations like Kenneth Waltz would make many years later. See his *Theory of International Politics* (Lexington, Mass.: Addison-Wesley, 1979).

102. Bhabha, Presidential Address, pp. 126–8.

103. For an example of the social way that scientists grew to trust each others' published results and experimental records, see Steven Shapin, *The Social History of Truth* (Chicago: University of Chicago Press, 1994).

104. These terms, 'nationalists', 'developmentalists', etc. emerge from social encounters with atomic energy and the meanings attributed to it and do not precede it. For the discursive framing of these positions see Itty Abraham, 'Towards a reflexive South Asian security studies,' in M.G. Weinbaum and Chetan Kumar, eds., *South Asia Approaches the Millennium: Reexamining National Security* (Boulder, Colo.: Westview, 1995), especially pp. 30–37.

105. This insight comes from Bruno Latour. See his *Science in Action: How to follow scientists and engineers through society* (Cambridge, Mass.: Harvard University Press, 1987).

106. Itty Abraham, 'Science and Power in the postcolonial state', *Alternatives*, vol. 21, no. 3 (July–September 1996).

4

LEARNING TO LOVE THE BOMB:
THE 'PEACEFUL' NUCLEAR EXPLOSION
OF 1974

The desire to produce a nuclear reactor in India leading to the tangible public demonstration of scientific achievement embodied in *Apsara* led to a number of unintended consequences. Most prominent among them was the resultant sense of national pride and achievement among the Indian political élite, which on seeing this demonstration took it as self-evident that the atomic energy complex was now fully functional. This led to the expectation that the atomic complex would soon be fulfilling the explicit and latent promises made when the desire to control this technology was expressed, at the very least the provision of cheap electricity. Yet the Indian atomic scientists were nowhere near being able to fulfil this expectation. This led to a frantic search abroad for a vendor of proven nuclear technology: eventually the United States sold India a safeguarded enriched uranium reactor. The AEC had managed to overcome their anxieties for the moment, but US reactor technology was not going to further in any way their articulated goal of self-reliance and national development.

This chapter takes that story further and argues that the next decade marks a crucial shift in the relations between atomic energy, as institution and object, and the Indian state. The contradictions emergent from the conditions of urgency that had driven the atomic scientists were now resolved by a wall of secrecy, materially derived from the Atomic Energy Bill passed by the Lok Sabha in 1962. The atomic energy complex was fully insulated from all scrutiny by the provisions of this Bill, giving them time to reassess their position, reorient their objectives, and consolidate their influence. But the allure of the sign of atomic energy as a historic response to the times had dimmed. All over the world it was beginning to be realised that atomic energy was not the panacea it was once proclaimed to be. The ability of atomic energy to ensure economic development was not as assured as it had seemed just a decade before. In spite of the large sums of money spent by the atomic energy establishment to set up working nuclear reactors, they were not yet generating electric power for public consumption. Owing to the origin of the reactors, the sense of indigenous accomplishment was still very fragile. But the successful creation of an 'Indian' atomic reactor, the apparent fulfilment of postcolonial ambitions, greatly raised public expectations. The AEC scientists had to cope with this challenge and transform atomic energy again into a form consistent with national objectives and their own institutional interests and abilities.

In describing that process, we find that a paradox emerges in relation to the context within which these changes were taking place. Simply stated, why did India not respond to the Chinese development of nuclear weapons in the mid-1960s by building its own nuclear arsenal? We find that all the preconditions for India's (in)action were in place: public support, technical ability, institutional desire, nuclear raw materials, and superpower acquiescence. Yet India did not take the step of responding to the Chinese 'threat' in a currency the international system would have understood. Why? This alleged paradox, it should be noted, emerges from a particular, but consequential, way of thinking: the foundational presumptions of 'realism' in international relations locate the 'reason' of a state in seeking security and self-preservation above all else. According to that logic, a Chinese bomb should have led to an immediate Indian response of some kind. It did not. But India would eventually explode a nuclear device in 1974, nearly a decade after it could/should have. This chapter seeks to explain both the initial inaction of the Indian state and its later action, according to a different logic.

THE 1962 ATOMIC ENERGY ACT

'*Es Bill ko "pass" karne ki jaldi kya hai?*' ('What is the hurry to pass this Bill?').[1] These words, uttered by Mr Baday, Member of Parliament from Khargaon, during the Lok Sabha debate on the Atomic Energy Bill in August 1962, have an ominous ring to them when read three decades later. The bill, which sought to concentrate in the Indian Atomic Energy Commission (AEC) even greater powers than those awarded by the 1948 Atomic Energy Act, was presented to the lower house of the Indian parliament under unusual circumstances. Contrary to usual procedure, the draft Bill had been circulated only a few days before being formally presented to the Lok Sabha, and hardly any members had had the chance to examine it carefully. The timing of the debate on the Bill had been changed at the last minute, supplanting a discussion on the Land Acquisition Act, which had left a number of MPs unprepared or unable to attend. The time limit on debate had been set for three hours – hardly sufficient to address the range and magnitude of issues being addressed by this Bill in any detail – and it was with considerable reluctance that the Speaker of the House agreed to increase the length of debate by an hour. Also unusual was that while the normally loquacious Prime Minister, also Minister in charge of atomic energy, had presented the Bill to the lower house, the Law Minister, A.K. Sen – who by his own admission was no scientist – had responded to practically all the questions raised in the debate. The Prime Minister's brief opening statement gives us a hint that this attempt to restrict debate and hurry through the passage of this legislation was not innocent of larger significance. In his opening statement Nehru repeated, as if to convince himself, 'This Bill, broadly speaking, I should imagine, is hardly controversial; in fact it is not controversial at all.'[2]

Given these repeated protestations of normality and the special circumstances surrounding its introduction, even if we did not imagine the Bill to be of particular importance, it is difficult now not to examine it more closely. This scepticism is deepened when we realise that Mr Baday, quoted above, was not a critic of the Bill *per se*; his view was that the Bill did not go far enough. The proposed legislation was to Baday and others quite unrealistic, as it stopped short of announcing the true character of the Indian atomic programme. As he put it, when he went to his rural constituency, even simple villagers could not understand how the government could credibly confront deadly enemies – a China or a Pakistan armed with atomic weapons – with mere slogans for peace. '*Apna raksha karne ke vaste yadi hum "atomic energy" se apne "defence" aur "military weapons" tiyar karen, to usmen kaun sa gunah hai, kaise veh shanti ke khilaf jata hai, yeh cheez mere samaj mein nahin até.*' ('If we develop atomic energy for our defence and military weapons in order to keep us secure, what's wrong with that, how can it be antithetical to peace, that's what I don't understand.')[3] To even the most rustic of villagers, he suggests, to prepare for one's security was self-evident and necessary with so many known enemies out there. What choice was there for a responsible government but to use atomic energy in this way?

Note how the representation of atomic energy had changed: unlike the atomic energy debate in 1948, when Nehru at least made an effort to start the debate by repeating India's peaceful intentions, no one on either side of the parliamentary aisle responds to Baday's 'common sense' logic in 1962 except to repeat it approvingly. There is no question that attitudes had changed in the intervening 14 years: for one, atomic energy seemed more commonplace and was no longer invested with the awe it once received. Indeed, even non-scientists could speak of it now. But further, members' acknowledgement of Baday's concerns makes clear the obvious association of atomic energy with military ends. In other words, by the early 1960s, insisting on the peaceful uses of this substance was anachronistic. Let us turn to the debate itself.

The ostensible reasons for the creation of new regulations relating to atomic energy were to give 'certain rule making powers to the Atomic Energy Commission because in dealing with these radio-active substances it is very necessary to make very stringent rules to prevent any disaster from taking place'. Also, the government was serving notice that it would no longer recognise international patents in atomic energy, and in case of infringement of any of these rules, 'certain penalties' had been increased.[4] The government noted that atomic energy was no longer an experimental or infant industry as in 1948. In the last decade one atomic reactor had been installed, others were being constructed, still others being negotiated for. Given these changes, it was argued, a new atomic energy act was necessary. As if to allay any fears or doubts, it was quickly added that the new Bill was not controversial at all, but was simply bringing the legal codes governing atomic energy and the current state of the atomic complex into closer correspondence: the Bill 'was rather in a sense *urgently* required because the old Act [was] out of date'.[5]

The allegedly 'non-controversial' sense of urgency was soon undermined. A member of parliament we first encountered during the 1948 Constituent Assembly debates, H.V. Kamath, tried to prevent the 1962 Bill from being introduced. He noted that that the document being presented to the Lok Sabha did not have a financial memorandum attached, as required by parliamentary procedure. The government's response to this fairly straightforward, even if annoying, intervention is remarkable for its degree of hostility, stonewalling, and evasion. Mr Sen, the law minister, representing the government, retorted that the parliamentary rule of procedure referred to by Kamath required the government to give financial estimates for a Bill *only if possible*. Law Minister Sen said: 'Where it is not possible, it need not be given. It is enough if the Government says that it is not possible, because the requirement of a rule is requirement of what is possible, not of what is impossible'.[6] The Speaker of the House concurred with the law minister's remarkable reading of the law. The Speaker then proceeded to shut off debate on this question noting that the state had tried to give an estimate of expenses, 'but as it would depend on the pace and extent of the programme for atomic energy development' – which clearly could not be known in advance – it would not be possible to give any estimate at all.[7] It is difficult to state how ridiculous this defence is: the appropriate analogy is perhaps with a bookmaker who will not accept bets in advance because he does not know how the race will turn out. In other words, the government's position was that it had 'tried' to give an estimate of the expenses needed by the atomic energy complex for the next few years, but it could not because these expenses would take place in the future! The Speaker's bizarre and circular ruling was accepted by the rest of the House without further question.

On this note the debate proceeded. Even as the government tried to steamroller the Bill through, they did not succeed completely and a few pointed issues were raised. One set of questions related to the right of the government to control all the sites where atomic minerals were known to be present and where they might yet be found. Kerala was a principal source of one of these minerals, monazite, which brought the state considerable income. A number of MPs from this state pointed out that the Bill sought implicitly to alter the frame of existing relations between the Union government and the states – a serious constitutional issue – to the detriment of the states. Had the states been officially consulted, they wanted to know? The law minister admitted that the states had not been consulted, and then firmly averred that he saw no need for such consultation as, in his view, the rights of states were not at all affected by the Bill. This blanket statement, devoid of corroborating details or evidence, ended discussion on that issue. Others pointed out that under the provisions of this Bill, workers in the atomic complex would no longer be protected by the Factories Act, which protected the rights of labour. The Bill would, in effect, create an industrial enclave that was above regulations that applied across the country and that denied the legitimate rights of workers in this industry. One member noted that the bill, if passed in its present form, would give such a range of new powers to the Atomic Energy Commission that it could only be based on the laws of 'Fascist Germany'.[8]

Such overtly hostile interventions were few. Yet, given the overall acquiescence to the provisions of the Bill, the text of the debate makes it clear that even those members who were not hostile to the new atomic energy legislation seemed alarmed by the speed at which the government was proceeding. The MP from Khargaon and like-minded supporters of the Bill requested the government to step back, noting that a proposal to consult the public was not unreasonable. Others suggested creating a select panel of parliamentarians who would work to improve the deficiencies of the Bill and report back to the Lok Sabha in a few weeks. The government firmly rejected all these options. The Bill had to be passed in its present form, and at once. *Jaldi kya hai?* What was the hurry? Minister Sen explained:

It is necessary to inform this House the reason why this Act should be passed soon. The Government of India has decided to set up the second 200MW electric [sic] generating station to generate power by nuclear energy at Pratapsagar near Kotah in Rajasthan … It is absolutely necessary that the Government should be equipped with all the necessary powers. These are heavy undertakings and without the powers which the Act purport to give to the Government, it will be impossible to carry out these undertakings efficiently. It is therefore urgent that the Bill should be passed with out much delay.[9]

But was this sufficient reason to pass new legislation in this way? Reactors had been set up before and negotiations with foreign agencies conducted in the past: what was so different now?

Reading the record of the debate three decades later, what is most obvious is the generation of a discourse of urgency through which important legislation is being pushed through parliament, the strong-arm tactics being used to stifle debate, and the anti-democratic provisions embedded in the document. It seems clear that the government did not want this Bill to be discussed by the public, or its provisions carefully examined by a parliamentary select committee. Further, the degree of confidence expressed in the atomic energy programme had fallen from the halcyon days of the Constituent Assembly, when delegate after delegate got up to express the importance of this resource and to con- gratulate the government for having brought it to their attention in such a prompt manner. This is not to say that some MPs did not use this occasion to curry favour with the Prime Minister – they did – but merely to point out that both the scale and fervour of such speeches were greatly reduced.

The great silence in the debate was over any discussion of the 'peaceful uses' of atomic energy. The introduction of a new atomic energy act could have been a suitable moment for the legal enshrining of this principle, now that the government knew better both what its own capabilities were and what atomic energy was capable of accomplishing. As we have seen, this was an item of considerable importance in the 1948 debates, dividing the Constituent Assembly delegates down the middle. Discourse about the peaceful uses of atomic energy was very differently situated 14 years later. Apart from those who demanded that the state develop a nuclear military option at once, rejecting any discussion of peaceful uses, the government's only mention of peaceful uses was in the short preface to the Bill: 'That the Bill to provide for the development, control and use of atomic energy for the welfare of the people of India and *for other peaceful purposes* and for matters connected therewith, be taken into consideration'.[10]

In response to a question, the Speaker confirmed that this preface had no legal standing. It was simply language for the introduction of the Bill and could not be taken to be an accurate reflection of the state's policy on atomic energy. The Indian government had always proclaimed that, in marked contrast with other atomic energy-capable states, their own use of atomic energy was for peaceful purposes only. In other words, the absence of legally binding language within the official text of the Bill restricting India to peaceful uses of atomic energy, confirmed by the Speaker's comment, draws attention to what the Bill was *not* about.

We must return to the law minister for further confirmation of this suspicion. Toward the end of the debate, Sen, in a stern summation evoking much more the rhetoric of the criminal courts than a democratic parliament, said that judging from what he had heard, since neither 'principles' underlying the Bill nor 'controversy' about its provisions were in question, the government felt able to reject members' recommendations to create a select committee of parliamentarians or consult public opinion. In any event, he went on to say, these kinds of interventions were pointless: 'the *larger interest of the country* demands that the Central Government, *which alone is competent* to deal with atomic materials and the use of atomic energy … should be *in complete control* of all our atomic resources including the right to acquire such atomic materials as may be discovered and *which in the opinion of the Central Government* should be acquired'.[11]

The tone of the debate, especially the interventions of the law minister, make it appear that the government was doing parliament a favour by letting them approve this Bill. Sen's last statement makes it only too clear that the Bill, for all its initial mention of 'peaceful uses', sought to make the atomic energy complex above the law in the interests of the state. The lines were being clearly drawn so that no one, even the most rustic parliamentarian, could miss them. The heavy hand of the state was being deployed, in the most direct manner short of announcing a disavowal of the peaceful uses of atomic energy, to identify atomic energy with its 'larger interests'. No one was better able ('more competent') to decide what to do with atomic energy than the state: from the absence of discussion of peaceful uses, we may surmise that national development was not what the state had in mind. There seems little question, given the deliberate absence of legal reference to peaceful uses, confirmed by the Speaker, that the subtext of the Bill was the orientation of atomic energy with the state's 'largest' interest: national security. It is only by evoking the conditions of national security that the state's excessive claims to control all meaning and use of atomic energy have any rhetorical legitimacy. Only national security concerns justify the degree of centralisation and control written into the Bill in order to limit the spread of information about atomic energy.

Through the 1962 Act, atomic energy was for the first time being legally drawn into direct relation with the interests of the state and national security. India was now overcoming its initial qualms about nuclear weapons and becoming like all the other nuclear-capable states. But this still does not explain the speed at which it had to be done. *Jaldi kya hai?*

UNSAFEGUARDED FISSILE MATERIAL

To understand the full context of this parliamentary debate, and to appreciate the significance of the strategic silence around 'peaceful uses', we need to turn back to the 1950s. Some years before their first research reactor *Apsara* went critical in 1956, the AEC had been engaged in an internal debate about the type of nuclear reactors they should build in India. Even though choosing natural-uranium-fuelled heavywater-moderated reactors seems perfectly logical given their desire for self-reliance, this choice was apparently not always so evident. Raja Ramanna, later to become chairman of the Atomic Energy Commission and minister of state for defence, reports in his autobiography that there was some disagreement within the AEC on this issue, with Homi Bhabha less than fully convinced that the natural-uranium heavy-water reactors would be cheap enough or technologically viable in the Indian context. Ramanna suggests that he and others managed to convince Bhabha not to reject this option for the self-reliance reason: 'because [it] would make us less dependent on foreign resources'.[12] However, Ramanna goes on to note that these reactors also produced plutonium in the fuel cycle, a nuclear raw material which would be necessary if India was to retain the 'option' to develop nuclear weapons: 'Further, natural uranium reactors gave us the nuclear option, as India's relationship with several [unnamed] countries was strained.'[13]

Notwithstanding the retrospective quality of this statement – in the 1950s India had hardly the number of enemies it would have ten years later – let us assume that the internal AEC conversation had included the option of nuclear weapons as an important factor in determining the choice of which reactor to acquire. Even though Ramanna's use of the term 'option' was not in common usage at the time, the case appears to have been made explicitly in the AEC during the mid-1950s that an important consideration influencing the choice of Indian reactors was the possibility of developing weapons. What other evidence is there to show that the weapons option was being considered seriously at this time?

We turn to the Canadian offer of a 40MW NRX reactor, 'CIRUS', made just before the 1955 UN conference in Geneva. The reactor began to be constructed in Trombay in late 1956. It went critical in July 1960 and was producing its full power component by October 1963. The initial understanding was that the CIRUS reactor would be fuelled with Canadian-supplied fuel elements. However, Indian atomic scientists were able to produce fuel rods in their Trombay plant just in time to be used in the reactor's first loading. Raja Ramanna notes with glee that the Canadians were amazed at the quality of the Indian product.[14] National pride apart, there may have been another reason to include Indian fuel elements in the reactor from the onset of operations, namely, access to plutonium produced in the course of normal reactor operations.

The strong Indian position on safeguards on nuclear reactors was that materials (including equipment) belonging to or leased from foreign countries could sometimes be placed under safeguards, as they did not strictly belong to India. Based on ownership criteria, it was possible to override the question of sovereignty and acknowledge that a lease or loan did not give India full rights over the system. As far as possible, however, Indian negotiators insisted that the product of reactor operations, whether electricity or material by-products, should belong wholly to India. This was a claim rather than a fully supported legal position, but the argument became substantially reinforced when at least some of the inputs were Indian in origin. The claim to ownership of the output was logically much stronger if some of the input was undeniably Indian. If the CIRUS reactor, with its Canadian design, equipment, and fuel, and US-supplied heavy water, did not contain any Indian inputs at all, it could be argued that the output produced by this reactor also did not belong to India but had to be either returned to Canada or placed under an international inspection regime. Using Indian fuel elements from the very beginning finessed this possibility.

The Canadians were eventually made aware of this loophole, but owing to the absence of international norms on nuclear exchange at the time, their inexperience, and their eagerness to make sure the deal with India went through, they were not sure what to do. Faced with the tactical intransigence of Indian negotiators, and reminded constantly of India's alleged other options, they finally agreed to waive most safeguards on the NRX reactor. The Canadians were aware that this agreement could set an unfortunate precedent for the international atomic energy regime then in the process of being set up, but were not sure how to mitigate this. They suggested weakly that the agreement between the two countries be re-evaluated when the IAEA regime was finally in place. But this would never happen. In an extraordinary turn of events, the principal negotiators, 'Pearson [of Canada] and Bhabha decided that the nuclear co-operation agreement between their countries would be "silent" on the provisions of fuel in order to avoid the creation of a precedent'.[15] They even went to the extent of agreeing that the minimal restrictions agreed upon would not be formalised in the official treaty but added in a secret annex. Canada's Legal Department later pointed out that, as a result, 'its actual implementation would be based only on the willingness of the parties to fulfil their obligations since logically it could not in practice be invoked nor enforced by national or international tribunals'.[16] In other words, the Indians managed to ensure that safeguards to monitor fuel records or stockpiles were never written into the formal public agreement. The Canadians had been out-manoeuvred completely. Putting together Ramanna's report of an internal discussion on the implications of reactor choice in 1954 and the behaviour of the Indian negotiators a year later, it seems quite clear that from the very beginning, Indian negotiations for the CIRUS reactor had been conducted with an explicit awareness that this reactor could produce the materials necessary for a weapons option, and that, as a result, the reactor and fuel should be as unsafeguarded as possible.

The Canadian-designed NRX reactor had an additional advantage over competing reactor designs from the viewpoint of extracting plutonium (Pu) for weapons use. An important consideration in bomb design is 'reliability': will it go off with the expected yield? Yield depends on the quantity of plutonium with atomic number 239 relative to higher isotopes of plutonium (atomic numbers 240 or 242) in the explosive device. The proportion of these latter isotopes must be minimised in order to ensure that the device will produce the expected yield. In general, once uranium fuel rods are bombarded with neutrons in a reactor, uranium transmutes into plutonium 239, along with other isotopes. However, if these fuel elements are left in the reactor for long, the proportion of the 'undesirable' isotopes Pu-240 and Pu-242 tends to increase. Hence, if there is a desire to maximise the quantity of 'bomb-ready' plutonium, irradiated fuel elements must be removed frequently from the core, spent uranium and plutonium extracted, the fuel elements rebuilt and then replaced in the reactor. In the typical enriched-uranium light-water reactor, the reactor must be shut down each time fuel elements are removed; in the Canadian design, however, fuel elements can be extracted and replaced as the reactor is running. This feature obviously makes it easier to reprocess fuel elements more rapidly and thus minimises the build-up of contaminating isotopes of plutonium.[17]

At the same time as the CIRUS reactor was being set up, Bhabha announced the building of a plutonium reprocessing plant at the

Trombay complex, to be headed by Homi Sethna, an engineer who had helped build the first monazite processing plant. This plant was to extract plutonium from irradiated fuel elements that had been through a reactor cycle. The objective was to have it ready in time to absorb fuel elements from the CIRUS reactor. The plant was completed in June 1964 with a nominal capacity to absorb 30 metric tons of irradiated uranium fuel rods annually.[18] In other words, by the middle of 1964, the AEC had an unsafeguarded reactor producing plutonium and a reprocessing plant capable of converting that plutonium to weapons-grade bomb material.

The US Office of Technology Assessment estimates that 'about 5 to 10 [kilograms] of plutonium' are needed in order to build an explosive nuclear device.[19] Using the higher end of this estimate, and making the conservative assumption that the Indian plutonium reprocessing facility had not produced any plutonium before being formally commissioned in 1964, this plant would produce about 8 kg of weapons grade plutonium metal annually, roughly the amount needed for a single explosive device.[20] We know that the CIRUS reactor had reached full power by October 1963, and that the plutonium reprocessing plant was more or less fully functional by June 1964. If the plant started producing weapons-grade plutonium no later than this date, the AEC would have had a quantity of plutonium adequate to produce one explosive device by June 1965, just eight months after the first Chinese nuclear test. Even if the AEC had wanted to build up a suitable stockpile of weapons-grade material before testing its first device so as not to use up its entire supply, it could have done so by 1967, roughly three years after the first Chinese nuclear explosion and soon after their first thermonuclear test. This estimate is confirmed by US intelligence statements of the time, which though not completely reliable as they do not disclose their sources, provide an added measure of confidence to this assessment.[21]

By the time the Atomic Energy Bill was presented to parliament in October 1962, the AEC was in a position to know with confidence that in no more than a few years they would have, at the very least, the means to conduct one nuclear test. At best, they would have enough fissile material to conduct a test and still have some material left over for later weapons fabrication. Given this reasoning, the haste with which the Bill was being pushed through parliament suggests that the government was concerned to have all the legal niceties in place, especially restrictions on information about the state of development of the atomic programme, before a decision was made on whether to begin a weapons-oriented nuclear programme. All these conditions were in place, it must be stressed, prior to the outbreak of hostilities between India and China in 1962. In

sum, India's initial decision to prepare the ground for a weapons programme seems to have had little to do with any overt external condition
or threat. This argument is confirmed by evidence from the international
context.

INTERNATIONAL CONFLICT

The early 1960s were good times for war correspondents and arms industries alike. The Cold War had heated up again with the Soviet Union
and the United States first locking horns over Berlin, eventually leading
to the building of the Wall, and then facing off – the fortunately aborted
nuclear 'showdown' – over the installation of Soviet medium-range
missiles in Cuba. The new US president, John F. Kennedy, proved to be
no Democratic dove and called for the elimination of an alleged 'missile
gap' by qualitatively increasing military spending over previous budgets.
Asia was a particular focus of the latest international tensions. The US
sent military advisers into Indochina to prop up the failing South Viet-
namese regime and encouraged the South Korean military to take over a
state that seemed to be vulnerable to left-wing political forces. China
and the Soviet Union, socialist allies since the Chinese Revolution,
appeared to be drifting rapidly apart – the former partners in international communism were now turning their weapons on each other,
heightening the overall tension.

This global sense of unease and insecurity became manifest in India
in late 1962. A series of border skirmishes between Chinese and Indian
troops over territories claimed by both states became a larger event by
late October, drawing in the armies of both countries in a brief and
bloody war. The under-equipped and unprepared Indian troops were
easily defeated by Chinese forces in a series of battles. In November
1962 the Chinese declared a unilateral cease-fire and ended the three-
week conflict. This is not the place, obviously, to delve further into this
issue; what is important is how this event was perceived and made sense
of within India and elsewhere.

For Indian militarists, this was the moment of truth. The norms of
peaceful co-existence and non-alignment underlying India's foreign policy
were shown up to be idealist and sentimental notions deriving from a
utopian vision hardly tenable at home and totally unsuited to modern
international politics. Earthy peasant wisdom about the obvious need for
security in order to confront hardened enemies, the views of parliamentarian Baday's village constituents, seemed quite vindicated. The
government's immediate response to the barrage of criticism that followed
the Chinese débâcle was to fire the controversial Defence Minister and

close ally of Nehru, Krishna Menon, and steadily to increase military spending for both equipment and personnel in the next few years.[22] Military expenditures had begun to increase in the years preceding the Chinese war, but the rate of increase now went up as well.[23]

Most characteristic of the times were themes of humiliation and betrayal. A number of commentators pointed out how India had spared no effort to acknowledge China's importance in the world at a time when she was not included in most multilateral gatherings, that India had worked hard and in good faith to develop bilateral relations between the two countries. The Prime Minister, Nehru, was the target of much of this outrage as he had been primarily responsible for these policies, as indeed for all Indian foreign policy. And, for the first time, Nehru seemed vulnerable to this criticism in a way he had not before. It is remarkable that just at the moment when West European nations had begun the final stages of giving up their remaining colonies in Africa and Asia, an act that Nehru had been demanding in every international forum since India's own independence, he seemed unable to take any pride or comfort in that considerable achievement owing to the Chinese fiasco.

Yet India's China war, for all the turmoil it caused in the defence ministry, did not lead at once to a widespread call for the development of atomic weapons to protect India against China or other enemies. That shift in élite opinion had to wait for another two years, until 16 October 1964, when China conducted its first nuclear test at a marshy site in Xinjiang province called Lop Nur. Following the first Chinese test, Indian domestic reaction was fast and furious.[24] There were repeated calls from all over the ideological spectrum demanding an appropriate Indian response to this belligerent act. But what was appropriate? There seemed to be three options facing the new government of Prime Minister Lal Bahadur Shastri (Nehru had died in May 1964): the first, which would be political suicide, was to do nothing; the second, to obtain nuclear protection from another state; the third, to build an Indian bomb.

Shastri plumped for exploring the second option and made a secret overture to the United States later that year.[25] The informal request sought the possibility of being given a formal guarantee of US assistance in the event of a nuclear attack by China, offering in return that India would not begin its own weapons programme.[26] In other words, Shastri had also chosen this option in order not to take the third path – development of an Indian bomb. The US prepared a special report on the question of possible US security guarantees for India, following the issuing of National Security Action Memorandum 355, and sent Ambassador Averell Harriman to India in March 1965 to discuss further the question of guarantees. Not surprisingly, there was considerable opposition in the Indian Atomic Energy

Commission to the idea of acquiring a US guarantee. Bhabha was a leading proponent of the idea that India should develop an independent nuclear
capability.[27] But Bhabha and others were strategic enough to realise that
a statement of US support would be useful in order not to get caught up
in a nuclear arms race with China, and furthermore that explicit US
assistance could speed up India's bomb making abilities considerably.
Hence, in conversations with Under-Secretary of State Ball in February
1965 he tried to get the US to understand that for their own strategic
interests vis-à-vis China, a nuclear India would be a good idea.[28] Bhabha
made his case in Cold War terms, drawing on the contrast between a
democratic India and a communist China, both offering powerful models
for other third world nations to emulate. He stated that 'India needed to
make some dramatic peaceful achievement to offset the prestige gained by
Communist China among African and Asian countries [after exploding
their bomb].' He noted that 'if India was to maintain its prestige relative
to the Chinese in the fields of science and technology, two things must
be done, (a) ways must be found for it to demonstrate [India's scientific
achievements] to other African and Asian countries and (b) a greater
awareness of Chinese indebtedness to the Soviet Union for its nuclear
achievements must be created'. He ended by noting that 'if India went all
out, it could produce a bomb in 18 months, with a US blueprint it could
do the job in 6 months'. Noting that it was the stated policy of his government not to make nuclear weapons, he argued however that 'ways had
to be found' to allow India to 'gain at least as much by sticking to peaceful
uses as it could by embarking on a weapons programme'.[29]

There were other pressures as well urging a decision to embark on an
independent Indian weapons programme. With another war brewing by
April 1965, this time with Pakistan, both the US and UK froze arms
shipments to South Asia. This embargo took care of what little élite
support there may have been for a policy searching for superpower allies
who might protect India under their nuclear umbrella. Not surprisingly,
in September 1965, nearly a fifth of members of parliament from all
parties urged Prime Minister Shastri to begin an open nuclear weapons
programme.[30] But the political leadership shied away from any public
response: careful diplomatic statements were crafted that while India
could, if it so chose, become a nuclear power, the country's current
policy was not to take that step.

Other events followed that furthered Indian anxieties about the future
of their country. In 1966, with huge deficits and balance of trade problems, and facing considerable pressure from the World Bank and foreign
donors, the government under new Prime Minister Indira Gandhi mas-
sively devalued the rupee. The sense of impending doom was furthered

by the disastrous harvests of 1965 and 1966 which, apart from the need for massive emergency food aid from abroad, would result in the post-colonial state's main development apparatus sustaining an important symbolic blow: the suspension of the Five-Year Plans for three years.[31] The insecurity of these years was soon felt in the political arena. In the 1967 general elections, the ruling Congress party did worse than it had ever done. It 'lost power in eight large states and almost did so nationally: two years later, it split for the first time'.[32]

Yet Indian foreign minister Swaran Singh, after a potentially even greater provocation than the first Chinese atomic test, namely the first thermo-nuclear 'booster' test explosion in May 1966, remained remarkably restrained in his ensuing statement to parliament: '[The] government still feels that the interests of world peace and our own security are better achieved by giving all support to the efforts for world nuclear disarmament than by building our own nuclear weapons.'[33] Even the US government now appears to have taken the position that an Indian bomb was a *fait accompli*. By July 1966, Dean Rusk, Secretary of State under Lyndon Johnson, recommended to the US president that 'no dramatic steps to discourage the Indians from starting a nuclear weapons programme [be taken]: this is because we have been unable to devise anything dramatic which would not cost us more than any anticipated gain'. Yet no Indian bomb followed.

Looking back over those years, the option chosen by the political leadership appears to have been the first one, the option I had supposed would lead to political suicide – to do nothing. This is surprising. We have already noted that the 1962 Atomic Energy Bill seemed determined to confirm the Indian move toward military ends. We know that the AEC had the means and materials to conduct a nuclear test from 1965 onwards. Under the implicit codes of the contemporary international system, an Indian nuclear test would have been read as a straightforward and appro-priate response to Chinese nuclear tests from 1964 onward. Additionally, given the state of American and Soviet relations with China, an Indian nuclear test at that moment would have hardly had the international response it was to have a decade later; indeed, an Indian test in 1966 would have been conducted with tacit superpower approval. Yet no Indian bomb followed. How do we make sense of this?

THE UNCERTAINTY WITHIN

The next two sections attempt to place an absence – the apparent deci-sion not to go ahead and develop nuclear weapons – in proper context. We explore the changes under way in two principal sites: within the agencies of the state, and in the international arena, particularly at the negotiations helping to create an international regime around nuclear energy. A certain caution in framing the problem above, to wit, the 'apparent' decision not to go nuclear, seems sensible at this stage: we cannot tell whether a decision was just not made at all, or a deliberate decision was made not to go nuclear.

The focus of this section is on the question of the changing balance of power within the two nodes of state power that had dominated atomic energy policy since independence: the Atomic Energy Commission and the office of the prime minister. Intertwined with and producing the shifting importance of these state agencies is the more fluid condition of the quality of leadership. As we follow the movement of individuals in and out of these key positions of state decision making, we see that notwithstanding Bhabha's ability to guide the atomic energy complex down a particular path of development, that path could be changed, almost overnight, by a different leader with a different vision, using the same instruments of institutional power that Bhabha had helped lay down. By the same token, we also see that as a powerful and imaginative leadership departs the scene, the once-powerful AEC begins a period of institutional stasis, seeking only to preserve its position and status in nominal terms.

If the 1960s were, from one view, a time of international conflict, it was also a time of great disruption within the atomic energy organisation. Rapid changes in leadership, the introduction of different trajectories and goals, and the potential loss of executive authority and state protection all combined to make the period between the wars with China in 1962 and with Pakistan in 1971 a period of change and considerable uncertainty. This decade, a period of great import in the chronology of Indian international relations, was marked above all by the deaths of nearly all the leading characters in this story so far. The first death, perhaps the one most expected, was Nehru's, in May 1964. Accompanied by many, particularly foreign, prognostications of India's imminent decline into anarchy as a result, Jawaharlal Nehru is usually seen as a spent force politically by this period: 'weary and chastened' is the Rudolphs' phrase;[34] 'spiritually shattered' is Robin Jeffrey's.[35] His passing was mourned, but the succession was relatively quick; many observers characterise the nomination of Lal Bahadur Shastri as the next prime minister as a holding action while the 'real' political battles were fought off stage.[36]

Shastri proved to be more determined than most give him credit for, especially given that his brief tenure as prime minister (1964–66) was not made easier by a war breaking out with Pakistan, initially over the territory of the Rann of Kutch, but soon expanding into Kashmir. The Soviet Union stepped in to mediate an end to the conflict, and helped the two belligerents to sign a peace accord in Tashkent. Shastri was far less positive about the atomic energy programme than Nehru had been. Reacting to the growing pressures within the AEC toward a policy of overt nuclearisation, Shastri resisted this tendency by approaching the United States to discuss the possibility of an American nuclear guarantee. Eventually when faced with the lack of élite support for this option, he reluctantly agreed to allow the AEC to begin studies on the feasibility of underground nuclear explosions.[37] Just hours following the successful negotiation of a Soviet-brokered agreement ending the war with Pakistan, Shastri died suddenly in Tashkent on 11 January 1966.[38]

The next prime minister, again erroneously expected to be a transitional figure, was Nehru's daughter, Indira Gandhi. With this second change, however, doubts that had built up around the question of continued executive protection for the AEC as a result of Nehru's death, and which had continued with Shastri's tenure in the prime minister's office, appeared to be resolved. Indira Gandhi was as fervent a supporter of the nuclear complex as her father had been, and she had a close relationship with Homi Bhabha, whom she knew well and trusted implicitly. But just a few days after Shastri's death, Bhabha died. He had been flying to Vienna for an IAEA meeting when his aeroplane crashed into Mont Blanc. There were no survivors.

This tragic event came as a complete shock to the Indian atomic scientists. There could be no thought given to questions of leadership change while Bhabha was alive, and now that he was dead, it seemed impossible to replace him. Thinking of his successor(s) was no easy task. At the time of this death, Bhabha had been director of TIFR, director of the Atomic Energy Establishment, Trombay, chairman of the Atomic Energy Commission, and secretary of the Department of Atomic Energy, the senior civil service position in the government. Eventually, the leadership of TIFR went to M.G.K. Menon, a cosmic ray scientist who had trained with C.F. Powell at Bristol, and who, as deputy director under Bhabha, was already in charge of most of TIFR's everyday activities.[39]

After a short interregnum, when the atomic energy complex was overseen by the Cabinet secretary, Dharam Vir, Vikram Sarabhai was invited by Indira Gandhi to be the second chair of the Atomic Energy Commission, to serve as the secretary to the Department of Atomic Energy, and to take over as chairman of the Electronics Commission, another post held by Bhabha. A decade younger than Bhabha, Sarabhai appeared to have much in common with his predecessor. He too was a child of wealth and privilege, had studied physics at Cambridge, and had spent time at the Indian Institute of Science during the Second World War. After completing a doctoral dissertation on cosmic rays in 1947, he returned to his natal home of Ahmedabad where he started, among other institutions, the Physical Research Laboratory (PRL) – the seedbed for India's eventual space research programme. Sarabhai was a stranger to neither the AEC nor national science policy – he had been a member of the Atomic Energy Commission since 1965 and had chaired the National Committee for Space Research (INCOSPAR) since 1962 – but he did not belong to the original team of scientists that Bhabha had nurtured.[40]

Sarabhai may appear to have had a lot in common with Bhabha, but it is important to place this congruence, and some important differences, in the appropriate frame. In particular, it is worth noting that Sarabhai's rhetorical understanding of the uses of atomic energy – whether for development or for defence – was far more carefully calibrated than Bhabha's. Where Bhabha would speak in grand sweeps of the 'historic' and 'necessary' uses of atomic energy for development, Sarabhai employed detailed and systemic proposals for the utilisation of nuclear power in different settings, especially for integrated rural development. While Sarabhai knew of course of the military potential of the Indian nuclear programme, unlike Bhabha he sought both to demystify the opacity of Indian nuclear policy and explicitly to eschew the use of nuclear weapons as an instrument of foreign policy. Most notably, in the press conference following his appointment as head of the Atomic Energy Commission, when he was asked by journalists about the atom bomb, Sarabhai was categorical that atomic weapons were not a solution to India's problems as he saw them. He ended his long response saying, 'I fully agree with the Prime Minister. [...] It is perfectly correct, when she says that an atomic bomb explosion is not going to help our security. I fully share this feeling.'[41]

It is quite significant that the new head of the AEC was drawn from an institutional base outside the atomic complex. The political leadership were clearly seeking to replace Homi Bhabha – in terms of scientific eminence and public respect – rather than trying to provide the institutional continuity that would have been their primary consideration if they had wanted simply to ensure the replication of the organisation. After all, Homi Sethna, Raja Ramanna, or M.G.K. Menon could easily have been asked to lead the organisation. Instead Sethna was made head of the Trombay atomic complex, now called the Bhabha Atomic Research Centre (BARC), in honour of the fallen leader. The atomic scientists did not try to resist this appointment for long. While Sarabhai was not a nuclear physicist by training, the Trombay scientists soon realised that he was not going to be beholden to their expertise or in any way be subordinate to them. Raja Ramanna notes ruefully, when informed of the appointment of Sarabhai as head of the AEC, 'I had some doubts as to whether Vikram [Sarabhai] would be able to get a grip on atomic energy developments here and abroad, and be able to give it special orientation.... [But in only a few months] he was able to participate in the deliberations of all the decision-making bodies in an effective and constructive way.'[42] The civil service, which had historically been subordinated to the atomic scientists, could have used this moment to try and reassert its authority over this enclave, but did not. It appears that for Indira Gandhi and her decision-making coterie, it was more important that India's atomic programme be headed by a person with the appropriate credentials to maintain the respect this programme was held in, domestically and internationally, than further institutional continuity. Vikram Sarabhai, apart from his other qualifications, filled that bill very well.

While Sarabhai may have been an outsider in terms of immediate institutional history, he was in other important ways a part of the larger ambit of the Trombay scientists. His scientific roots in India, like Bhabha's, lay in the institutions centred upon the Indian Institute of Science, Bangalore, and C. V. Raman. He shared his mentor's view of science as the primary symbol of modernity and its privileged means of transformation, and saw science as an élite activity. Sarabhai did not, for instance, seek to modify the legislation that protected the AEC from scrutiny or open up the organisation to scientists in other parts of the country, as had been intermittently called for. Rather, he worked to maintain the insulation of the atomic enclave and, leaving us in no doubt that he knew what he was doing, copied this model explicitly to build the new Indian space centre in Trivandrum. Although Sarabhai did not see the bomb as a means to security, he did not change the characteristics of Indian 'big science' or the ideology of modern science that marked the AEC. If anything he took that vision further, even as he marked his difference from the logic that had governed those processes in the past.

While reinforcing the ideological perspective framing existing practices, Sarabhai did bring to the organisation a set of ideas about atomic energy that differed in important ways from existing norms. The degree of continuity and change these ideas represented is best seen in the document he prepared in the name of the AEC, 'Atomic Energy and Space Research: A profile for the decade, 1970–1980', published after he had been in office for nearly four years, in May 1970.[43] This document sought, first, to identify and justify the concepts of atomic energy and space research as the key technologies that would transform India's political economy. By juxtaposing space research with atomic energy,

Sarabhai was mobilising support for his pet project through the already well-established national atomic energy programme. At the same time, however, his approach shifted away from the existing discourse legitimating the value of atomic energy. This former discourse, epitomised by Bhabha's speech to the UN conference in 1955, rested on a neo-Malthusian logic of estimating future energy needs based on current norms, 'proving' that there would inevitably exist a gap between future demand and supply, and thus opening the door for the solution, atomic energy.

Sarabhai noted in the 1970 AEC document that:

> [t]he traditional approach of planning to provide things like electric power or telecommunication services for a national infrastructure *based on projections of growth* is inadequate. An alternative approach lies in creating consumption centres alongside facilities for supply, as for instance an agro-industrial complex served by a large nuclear power station or a programme for television to the entire countryside using a direct broadcast synchronous communications satellite. Indeed there is a *totality* about the process of development which involves not only advanced technology and hardware but imaginative planning of supply and consumption centres, of social organisation and management.[44]

This was a radically new conception of the role of nuclear power, but one which is less liberatory than it might seem at first glance. Even as it seemed to recognise the existence of society for the first time, this conception in no way diminished the power and reach of the state in controlling the lives of its people. If anything, this project had far more in common with the intrusive development programmes of the 1950s and 1960s, especially the community development and integrated rural development programmes, than the relatively hands-off atomic energy strategy of the time. There was no mention, for instance, of including within the purview of decision making any input from the communities being affected in this way: Sarabhai may have recognised society, and indeed may have been driven by a greater sense of the need to overcome poverty and underdevelopment, but there was no room for local knowledge or non-expert thinking within this system.

Sarabhai was working at two levels. On the one hand, his was a truly technocratic vision: he sought to make a clean break with the scientific queasiness exhibited by the AEC in not wanting to get their hands dirty solving real world problems. Sarabhai rejected the osmotic model of atomic energy as originally imagined by the postcolonial leaders. He refused to wait for the benefits of modern technology to seep into the collective unconscious, but rather deliberately and consciously forced an engagement between man and machine. On the other hand, by moving atomic energy away from the industrial grid and into the lived texture of people's existence, he proposed a more sustainable future for the atomic energy programme *qua* institution.[45] Sarabhai suggested that the means to save the atomic energy programme was to integrate it into an all-encompassing ensemble of technologically sophisticated artefacts which would provide and constitute modernity in India. Each power station would be surrounded by social and industrial consumption centres, producing a totality which would be autonomous yet interdependent. By integrating atomic energy into a bounded field of self-contained modern artefacts, it could be said that atomic energy was now being justified by producing its own consumers. Under the new scheme, instead of producing energy for social consumption, as originally planned, the social world was being brought into the domain of atomic energy in order to be serviced by it.

In more prosaic manner, the 1970 AEC document argued for an enormous expansion in the scope of atomic energy and space activities in India. Not only would India seek to build 500MW reactors, double the capacity of each unit it had undertaken to build thus far, but the overall programme of expansion included the development of gas centrifuge technology for uranium enrichment and the speeding up of the fast breeder reactor programme. By this plan, India would have 43,000MW of installed nuclear power by the year 2000, compared with less than 400MW actually operating in 1970 – an exponential increase which would be prohibitively expensive. This change in the reactor profile – building larger unit capacities and employing enriched uranium – suggests first that the AEC had not managed to bring down significantly the unit cost of producing electricity, and second, that increasing expenses had become a significant factor inhibiting the installation of more CANDU reactors. Sarabhai's response to the sluggish state of the atomic energy programme appears to have been a classic bureaucratic one – to spend more as soon as possible in order to overcome the problems, especially financial problems, of the past. His reasons for undertaking a decade-long project were straightforward: to get investment started right away. He had little doubt it could be done: 'It is hardly necessary to emphasise that for projects that take five to seven years to complete, we have to look at least ten years in advance if our progress is not to be halting and our results mediocre. The programme that we envisage is ambitious, but achievable.'[46] Sarabhai's 'ambitious but achievable' strategy drew heavily on the political capital he had built up, the sense that the atomic energy programme was in a rut, and the audaciousness of what he proposed. Even though enriching uranium is an extremely expensive technology to master, enriched-uranium reactors are cheaper than natural-uranium reactors in terms of physical capital costs, and, larger reactors at least hold out the possibility of lower electricity costs per unit. As long as decision-making is based on a strict cost–benefit basis, being able to present numbers that appear to prove that the long-term gains of current investment are an improvement on current returns allows a determined leader to argue that the shortcomings of the present can be swept aside as not relevant.

Sarabhai had taken a few years to get settled in as head of the AEC and had spent much of this initial period getting his ideas, especially in relation to the space programme, institutionally ensconced.[47] By 1970 he was ready to deploy his vision of the growth of these two programmes in tandem. This was a vision that was still within the established parameters of state science projects, but was explicitly social in its ends. Sarabhai seems to have realised that the principal problem facing postcolonial projects like atomic energy, both as material technologies and as ideological forms, was the distance between traditional society and modern technology: his solution to the problem was to force a connection between daily life and these technological mega-projects. His was the apogee of the rationalist view embedded in the atomic energy project as first conceived; within this system there would be no distinction between the instruments of development and its subjects – it would constitute a totality of modernity. Over time, as he saw it, atomic power, space satellites, and Indian society would enter into and produce a mutually constitutive relationship with each other. But any manifestation of this new Atlantis ended abruptly when Sarabhai died in his sleep at the age of 53, on 30 December 1971, just after the end of the third India–Pakistan war and the creation of Bangladesh.

After nearly two decades headed by the same person, the atomic energy complex now faced another major change of leadership in the span of five years. The question of leadership is crucial for organisations like the AEC, which had always been dominated by a single figure; this organisational characteristic in fact suggests that, had Sarabhai lived, he would have probably been able to carry out a substantial transformation of the atomic energy complex, even though his plans did not mimic the initial vision of the organisation. This time around, however, the new leadership was chosen from within the original coterie of Bhabha-mentored scientists. During Sarabhai's time, the membership of the Atomic Energy Commission was as follows: Sarabhai (chair), I.G. Patel of the Finance Ministry as member for finance, Homi Sethna, head of BARC, member for research and development, P.N. Haksar, of the Prime Minister's secretariat, J.R.D. Tata, the industrialist, and Satish Dhawan, director of the Indian Institute of Science, Bangalore. T.N. Seshan, of the Indian Administrative Service (IAS), was director of the department of atomic energy and secretary to the commission (a non-voting position). Following the tradition set by Bhabha, scientists dominated the Commission numerically, but only one of them, Sethna, came directly from the TIFR/BARC system. The newcomer Dhawan was not a nuclear physicist and would eventually become secretary to the Department of Space when it was set up in 1972: he was Sarabhai's protégé.[48]

Once Sarabhai died, the composition and the balance of power of the commission shifted. Sethna was appointed chairman of the AEC and Raja Ramanna, who had succeeded him as director of the Bhabha Atomic Research Centre (BARC), became member for research and development, and would eventually serve as Minister of State for Defence. Satish Dhawan was still a commissioner, but in mid-1972 he took over as chair of the newly formed Space Commission and secretary of the government's Department of Space. The Indian Space Research Organisation (ISRO), which had been chaired by another member of the original Bhabha group, M.G.K. Menon, also director of TIFR, was folded into the new umbrella organisation for space, the Space Commission. With these organisational changes, Dhawan would be in complete control over space activities and his active participation in atomic energy policy making commensurably less. Menon would go on to hold various governmental positions, including Minister of State for Science and Technology, and would chair various governmental commissions. M.G. Kaul took over from Patel as finance member and R.C. Sharma from Seshan as secretary to the AEC. Tata and Haksar, representatives of the private sector and the prime minister's office respectively, remained in place. The Trombay scientists were back in control of atomic energy and they were quick to suggest their unhappiness with the details of Sarabhai's vision, even as they agreed wholeheartedly with the demand for increased funding to atomic energy.

In a speech soon after becoming chairman of the AEC, Sethna indicated he was not in favour of the 500MW reactors or the enriched-uranium route proposed by Sarabhai for a variety of reasons, including the bogey of foreign dependence. He stated:

> As far as India is concerned, the 200MW nuclear unit is the largest single unit size and this is bigger than any thermal reactor operating at present. Should we then go in for bigger units? It is true that the cost of power is lower for large units, but this economy is possible only if there is a big enough base load so that the large units can function at say, 80% of their rated capacity.... Whilst enriched uranium systems are not as capital intensive [as natural uranium reactors] they call for the import of enriched uranium, *which could be cut off*. If, however, we decide to manufacture enriched uranium in this country (and we are investigating this problem) we are faced with the question of energy and costs.

All methods of separation of uranium, i.e., enrichment, involve large consumption of energy [Sethna then develops the theme of energy-consumption]. As I said, we are working on this method of separation, but it will be some time before we get the answers which would permit us to take a decision.[49]

Likewise, Raja Ramanna, in an article first published in *Electronics Today* around the same period, repeats almost the same criticisms, also invoking the danger from abroad. Discussing Sarabhai's ten year profile, he said,

The document itself points to all the difficulties in a country like India, though this was not said in so many words.... Should we go on building 200MW CANDU type reactor until our industry has stabilised ... or do we go next to ... building large scale systems of the order of 500MW on the basis that electricity become cheaper with larger unit size. If this is so, do we stop at 500MW units or go on to 1000MW units and so forth.... Do we even have a transport system which can handle such equipment and move it to remote places where nuclear power stations get located due to various considerations? Is the cost of such development a part of nuclear power cost or part of national development? *Such expenditure is perhaps more justified in a peaceful world, than say, expenditure on border roads....* The advantages of enriched uranium are obvious in any power station, but unfortunately the enrichment process is costly and the new technologies like centrifugation, though they have been widely talked about, are steps in the dark. How much risk does a country take in the interests of the future?[50]

How much risk indeed? There were words that struck a very different chord than the statements typical of the early leadership of the AEC. For Homi Bhabha and Vikram Sarabhai, brimming with boundless confidence in themselves and in science, any risk was worth taking even if success was not assured. For them the task of building an entire scientific complex from scratch, whether for atomic energy or for space, was always worth the risk because of the challenge of the project, but also because the price of not doing these tasks, in social terms, was too high. For the new leaders of the atomic complex, Sethna and Ramanna, caution was called for when thinking about the future of atomic energy. They were in favour of the continued growth of their institution, but preferred growth without risk. They would continue to push for an expansion in the number of reactors and for the increased utilisation of atomic energy, but their statements suggest that the period of technical and institutional innovation was over. As they saw it, great expense and effort had eventually made possible mastery of the technology of the 200MW CANDU reactor. Research on the next stage of the three-stage plan originally laid down by Bhabha, namely the development of fast breeder reactors, was proceeding in collaboration with the world's experts on this technology, the French. What need was there to court failure, and possibly raise questions about their expertise, by calling for the development of new, untested technologies – whether 500MW reactors or enriched-uranium systems?

Also to be noted from these statements is the alignment of the atomic energy programme alongside the discourses of fear and threat. Both Sethna and Ramanna assert, in almost the same words, that atomic energy cannot be seen simply as a instrument of national development. They argue that an atomic energy project inevitably spills over the national frame and becomes an object of international attention. Sethna suggests that some nations may seek to curtail Indian development in this field because of its military potential, while Ramanna argues that we live in a world of insecurity, making some decisions unrealistic owing to this natu- ralised condition. Through these moves, atomic energy is being firmly located in relation to the discourse of state fear and anxiety, of national security. Unlike Sarabhai who sought to move atomic energy away from this nexus, Ramanna and Sethna indicate they are more comfortable with an orientation where atomic energy marks a limiting condition between development and security and habituates a range of well-worn state and institutional practices. The AEC was no longer in the business of institutional innovation: it was time to hold on to what was in place and look for strategies of institutional maintenance.

NON-PROLIFERATION STRUGGLES

By 1972, when Sethna took over the AEC, marking the return of the original AEC scientific core, the anxieties of the previous decade had never seemed so distant. The country's economic situation had stabilised somewhat, and the once 'transitional' Prime Minister, Indira Gandhi, had successfully split her party and, following that, received a huge electoral mandate for her action. In December 1971, India had delivered a crushing military blow to its main regional rival, Pakistan, overcoming the ambivalent memories of the 1965 conflict and even perhaps, by extension, the humiliation of 1962. From the national security point of view at least, India seemed quite dominant.[51] A geographic peculiarity of South Asia, namely, that while India abuts all the countries of the region, none of them share borders with each other, now appeared to have a political correlate. After 1971, all roads to South Asia, so to speak, would lead through New Delhi. In the world view of the mandarins of the South, at last the 'natural' order they had been waiting for seemed to be falling into place; so too with the atomic energy establishment.[52]

But even if the regional order was settling into place thanks to military might, Indian diplomacy was fighting a very different battle on the global front. We turn to explore this arena, hoping through an examination of Indian behaviour to ascertain whether signs of a systematic nuclear policy or clues to understanding Indian restraint emerge. From the onset of the negotiations that would eventually lead to the formation of a non-proliferation 'regime', formalised by the Non-Proliferation Treaty (1970), Indian efforts had shuttled between closing some legal loopholes to the development of nuclear arms, while keeping open others. In general, the Indian position was to agree that while nuclear weapons, and the possibility of nuclear war, was one of the most serious problems facing the international community, the greater threat to world peace came not from an increase in the number of countries possessing weapons but from the enormous nuclear arsenals controlled by the US and USSR.[53] The baseline position of Indian negotiators, a position that dated to Bhabha's first days on the Scientific Advisory Committee of the IAEA, was that any regime seeking to control the spread of nuclear technologies had to be applied equally to all states. In Indian parlance, 'horizontal' proliferation could not be given precedence over 'vertical' proliferation, or, nuclear weapons powers could not be allowed to continue their arms build-up (vertical proliferation), while non-nuclear weapons countries found themselves facing a range of restrictions as they attempted to de-velop atomic technology in their own national interests (horizontal growth). Running parallel to this argument for equal treatment before international law was an articulation of national sovereignty. Nuclear weapons states were attempting to apply restrictions to the behaviour of non-nuclear weapons states, in effect, informing them of what they could and could not do to further their own national goals and objectives. This was a restriction that no self-respecting state could accept, especially if they had no intention of using atomic technology for military purposes.

This combination of arguments – the re-definition of the problem of proliferation and the elevation of national sovereignty to foundational status – allowed the Indian state to stake out a diplomatically singular and occasionally moral high ground in the UN Conference on Dis-armament, and drove two bargaining positions.[54] The first was to link any effort at controlling nuclear proliferation among 'new' countries to reductions in the arsenals of the superpowers, the second was to reject all conditions that might close off, legally or technically, Indian options with respect to 'peaceful' uses of atomic technology, however vacuous the term 'peaceful' would soon grow to become. These tactics were politically effective in a number of ways. First, they helped to buttress paternalist Indian claims to leadership of the non-aligned movement and the third world more generally by speaking for those countries who were not yet able to speak for themselves. Second, by couching these arguments in the idiom of a discredited image, that is, by implying that the North, or the nuclear 'haves', were guilty of international neo-colonialism, India could immediately split the coalition of nuclear weapons states and put them on the defensive. On hearing the accusation of neo-colonialism, the Soviet Union had of ideological necessity to identify with the 'progressive' Indian position in order to distinguish itself from 'capitalist' nations, while the West equally sought to separate themselves from the actions of their own past, while maintaining that these negotiations did not, somehow, create two classes of states. Under this attack, claims that selective nuclear restraint was for the greater good of international society began to sound a little hollow. More subtly, taking this seemingly principled position reminded other states of India's difference through its claim to uphold another image of international relations – of non-alignment from existing antagonistic blocs and peaceful co-existence as a norm of international behaviour.[55] This difference, it was hoped, would allow it thereby to assert a claim to membership in the élite group of states that set the rules and established norms for the international system.

Ironically, the Indian argument would soon lead to a double bind. A great measure of India's credibility in these international gatherings came from its ability to claim that it had the knowledge and technology to become a nuclear weapons state, if it so chose, but had self-consciously decided not to. India could point to its restraint in this regard even when provoked by repeated nuclear testing by its rival China. In other words, the strength of the Indian position lay in the argument and example that nuclear *weapons* proliferation was not inevitable even once the technical ability to do so was established. If nuclear restraint led to inclusion in the group of Great Powers, this strategy would be successful. But if it did not, and India went ahead and developed weapons in order to be included in the nuclear club, it would be shown up as hypocritical, and the basis of its original point of difference undermined. Thus, the Indian position could be too successful in that the very success of the strategy of self-restraint would prevent it from developing nuclear weapons, in order to be consistent with its strident international position.[56]

Two legal loopholes were employed in order to keep the 'option' open: first, the distinction between nuclear weapons powers and non-nuclear weapons powers, and, second, the distinction between nuclear tests for military purposes and 'peaceful' nuclear explosions. By claiming that adequate recognition did not exist for a state that was nuclear-capable but did not want to develop nuclear weapons, India created a space for itself to be a part of any international agreements about nuclear issues, without declaring itself a nuclear weapons state. It could legitimately stay out of the NPT regime by claiming that the discrimination it had called attention to had not been resolved to its satisfaction. India could say it was not signing the NPT, not because it wanted to develop weapons, but as a matter of principle. The first distinction, in the words of the Indian representative to the United Nations, V.C. Trivedi, was in order to 'destroy the impression that membership of the exclusive "nuclear club" is a desirable objective'.[57]

Further, by making a distinction between 'peaceful' and other nuclear explosions, it left the possibility open of demonstrating the capability to produce nuclear devices, in effect testing weapons, without appearing to fall into the category of a nuclear weapons state. Two factors aided this position: first, there is no determinable difference between a 'peaceful' test and a 'military' test from a technical point of view, and, second, there had been an extensive programme of peaceful nuclear explosions both in the United States (the 'Plowshare' programme) and the Soviet Union, which India could point to as other international examples of the validity of the notion of 'peaceful' nuclear explosions.[58] The need to keep this loophole open, employing all the discursive tactics mentioned above, is perfectly captured by V. C. Trivedi when he said to the Eighteen Nation Disarmament Commission in 1967:

> I would like to say a word or two on the ... question of peaceful nuclear explosives.... The civil nuclear Powers can tolerate a nuclear weapon *apartheid*, but not an atomic apartheid in their economic and peaceful development.... The Indian delegation does not deny that the *technology involved in the production of a nuclear weapon is the same as the technology which produces a peaceful nuclear device*, ... [but] technology in itself is not evil. Dynamite was originally meant for military use. Aeronautics, electronics, even steel fabrication – these are technologies which can be used for weapons as well as for economic development. That does not mean, therefore, that only the *poor and developing nations* should be denied all technology for fear they may use it for military purposes ... the solution of the problem must not be sought in the renunciation of the *sovereign right* of unrestricted development of [atomic] energy by some countries only ... we must not throw the baby away with the bath water.[59]

Arguing both for and against nuclear weapons in this way was not a stable position to be taking in the long run, but it was an effective tactical stance. What was important for India in the short term was to retain its position in the inner circle of international clubs like the Commission on Disarmament, and to ensure that, legally, it retained the possibility of carrying out nuclear tests at a time of its choosing. India had found a way of staying outside the NPT regime without losing support for its position, indeed it sought to convert weakness into strength by making its position appear principled. India could fall back on the super-powers' history of peaceful nuclear explosion programmes to justify its own. It had managed to stay free of an inspections regime imposed upon signatories to the NPT. Finally, by making its case on the basis of the foundational notion of 'sovereignty', it reaffirmed its acceptance of the dominant norms of international relations, even as it appeared to question them on the basis of fairness and equal treatment. The evidence thus leads to an ambiguous conclusion: India could, if it had wanted to, have conducted a nuclear test under the guise of a 'peaceful' nuclear explosion, yet, at the moment when the test would have seemed most logical, according to the norms of realist international relations, it did not. We are still no closer to understanding whether there was an ex-plicit policy not to develop weapons, or why there was such a hurry to get the 1962 atomic energy act in place: *Jaldi Kya Hai?*

DEMONSTRATION, OR THE NUCLEAR EXPLOSION OF 1974

'After Vikram Sarabhai's death in 1971, India began to seriously consider conducting a Peaceful Nuclear Explosion (PNE).'[60] These words tell one tale and ignore another. In his autobiography, Raja Ramanna, former director of the BARC and member of the Atomic Energy Commission, describes how the Pokhran explosion of 1974 came to pass by locating it as one of a series of events that began after he and Homi Sethna, AEC chair from 1972, came to power. He suggests that the institutional direction in which the atomic complex had been heading during the 1960s, just before the death of Bhabha, were set back on track. Is that all there is to it?

There had always been regional suspicions about the Indian desire to conduct an atomic test; Pakistan had raised this question in international gatherings at least since 1966, and her diplomats had been following the Indian acquisition of nuclear technologies since even earlier.[61] Around this time, discussion of this issue expanded into other arenas and became more public. To take just one example, in November 1972, the Prime Minister replied to a question in the Lok Sabha saying, 'The Atomic Energy Commission is studying conditions under which peaceful nuclear explosions carried out underground could be of economic benefit to India without causing environmental hazard.'[62] Knowledge of the debate had also spread beyond the region. Lincoln Bloomfield, a professor at MIT's Centre for International Studies, wrote to a friend in the US Arms Control and Disarmament Agency (ACDA) in May 1971 that he had been visited by a senior civil servant from the Indian defence ministry, Srinivasa Krishnaswami. Krishnaswami had informed him that a debate was under way in the Indian government over the pros and cons of going nuclear. While the external affairs ministry was opposed to a PNE, the Atomic Energy Commission was in favour, he noted, implying that the defence ministry would have the 'swing vote'. Krishnaswami appeared to be getting the benefits of Bloomfield's analysis of this decision, even as he was informing the US government through an informal channel that India was considering such a move: they were sending up a 'trial balloon' to gauge potential international reactions to such an event.[63] When the Canadians heard of this possibility, they warned the Indian government that there would be economic and political repercussions should India decide to carry out an explosion.[64]

As this debate went on, with its suggestion of a choice yet to be made, for the atomic scientists the decision to go ahead with a PNE was already a *fait accompli*. They were involved in the details of bomb production: finalising the design for the explosive, producing the trigger and supporting electronics, and preparing the plutonium device in the requisite shape. *Bombmeister* Raja Ramanna reports close collaboration with the Defence Research and Development Organisation (DRDO) laboratories from 1972 onwards, a first for the AEC and the Indian defence ministry.[65] The DRDO was necessary because only they had the necessary expertise to produce the conventional explosives necessary for the implosion device. For the bomb to work, conventional explosives would go off first, forcing the plutonium to the centre of the device, where it would form the critical mass required for a nuclear reaction to occur. By 1973, according to Ramanna, all the necessary technical problems had been solved. A site was found in the Indian army's test range in the Rajasthan desert, in the north-west of India, a 'closed area with a sparse human population'.[66] The time for final decision-making soon came, Ramanna reports, again suggesting the decision could be revoked, while he at once adds that it was a foregone conclusion, as the bomb – the 'plutonium alloy' as he calls it – had already been moved to the test site. Even though there was some opposition in the small group of advisers to the Prime Minister up to the last minute, 'Mrs Gandhi decreed that the experiment should be carried out on schedule *for the simple reason that India required such a demonstration.*'[67] 'India' duly conducted an underground nuclear explosion on Saturday 18 May 1974.

The Indian atomic programme as well as the country as a whole went through turbulent times during the 1960s. While the atomic complex had been consolidated, legally, economically, and institutionally, it had had to adjust to the loss of both its scientific founder, Homi Bhabha, and its greatest political resource, Jawaharlal Nehru, in quick succession. By the end of the decade, and certainly by the early 1970s, the possible change in institutional direction started by Vikram Sarabhai had been arrested and the original Trombay scientists were back in control. I have argued that Sarabhai had sought to introduce two new directions to the atomic programme: his desire to go in for the production of larger reactors and enriched uranium facilities, and his definition of specific social ends, most concretely an image of rural transformation that integrated demand and supply 'centres' in harmonious co-existence. However, there is an additional aspect to the Sarabhai vision that needs to be addressed, especially in relation to atomic weapons. Earlier, quoting the press conference announcing Sarabhai's appointment as chair of the AEC, I noted that he had been categorically against atomic explosions, as they would not 'help our security'. His reasons for this decision are worth examining in detail in order to contrast his view to that of the Trombay scientists.

Contrary to the pacifist position he is often thought to have held, Sarabhai did not reject atomic weapons outright as a means to national security. What he was adamantly opposed to was the appearance of an aggressive military posture without the necessary infrastructure and means to back this position up. But he also distinguished between threats that appeared to emanate from within to those that appeared to come from abroad. For Sarabhai, it was not clear which source of threat was more serious for the country: 'I would like to emphasise that security can be endangered not only from outside but also from within. If you do not maintain the rate of progress of the economic development of the nation, I would suggest that you would have the most serious crisis, something that would disintegrate India as we know it.'[68] Of course, these words were being spoken at a time of considerable economic and political turmoil in India, but the point is that Sarabhai was setting up a familiar dichotomy for national policy makers to choose from. Was internal development going to be the priority, or was external defence? To quote him, 'So the real problem in this whole question relates to the utilisation of national resources for productive and social welfare against the burden of defence expenditure which a country can bear at any particular time.'[69] What did the 'either guns or butter' argument mean in this context? Speaking of nuclear weapons, Sarabhai pointed out that 'paper tigers', a term borrowed from Chairman Mao, did not provide security, 'that is, you cannot bluff in regard to your military strength'. But in order to provide for credible military strength for successful deterrence:

> that is not achieved by exploding a bomb. It means a total defence system, a means of delivery in this case. You have to think in terms of long range missiles;

it means radars, a high state of electronics, a high state of metallurgical and industrial base. How do you develop such a system? ... It requires total commitment of national resources of a most stupendous magnitude ... I think India should view this question in relation to the sacrifices it is prepared to make, viewing it in its totality.... [That is why] an atomic bomb is not going to help our security.[70]

Sarabhai was arguing, first, that India could not afford an atomic deterrent in order to be secure from external threats, as nothing short of a full-fledged atomic weapons arsenal with all its concomitant systems (delivery systems, second strike capability, command and control infrastructure) would provide that security. Second, and more subversively, he suggests that perhaps the more serious threats to national security came from within the country – and atomic weapons were certainly not going to be of help there. In other words, Sarabhai was denying the correspondence between the possession of atomic weapons and the particular meanings that the state and the Trombay scientists wanted to attribute to particular manifestations of atomic energy. He saw an atomic explosion as having no significance as an instrument of foreign policy because it was a 'paper tiger' and was not backed by the complete infrastructure of deterrence. Further, it had no relevance as an instrument of domestic policy because it did not further economic development, the only response to India's 'true' crisis of security. By providing these alternative arguments, he rejected completely the idea of conducting an explosion for demonstration, just to show that Indian scientists could do it. His realist approach, which sought to frame problems in the starkest binary fashion – development or security – could not fathom the point of demonstration. The idea of demonstration was pointless as it had no instrumental value in itself and was positively dangerous as it suggested that India had all the concomitant resources of nuclear deterrence. Sarabhai refused to acknowledge the ambivalence made possible through the detonation of a nuclear explosive, how it could link the internal domain with the external, and tie development to security.

The Trombay scientists did not share this view. Apart from distancing themselves from Sarabhai's challenging and risky technological choices, they also rejected his totalising approach to public policy. They could not accept his sharply divided worlds of meaning, internal from external. From a purely tactical point of view, the Trombay scientists would not see issues in either/or terms, for that constituted an enormous constraint on their options. They had not achieved their level of institutional success by being fixed to unchangeable positions; quite the contrary, it had been their flexibility that had aided their survival. Thus for them the idea of 'demonstrating' mastery of technology fitted into a different register of affect. It was a register that replaced ends with means, that defined success not in terms of the welfare such technologies would provide when in common use, but in terms of the more prosaic and controlled placing of technological artefacts in the public sphere for admiration – as a state fetish. Their objective was precisely to produce a linkage between the various meanings attributed to atomic energy, especially between security and development. National development was to be reconfigured to mean national security, and the explosion of an atomic bomb was to be the index of security. For the AEC, an atomic explosion was the surest way of demonstrating this connection.

JALDI YEH HAI?

Perhaps now we are in a position to appreciate the government's hurry when it came to the Atomic Energy Bill of 1962, and why in spite of the rush, 'nothing' happened. This chapter has shown that, first, the atomic energy establishment began the process, through certain strategic choices, of ensuring the ability to produce nuclear weapons from as early as the mid-1950s. Second, following the Chinese nuclear test of 1964, élite opinion shifted markedly in the direction of arguing the need for an independent Indian nuclear weapons programme. Third, Indian international negotiating postures were always careful to ensure that India would retain the possibility of conducting nuclear explosions/tests through their conceptual separation of the idea of the 'peaceful' nuclear explosion from the military test. According to the logic of realism, all of these factors, coupled with the urgency surrounding the Atomic Energy Act of 1962, should have forced India to become a (*de facto* or otherwise) nuclear state well before 1974. That it did not is a paradox within the dominant logic of international relations.

A very different interpretation can be found by weaving together a narrative operating at three levels: institutional, national, international. I have already suggested above what was at stake for the atomic scientists as institutional figures. The AEC had begun to shift its institutional orientation from that of an organisation whose stated objective was the production of cheap electric power through atomic energy to that of one in the business of enhancing national security through the development of nuclear weapons capability. This orientation was always latent in the conception of atomic energy employed by the Indian state, as I have shown from the analysis of the Constituent Assembly debates of 1948. For the AEC, the Chinese test came along at a moment which reinforced their own institutional direction. The Chinese test did not create a new condition forcing an appropriate response, rather it allowed the atomic scientists to identify and mobilise new social allies for a project that was already well under way. From the institutional point of view, as I have shown, not taking the final steps toward building nuclear weapons is most clearly related to sudden changes in leadership. Rapid and unsettling changes during the 1960s left the nuclear project in suspended animation as it waited for a semblance of institutional continuity to return.

If changes in leadership stymied the AEC, a very distinct set of conditions were being played out abroad. This was the diplomatic position established by the Indian state in multilateral negotiations. I have already pointed to the double bind the Indian position on nuclear proliferation had led them into, the bind that prevented them from testing in order to remain consistent to their position, even as they kept the possibility open by arguing that peaceful nuclear explosions were not identical with a military test. Yet the crux of Indian difference, the basis of their power as it played out in these settings, was the *restraint* they had shown in not conducting a test, especially when they were directly provoked and when it became clearer and clearer that they were capable of conducting a test. But this restraint was not derived from conscious decision-making. It came from indecision and uncertainty.

How do we explain this restraint? Indian foreign policy was in a peculiar position until 1974. Thanks to the moral stature of Mahatma Gandhi, to the timing of independence, to the size of the country, and to the figure of Nehru and the third world that he articulated and represented, India in foreign affairs had played a role far in excess of the raw economic and military power it brought to the table, the bottom-line calculus of relative importance in the international system during the Cold War. Their advantage was that as long as the 'realist' norms that underlay the post-1945 international system had not yet become absolute, the articulation of alternative norms could not be ignored. This moment and these conditions allowed India to become a relatively influential player in this system for a few short years following its independence, notwithstanding its 'real' status as an economically poor, militarily weak country. India's zenith as a maker of international order may well have been reached during the armistice negotiations during the Korean war, even though its visibility remained high during the 1950s and the beginnings of the Non-Aligned Movement. But after Suez and the beginning of British decline, India's international standing uncannily followed suit. By the early 1960s and especially following the Chinese conflict in 1962, India's original foreign policy positions of peaceful co-existence and equal distance from all blocs was in tatters. The decline of India's standing was not separate from the strengthening of the norms of realism: as the Cold War intensified, and the United Nations became less relevant, less attention was paid to a country that argued for an international system based on principles that rejected raw strength and power. India could not remain immune to this trend; its ability to stand apart seemed ever more compromised when its unique mixed economy appeared to be failing, when it requested more aid from those it castigated for moral flaws, and when its security was imperilled from within and without the region. Under these circumstances, the denouement came when India was tested according to the dominant norms of the international system, and came up short according to those standards. For cynically minded realists in the international system, the Indian war with China in 1962 was the moment when the philosopher-kings of India were shown to have no clothes.

However, even as India's relative position declined, Indian élites never stopped thinking of their country as one that deserved to play an important role in the international system. The more 'realistic' of them realised the sooner that continued influence might not be separable from increased military power (in the days of the Cold War), but this was by no means a mainstream position. No one was more seduced by the flights of Indian rhetoric than Indians themselves, which is why Indian élites have never quite fully understood why the country is not given the importance it naturally deserves in the world. Hence, to continue to hold a number of important positions in international meetings, not the least of which was the UN Conference on Disarmament, was very important both for the self-image of the Indian foreign policy élite as well as for the country that had told itself that it was held in the highest esteem internationally. The rhetoric expressed in these meetings had less and less effect on the course of action of the most powerful states in the international system, but it was still powerful in India: officials of the External Affairs ministry expressed over and over again the uncertainty of what might happen if they changed their behaviour. Indian nuclear restraint was the outcome not of holding fast to a principled position in the international system, but rather of the fear of what might happen to India's international position if it decided to change it. No change would be more dramatic than conducting a nuclear explosion. It was a decision that no one was willing to take; indeed, most never knew that it was a decision possible to take.

The 1962 Atomic Energy Act can now be seen in very different light. If the 1948 Act governing atomic energy was passed in order to conceal from the Indian public that their most highly regarded indigenous post-colonial project was in fact deeply imbricated in an external economy of trade, exchange, and barter, its public justification was precisely the opposite. It was argued that the secretive provisions of this law were necessary for the protection of this enclave from external threats. In fact the 1948 law was put in place in order to prevent domestic forces from becoming aware of the relative lack of local knowledge and technology within the atomic energy system; the Act was defined in order to make impermeable the boundaries between the state and domestic society even as it opened the atomic complex up to the outside world. The 1962 Act performed precisely the opposite function. Even as it appeared that the thrust of the provisions of this law were directed against a domestic audience, against the many regions whose resources it would appropriate, against the workers whose safety it would disregard, the more compelling reasons for its enactment lay elsewhere. This Act was passed, urgently and with considerable arm twisting, in order belatedly to shore up the boundaries between the domestic and the foreign, between inside and outside. At the moment when the Atomic Energy Commission was close to completing the technical conditions allowing for the development of nuclear weapons, it became critical, for the reasons outlined above, not to let the outside world know what was happening. It may be recalled that the 1948 Act already legalised most of the provisions the 1962 Act would re-emphasise. The domestic public was already at arm's length; the security surrounding the atomic enclave was already tight; the state could already appropriate any mineral and other resources it needed. The principal weakness for the atomic complex came from outside. Sealing that point of access was the purpose of the 1962 Act, in order for the institutional shift toward nuclear weapons and national security to be hidden from the gaze of the outside world, which had helped India obtain most of the materials it needed for a military project, to protect India's diplomatic position from breaking down. Thus, in contradictory fashion, what we call *restraint* cannot be separated from the imposition of a formal, legal, coercive barrier between India and the outside world.

Finally, we come to the position embodied by Sarabhai. I have already shown that he could not countenance the idea of a demonstration of nuclear capability without the resources and will necessary to commit India to a full-fledged nuclear arsenal. From his realist standpoint, this was at best meaningless; at worst, it was a foolhardy decision likely to provoke the wrath of countries that would see India as a problem that would have to be dealt with in the same coin. It would create, not solve, Indian security problems. This position was in marked contrast to the position of AEC scientists like Sethna and Ramanna, who saw no conflict in conducting the experiment of a nuclear test even if it was never going to lead to anything else. For one thing, conducting a nuclear test excited them as scientists. To know whether they could carry it out, to feel what the great Manhattan Project scientists must have felt, to do science for the state: all these factors must have made this experiment seem an exciting and worthwhile task. As institutional figures, however, they also saw the nuclear test as a symbol of the changing fortunes of the atomic energy establishment. If the establishment was undergoing hard times, if people had lost faith in atomic energy, if filling the shoes of giants like Sarabhai and Bhabha was weighing heavily on them, what better example of their own ability would there be than to conduct an activity that only five other countries had carried out successfully? Not only that, this would truly be an indigenous project. No country was going to help India carry out a project of this kind. All the questions they had faced about the authenticity of the Indian nuclear programme would be resolved by this test: better still, even if they failed, there was good chance that they would get away with it because of the enormous degree of secrecy covering their every action. What did it matter if it never led to anything? This event would take care of their institutional needs for many years while they basked in the fallout of that explosion.

For the political leadership, especially Indira Gandhi, the nuclear explosion was similarly above all a symbol. India's long transition, starting before the death of Nehru and running through the 1960s, appeared finally put to rest after the 1971 military defeat of Pakistan and the creation of a new country out of what was once East Pakistan. By seeming to show that Islam was not sufficiently mobile as a political ideology to keep the two wings of Pakistan together, India's own official ideology of secularism seemed reinforced. For the country struggling to define a clear identity for itself after the first flush of independence, the nuclear explosion was a symbol of a new beginning, of putting to rest the ghosts of the past. The restraint of the past, a restraint that I have argued was born of indecision and concealment, could now be replaced with an irreversible action demonstrating a new India that would have to be taken seriously by the international system. After all, if the world's pecking order was defined above all by the existence of nuclear capability, who could any longer deny that India deserved to be in its highest ranks? From Indira Gandhi's point of view, the nuclear explosion was conducted from a position of great strength. It thus became a metonymic condition for India's renewed strength, first proven on the battlefield and then confirmed beneath the Rajasthan desert. And this is how it was seen by Indian élites: proof of the importance of the country, a proof confirmed by the furious reaction of the Western powers to this action.

Demonstrations, however, like all second order signs, have one problem: by definition, they have a surplus of meaning.[71] Hence they can rarely be contained within the discursive frame of their 'original' sense. If the demonstration of an 'indigenous' nuclear reactor in the 1950s was meant to show, first, the virtuosity of Indian scientists, and, second, the ability of the postcolonial state to produce the means for a whole-scale transformation of the Indian landscape, that event became also the tangible proof that there was no longer any need to wait for the promise of development to come about. Domestic expectations of immediate change now escalated exponentially. The state's only possible response, given their inability to satisfy these expectations, was to clamp down on the representations of that demonstration through the use of state power.

Likewise, the 1974 nuclear demonstration: meant first to mark the rise of a new ruling clique within the AEC, and, second, to buttress India's claims to a renewed power and purpose, it became immediately much more than that. In particular, the sign of the nuclear explosion was equated internationally with the expectation that India was now going to produce a nuclear arsenal, just as every other state that had conducted such a test had done. This led both to Pakistan renewing its efforts to build nuclear weapons, in the best action–reaction scenario, and also for India to become the object of greater scrutiny and punitive action by the powers of the international system. The nuclear explosion had completely upset India's relations with its neighbours and changed its status, for the worse, within the international system. India neither reaped the benefits of taking this step – most obviously, being invited to serve as a permanent member of the UN Security Council – nor did it objectively improve its international standing or security. No one stopped to think, even in the wake of the oil crisis and the US departure from the gold standard, whether the codes of international power were still what they had been a decade before. By 1974, nuclear weapons were no longer the single, universally accepted and valorised currency of inter-national power. Yet 'restraint' continued to mark India's foreign policy, as if nothing had changed (recall, this was a 'peaceful' nuclear explosion). But now India had shown its hand. From this point on, India would be considered a nuclear power at (other's) will; not in order to give India the alleged benefits of membership of the nuclear club, but rather to punish it, to point to the dangers of proliferation, to use it as justifica-tion for military build-ups in the region. What happened in 1998 would reinforce that trend, as by then the modes of power in the international system had shifted even further. India first created an unstable regional environment, and then twenty-four years later acted to reinforce that instability.

NOTES

1. Member of Parliament Baday in the debate on the Atomic Energy Bill of 1962, *Lok Sabha Debates*, Third Series, Second Session, 20 August 1962, p. 2919.

2. Debate on the Atomic Energy Bill of 1962, *Lok Sabha Debates*, Third Series, Second Session, 20 August 1962, p. 2864.

3. Debate on the Atomic Energy Bill of 1962, *Lok Sabha Debates*, Third Series, Second Session, 20 August 1962, p. 2914.

4. Debate on the Atomic Energy Bill of 1962, *Lok Sabha Debates*, Third Series, Second Session, 20 August 1962, pp. 2864–5.

5. Debate on the Atomic Energy Bill of 1962, *Lok Sabha Debates*, Third Series, Second Session, 20 August 1962, emphasis added, p. 2865.

6. Debate on the Atomic Energy Bill of 1962, *Lok Sabha Debates*, Third Series, Second Session, 20 August 1962, p. 2870.

7. Debate on the Atomic Energy Bill of 1962, *Lok Sabha Debates*, Third Series, Second Session, 20 August 1962, p. 2872.

8. Debate on the Atomic Energy Bill of 1962, *Lok Sabha Debates*, Third Series, Second Session, 20 August 1962, p. 2882.

9. Debate on the Atomic Energy Bill of 1962, *Lok Sabha Debates*, Third Series, Second Session, 20 August 1962, pp. 2930–1.

10. Debate on the Atomic Energy Bill of 1962, *Lok Sabha Debates*, Third Series, Second Session, 20 August 1962, emphasis added, p. 2864.

11. Debate on the Atomic Energy Bill of 1962, *Lok Sabha Debates*, Third Series, Second Session, 20 August 1962, emphases added, p. 2925.

12. Raja Ramanna, *Years of Pilgrimage* (Delhi: Viking, 1991), p. 69.

13. Ramanna, *Years of Pilgrimage*, p. 69.

14. Ramanna, *Years of Pilgrimage*, p. 71.

15. Iris Heidrun Lonergun, 'The negotiations between Canada and India for the supply of the NRX nuclear research reactor 1955–1956: A case study in participatory internationalism', MA thesis, Carleton University, Ottawa, August 1989, p. 122

16. Lonergun, 'The negotiations between Canada and India', p. 155.

17. The rule of thumb is that the contaminant plutonium isotopes must be less than 7% of the total for a reliable yield. See Office of Technology Assessment (OTA), 'Nuclear Proliferation and Safeguards', Main Report, PB-275-843, Dept. of Commerce, Washington, DC (June 1977), p. 141; and Dietrich Schrooer, *Science, Technology and the Nuclear Arms Race* (New York: John Wiley, 1984), pp. 316–31.

18. H.N. Sethna and S.N. Srinivasan, 'Operating experience with the fuel reprocessing plant at Trombay', *Nuclear Engineering* (Chemical Engineering Progress Symposium series), vol. 65, no. 94 (1967), p. 24.

19. Office of Technology Assessment, 'Nuclear Proliferation', p. 30.

20. Schrooer, *Science, Technology*, p. 331. The plant's output is estimated at 9.4 kg annually in 'Analysis of six issues about nuclear capabilities of India, Iraq, Libya, and Pakistan', Report prepared for the US Senate Foreign Relations sub-committee on Arms Control, Oceans, International Operations, and Environment (January 1982), p. 3.

21. In 1965, a US inter-department group chaired by the State Department (the Gilpatric Committee) produced a report on factors influencing the decision

to acquire nuclear weapons. It stated that India has the 'capability of producing and testing a first nuclear weapon in one to three years after a decision to do so. A weapon deliverable by the Indian Air Force's Canberra bomber could be produced about two years after the first test.' p. 2. South Asia folder, Nuclear Non-Proliferation documents, National Security Archive, Washington, DC.

22.   T.J.S. George, *Krishna Menon: A biography* (Bombay: Jaico Publishing House, 1966).

23.   Itty Abraham, 'Civilian Scientists and Military Technologies: India's Strategic Enclave', *Armed Forces and Society* (Winter 1992); Raju Thomas, *Indian Security Policy* (Princeton: Princeton University Press, 1988).

24.   For a sampling of contemporary domestic views on the nuclear question (though not on the question of guarantees, which were secret), see Raj Krishna, 'India and the Bomb', *India Quarterly*, May 1965; Sisir Gupta, 'The Indian Dilemma', in A. Buchan, ed,. *A World of Nuclear Powers*, (New York: Prentice Hall, 1966); special issues of *Opinion*, vol. 7, no. 3, May 1966; *Science and Culture* vol. 30, no. 10, October 1964; *Seminar*, 83, July 1966; D. Som Dutt, 'India and the Bomb' *Adelphi Papers*, no. 30 (November 1966); V. Dutt, 'The Bomb and We', *Times of India*, 19 May 1966; Minoo Masani, 'The challenge of the Chinese Bomb', ICWA lecture, 8 December 1964 (mimeo).

25.   Memo of the committee on nuclear non-proliferation, 29 March 1965. South Asia folder, Nuclear Non-Proliferation documents, National Security Archive, Washington, DC.

26.   M. R. Srinivasan, former chairman of the Indian Atomic Energy Commission, in a recent op-ed, denies that India ever asked the US for assistance to test a nuclear weapon in the 'early Sixties', as stated by Daniel Ellsberg. Ellsberg says that Dean Rusk, then Secretary of State, in particular was not unsympathetic to this request. Srinivasan rejects this idea because, in his view, India would never have asked the US, of all countries, for assistance. Srinivasan bases his statement on having seen the official correspondence, which is not available to scholars or the public. As I have indicated above, available US documents show quite the opposite. Cf. 'Self Reliance is the Key', *Hindu* (Madras), 7 December 1995, p. 12.

27.   Chester Bowles to Secretary of State, State Dept. telegram, 26 October 1964. South Asia folder, Nuclear Non-Proliferation documents, National Security Archive, Washington, DC.

28.   Dept. of State memorandum of conversation with Dr Bhabha and B. K. Nehru. Others present, Robert Anderson, David Schneider, and Undersecretary Ball, 22 February 1965. South Asia folder, Nuclear Non-Proliferation documents, National Security Archive, Washington, DC.

29.   Department of State memorandum, 22 February 1965, Nuclear Non-Proliferation documents, NSA, Washington, DC.

30.   Sampooran Singh, *India and the Nuclear Bomb* (Delhi: S. Chand and Co., 1971), p. iii.

31.   See Pramit Chauduri, *The Indian Economy: Poverty and Development* (Bombay: Vikas, 1978), especially pp. 41–76.

32.   Lloyd I. and Susanne H. Rudolph, *In Pursuit of Lakshmi: The political economy of the Indian state* (Chicago: University of Chicago Press, 1987), p. 133.

33.   Swaran Singh quoted in J.P. Jain, *Nuclear India*, vol. 2, (New Delhi: Radiant Publishers, 1974), p. 178.

34. Lloyd I. Rudolph and Susanne H. Rudolph, *In Pursuit of Lakshmi: The Political Economy of the Indian State* (Chicago: University of Chicago Press, 1987), p. 133.

35. Robin Jeffrey, 'The Prime Minister and the Ruling Party', in James Manor, ed., *Nehru to the Nineties* (Delhi: Viking, 1994), p. 169.

36. Jeffrey, 'The Prime Minister and the Ruling Party', p. 169.

37. Raja Ramanna, *Years of Pilgrimage*, p. 74; Chester Bowles to State Dept. telegram, 'In discussion with EMBOFF Oct. 26 [1964], Gopal of [Ministry of External Affairs] said pressures within Government of India for India to develop its own bomb were building up. Bhabha was the leading advocate for this group and he was actively campaigning for India to go down the nuclear road. Gopal stressed, repeat, stressed that no decision had been reached and he personally felt that India would not reverse its nuclear policies. However, matter was under active debate and discussions had gone far enough for Shastri to authorise Bhabha to come up with what was involved in India's attempting an underground "explosion".'

38. For a useful study of this period see C. P. Srivastava, *Lal Bahadur Shastri: A life of truth in politics* (Delhi: Oxford University Press, 1995).

39. For details of Menon's continuing career as a 'state scientist' see C.R. Subramaniam, *India and the Computer* (Delhi: Oxford University Press, 1994).

40. INCOSPAR eventually mutated into the Indian Space Research Organisation (ISRO) in 1969. Further details of Vikram Sarabhai's life and activities can be gleaned from a hagiography, Padmanabh K. Joshi, ed., *Vikram Sarabhai: The Man and the Vision* (Ahmedabad: Mapin Publishing, 1992).

41. Quoted in J.P. Jain, *Nuclear India*, p. 180.

42. Raja Ramanna, 'Chairman, Atomic Energy Commission', in Joshi, ed., *Vikram Sarabhai*, p. 121.

43. *Atomic Energy and Space Research: A profile for the decade, 1970–1980* (Bombay: Atomic Energy Commission, 1970).

44. *Atomic Energy and Space Research*, pp. 1–2.

45. *Atomic Energy and Space Research*.

46. *Atomic Energy and Space Research*, p. 2.

47. See Table 1 in Abraham, 'Civilian Scientists and Military Technology'.

48. Parenthetically, the civil servants listed above are an extremely interesting group: larger in number than in Bhabha's day, they were all carefully chosen and already were (or in Seshan's case, would become) extremely influential. Patel would go on to become Governor of the Reserve Bank of India and director of the London School of Economics. Haksar was closely linked to Indira Gandhi and served as an extremely influential member of her circle of informal advisers. Seshan would eventually become Cabinet Secretary and acquire considerable notoriety as Chief Electoral Commissioner after official retirement from the civil service.

49. Homi Sethna, lecture to the Nuclear Physics and Solid State Symposium, BARC, Trombay, 3 February 1972, published in *Nuclear India*, vol. 10, 6 (February 1972), pp. 4–6.

50. Ramanna, *Vikram Sarabhai*, p. 122.

51. For a typical endorsement of this view see the opening pages of Robert Bradnock, *India's Foreign Policy Since 1971* (London: RIIS/Pinter, 1990), pp. 1–2.

52. For an insightful critique of India's 'rightful place' in South Asia, see Anirudha

Gupta, 'A Brahmanic Framework of Power in South Asia?' *Economic and Political Weekly*, 7 April 1990, pp. 711–14.

53. There is no single official policy statement to which one can point to substantiate this position, yet it can be observed in practice through the actions of Indian negotiators for the last forty years. For an intellectual rationale and for the most systematic explanation of this position see the work of the enormously influential Indian strategic thinker, K. Subrahmanyam, especially his edited volume, *Nuclear Proliferation and International Security* (New Delhi: Institute of Defence Studies and Analyses, 1985).

54. See the collection of speeches in Jain, *Nuclear India*, vol. 2 and Ashok Kapur's interviews with V. C. Trivedi in his *India's Nuclear Option: Atomic diplomacy and decision-making* (New York: Praeger, 1976).

55. See M. S. Rajan, *Non-alignment: India and the future* (Mysore: University of Mysore Press, 1970).

56. This makes the Indian position following the Chinese test of 1964 even more confusing. This could have been the perfect moment to 'go nuclear' and yet have a fail-safe reason according to the logic of international anarchy. But it did not.

57. Quoted in Jain, *Nuclear India*, vol. 2, p. 182.

58. Office of Technology Assessment, *Nuclear Proliferation*, pp. 144–5. PNEs were so popular not so long ago that Malaysia asked the Indian government whether they would be willing to use nuclear explosives to build a harbour in Sarawak. Letter from Dr Teh Hock Heng, Director of Malaysia's National Institute for Scientific and Industrial Research, to Gerald Johnson, US AEC, 5 May 1973. Victor Gilinsky Papers, Box 209, HI, Stanford, Calif.

59. Jain, *Nuclear India*, vol. 2, pp. 192–3, emphasis added.

60. Ramanna, *Years of Pilgrimage*, p. 88.

61. Memo on the visit of a Pakistani envoy to the US AEC to inquire about safeguards on the Indo-US nuclear agreement, 15 March 1963. Victor Gilinsky Papers, Box 211, HI, Stanford, Calif.

62. Quoted in Jain, *Nuclear India*, p. 327.

63. Lincoln Bloomfield to Phillip Farley, Deputy Director, ACDA, 11 May 1971. Victor Gilinsky Papers, Box 211, HI, Stanford, Calif.

64. Quoted in Jain, *Nuclear India*, p. 344.

65. An aside to this discussion is that interaction with the DRDO was, according to Ramanna, due to his friendship with B.D. Nag Chowdhury, Scientific Adviser to the Ministry of Defence. Yet Nag Chowdhury had been a student and colleague of Meghnad Saha, implacable enemy of the AEC. Obviously by this time the tension between 'Calcutta' and 'Bombay', between the two main academies of science in the country, had diminished considerably.

66. Ramanna, *Years of Pilgrimage*, p. 88.

67. Ramanna, *Years of Pilgrimage*, p. 89.

68. Quoted in Jain, *Nuclear India*, vol. 2, p. 179.

69. Jain, *Nuclear India*, vol. 2, p. 179.

70. Jain, *Nuclear India*, vol. 2, pp. 179–80.

71. Roland Barthes, *Mythologies* (New York: Farrar, Strauss, & Giroux, 1970).

5

FETISH, SECRECY,
NATIONAL SECURITY

FETISH

To say 'nothing happened' for 24 years after the 1974 explosion is to say that an expected narrative did not unfold to govern the usual meanings of a nuclear explosion. The histories of Indian nuclear policy since 1974 see that event as a beginning rather than as an end, and ask questions about the missing events expected to follow: where are the second and third tests, the delivery systems, the C^3I (command, control, communications, and intelligence) systems, the backup and safety parameters built into the nuclear complex, who is in charge, and so on. But these are the correct questions to ask only if the 1974 PNE was planned as the event to announce to the world that India was now a nuclear power, which is why they cannot be answered.

The challenge laid down by domestic critics of the atomic programme, notably Meghnad Saha, was to suggest that the AEC would not be capable of developing an atomic programme in India: in particular, they would not be able to create an atomic reactor, the quintessential sign of atomic prowess. The need to respond to this challenge, to keep domestic critics at bay, condensed the terms of the AEC's overall project from developing a full-fledged nuclear programme over the long haul into the concrete task of producing a nuclear reactor in the short term. Under the best of circumstances, of course, the reactor would have been purely indigenous. Thanks to the prevailing conditions of official secrecy, the AEC was able to get away with producing a reactor that at best can be described as hybrid. The AEC's first Indian reactor, *Apsara*, was based on an imported design, with British fuel rods and components, but was represented as a purely Indian achievement, the 'first in Asia'. The production of the *Apsara* reactor in 1956, while undoubtedly a scientific and technological achievement, was represented in terms that had little to do with science or technology *per se* and much more to do with the state's promise of modernity. The event was seen to create a new moment in the discourse of Indian statehood by inference, the modernity of the object, an atomic reactor, metonymically leading the country to the front rank of technologically developed states. By suggesting that it was quite indigenous, almost wholly the effort of Indian scientists, it re-articulated a vision of Indian statehood that equated technological achievement and sophistication with national development. But by the very token of its success as representation, this first reactor would trigger a set of demands on the system to fulfil promises made earlier.

Through demonstration, the production of the technological artefact which would stand in for development (or national security as the case may be), the state sought to produce a modern fetish. Inscribed with all the accoutrements of the postcolonial state's desire − science, modernity, indigeneity − the technological artefact was meant to stand out from the landscape of Indian history and tradition, bearing no trace of its origins, embodying the future, situated only in relation to other fetishised objects like dams, railways, steel mills and jet aircraft, aesthetically and practically the new face of India. The special, even sacred, aura of the state fetish produced through the difference it embodied, affirmed through its particular rituals of achievement and status, monitored by the high priests of the modern state (in this case the atomic scientists) was the demonstration, and, by displacement, the proof, of the postcolonial.

If, following Michael Taussig, the state as fetish seeks to mask the gaze of the public from political reality, the state fetish equally seeks to conceal the conditions of its creation, to marginalise questions of its origins, to naturalise the displacements of its production, to fulfil simultaneously all the multiple economies in which it circulates.[1] But the fetishised relation is always doubled, as Laura Mulvey reminds us. '[Fetishism] is the most semiotic of perversions. It does not want its forms to be overlooked but to be gloried in. This is of course a ruse to distract the eye and the mind from something that needs to be covered up. And this is also its weakness. The more the fetish exhibits itself, the more the presence of a traumatic past event is signified.'[2] In other words, the 'better' the fetish becomes in obscuring the conditions of its production, in exemplifying a new mode of scientific modernity and aesthetics, the more difficult it becomes to dispel the curiosity that underwrote the willing suspension of disbelief basic to the fetishised relation. In the case of atomic reactors, the ever increasing size, scale, and power of the reactor would engender ever increasing curiosity about its conditions of production: where did it come from, what was here before, who made it, whose aesthetics are these, does it perform?

The discourse of the postcolonial state had always been to present atomic energy as the privileged instrument of development, but due to the exigencies of urgency and secrecy – specific modalities of the post-colonial project – the instrument of development became its end. The very existence of an atomic reactor was tantamount to the promise of development. But it was merely a demonstration. The idea of demonstration could not be contained within its discursive frame due to the very conditions of production of atomic energy as a state project in the first place. If the AEC was able to produce a reactor indigenously, this meant that the scientists were now capable of carrying out their historic mandate, and, further, that the remaining elements of the postcolonial project would soon be available for public consumption. The resolution of the postcolonial dilemma appeared to be at hand. However, these were expectations that the AEC was clearly not able to fulfil. They had managed to produce *Apsara* as a demonstration of their ability to carry out the promises made in their institutional name, not to suggest that the whole project was ready for integration into the national development system. The state's only available response was to conceal, even more than before, the institution of atomic energy behind the barrier of state secrecy in order to postpone the emerging public denouement of unfulfilled modernity. All that was left was the idea of demonstration.

We realise that the greatest flaw in the making of the reactor-fetish was the conditions of production: the scientists in their laboratories. Unable, or unwilling to transform their practice, which in this context is likened to a craft, into the modernist parameters of industrial practice, which would have been a basic condition for the expansion of their complex, the reactor as fetish was always marked by the authorial presence of the scientist. Scientists *qua* members of the scientific institution could not but seek credit for their creation, thereby re-inscribing the marks of the scientific craft shop where they should have been seeking to erase all reference to the present, producer, and practice. The scientists had produced the notion of the demonstration as a way of vivifying the state's project. As long as they were able to produce a working model of the system they were meant to be creating, they could make the claim that this path was a strategic choice, that their programme was still on track toward its final objectives, and, most important for them, that they were still a part of the world community of scientists. Each working model, each demonstration, was marked with the signs of a scientific practice which did not – could not – follow the forms of the commodity. As a result, the curiosity engendered by the fetish always had something to hold on to in its search for the reality that lay beyond. The fetish was undermined in the conditions of its making: scientists, not engineers, produced it, demonstrations, not systems, were their goal. But for the fetish to 'work', signs of history, origins, and function were counterproductive for the state's ideological project. The state, facing these flawed representations of the postcolonial, had to install a process that erased its multiple social relations. Nothing short of gross power, of overt domination, would have to be used in order to erase these immodern traces. Ironically, this condition, the use of state violence to mask signs of scientific authorship, were in turn necessary to produce legitimate authority. This contradiction produces an escalation of greater violence as each recognition of the limits of the artefact would create more doubt and confusion. In order to eradicate these histories, the presence of other spaces, the signs of subversive meaning basic to the conditions of production, the state set into motion a process that was gravely compromised by the weight of its own contradictions.

SECRECY

We have argued that the curiosity engendered by the fetish always had something to 'hold on to' as a result of the conditions of its production. In other words, one cause of the breakdown of this project was generated by the atomic complex, the outcome of the necessity of opening itself up to the immodern gaze of the outside. How did those 'inside' attempt to retain their distinction under this assault?

The postcolonial project as a whole was to transform the external social landscape in order to be successful. This implies that the location of the modern boundary, the line between being and becoming, was always a constraint central to the self-understanding of those within the project.[3] This boundary was historically and socially produced. It could not be static but was always engendered under political forces; thus to know where it was, and to keep it in place was a vital component of the politics of the postcolonial. Not surprisingly, we find that establishing and controlling the limits of the modern was a source of much anxiety for those within the atomic energy complex. Let us explore some views of this struggle.

From the air, the main buildings of the Tata Institute of Fundamental Research (TIFR) are built in the approximate shape of an Orthodox cross. The building lines are perfectly straight, with all movement at right angles. At ground level, on approaching the building after passing through a manned guard post, the visitor on foot sees the building at the point where two wings meet. Apart from a few gardeners busily working, there is hardly anyone about, an uncommon sight. The building looms large and somewhat forbidding, with rows of columns on the ground floor like stilts supporting the overall structure. The general impression is of a modern industrial facility. Windows run regularly across the length of the facade marking each floor. There is no feature of visual relief from the outside, except for the occasional glimpse of gardens beyond the ground floor columns. The rigidity of this design is somewhat ameliorated by the setting, particularly by the movement of the sea, but even the landscaped gardens that lie between building and sea are carefully and formally symmetrical. This is a building in the best, that is to say, most rationalist, architectural modernist style.

What is remarkable about the TIFR building, notwithstanding the desires of its Chicago architect, is that it does not betray any obvious mark of physical location, only its place in time.[4] Perhaps this is not so surprising. Thomas Metcalf notes that public architecture in colonial Bombay was unusual in that it did not succumb to the imperial desire to find a mediating position between the Indian and the Western, a mediation which took its most distinct form in the 'Indo-Saracenic' style of architecture. Rather, the dominating architectural image of public buildings in Bombay was Gothic – especially the enormous Victoria Terminus train station, built 1878–87, which 'forever stamped Bombay as pre-eminently a Gothic city'.[5] Metcalf suggests that the predominance of this architectural form was emblematic of the city that 'sought to define itself as to some degree a European city, a trading and commercial city….[Bombay] looked outward'.[6] Like the massive public buildings in Bhabha's natal city, the TIFR building was not meant to evoke features appropriate to 'India'. In its outer shell, starkly modernist and formal, with primacy given to Cartesian norms of space, this structure represents a transformation of the ground it stands on, a concrete symbol of a 'scientific temper' that was not yet India but at some point would be. Modernity was the explicit project of the atomic scientists. This was a building of the future, producing an image of a modern India, making possible the idea of Bombay looking outward again, but to a different horizon. But, if this was a building of the future, how do we represent the present and the past? The TIFR building must also be read as an attempt to repress the memory of an alien, colonial presence, not past conquerors like the British, but rather the unscientific present. The postcolonial project was, at its heart, an attempt to overcome, and simultaneously to deny, representations of India that teemed with tropes of the irrational, unscientific, and immodern. If any building was to symbolise the future, it would have to address these shortcomings. But this is where history and geography displace each other. The building of the future had to confront the present, only to discover that it was impossible to contain traditional representations of India within the same space. These representations would push against the boundaries set up by this difference – colonial/postcolonial, immodern/modern – a pressure that is repeatedly evoked in representations of these 'temples of modernity' across the country.

The habitual presence of the non-scientific, traditional, and the im-modern along, together, around and even within the modern scientific institutions of the atomic energy complex made a confrontation difficult not to acknowledge. The view of the scientist that sought to erase the past and the non-scientific is further developed in official photographs of the Trombay atomic energy complex. These photographs, especially those dating from the 1960s, centre the iconic dome of the CIRUS reactor, showing it set in the middle of carefully landscaped gardens each conforming to an imposed geometry of two dimensions: a perfect circle and a rectangular form set within a triangular space. The gardens, sym-metrical in themselves, act also as a device to draw attention back to the perfect dome of the reactor at its centre. But the edges of this photograph betray the limits of transformation. The borders of the promontory on which the reactor is located are less clearly articulated in Cartesian space. They are scrublands, dry and spotted with unruly bushes. They mark the intransigence of the land, but, by the same token, denote the degree of human effort that has made this orderly and unnatural space possible.

The 'natural' spaces and gardens represented in this photograph are artifices deliberately designed to provide an appropriate backdrop for the primary object, the vivid and dominating man-made building. The idea was to have the modern building appear in harmony with its surround-ings: yet this degree of naturalness could come only from the careful and powerful application of symmetry, balance, and order to nature. The result was not a sympathetic mediation between man and nature – quite simply it was the modernist conceit of the effortless and natural rule of man over nature. The official photographs of the Trombay complex develop this conceit explicitly. Taken from a hillside above the reactor and buildings, they provide the only possible point of reference which demonstrates, beyond doubt, the order and symmetry that has gone into the design of the land. This panoptic view provides a unique gaze to the viewer: it 'proves' that atomic energy is dominant, orderly, and planned – and powerful. On the right-hand side of the photograph is a long horizontal structure, which contains pipes for the reactor cooling system. The struc-ture extends into the sea and forms a two-dimensional axis with a 400-foot high cooling tower at the edge of the water. The planar space thus defined extends out from the atomic energy complex, visually intersecting the island of Elephanta, site of an old Shiva temple, as if to slice it in half. The breakwater and its tower marks modernity's distance from its past/present. It defines a boundary between the old and the new, not a natural boundary that separates, but a forceful divide that seeks to erase what lies beyond the limits of the modern. In the face of this aggression, our sight is drawn back to the messy scrublands at the margin of the photograph. The visual and concrete difference of the atomic energy reactor now seems less so: we are confused and made uncertain by the signs of the immodern in the presence of the hypermodern.

Perhaps most vivid and violent in its representation of the rational, scientific modern emerging from the *tabula rasa* (or rather, the slate *made blank*) of the traditional Indian landscape is the following account by former chairman of the AEC, Dr M. R. Srinivasan. Srinivasan's narrative appears in the introduction to a volume containing his major public addresses, published in-house by the Department of Atomic Energy on the occasion of his 60th birthday. The young scientist-protagonist was looking for a site for India's first power reactor; he would eventually choose a small village called Tarapur. Srinivasan describes his trip as follows:

> Chakravarti and I [Srinivasan] made a reconnaissance visit of the west coast from Bombay to Dahej, on the Narmada river, close to where the river joins the sea. Three coastal sites appeared promising and one of them was Tarapur. Chakravarti and I set off to Tarapur by road. The Bombay–Ahmedabad highway had not yet been built. So we drove from Bombay to Bhiwandi and on to Manor. From Manor we proceeded to Palghar and then on to Tarapur. The Manor–Palghar stretch across the western ghats was deeply furrowed with the middle hump posing a hazard to the engine crank case. In fact our car did hit a high bump and there was an oil leak from the crank case. We had to have the State Transport bus depot at Palghar attend to the problem. It was the monsoon time and there had been a lot of rain. From Tarapur, Chakravarti and I got onto a bullock cart as it was the only way to reach the light house, just north of the coastal promontory which I had selected as a potential site from a study of the maps. We could go no further than the light house as there was no cart track even and the approach was very slushy and water logged. From the very first visit, I was convinced that Tarapur offered an ideal site for an atomic power station.[7]

This account explicitly evokes the genre of the pioneer or explorer, with intrepid travellers setting off on a journey that gets progressively more rugged and less civilised, with the everyday markers of modern life gradually growing more faint. They start by car, but some roads are missing and the rest are bad, so they take a circuitous route. At a suitable moment, when they are still far from their destination, the car breaks down. The next form of conveyance mentioned is the bullock cart, which appears as if by magic, but should be taken to represent the rustic state the scientists now find themselves in. How they had gone from Palghar to Tarapur (where they got into the bullock cart) is not mentioned in order to develop further the sense that 'Chakravarti and I' were proceeding deeper into the unknown, armed only with maps and faith in reason. The lighthouse appears at their worst moment, when even the appropriate technology of the bullock cart had failed and raw nature had done her worst to the 'slushy and water-logged' track. Its sight gives them both relief and refuge, and marks the limit of human transformation of the land. This transcendent moment is violently undone by the abrupt transition of the next sentence: 'From the very first visit, I was convinced that Tarapur offered an ideal site for an atomic power station.' Time collapses in the face of the promised land. In a moment, we are transported from the desolate and virgin promontory to the space of a modern functional atomic reactor many years later.

The movement from the arrival at land's end to the 'ideal site for an atomic reactor' is instantaneous; this abrupt move implies that whatever was there operates only as prehistory to the real event, the building of the reactor. The narrative takes us on an apparent journey in space, from metropolitan Bombay to the empty wilderness: once there, the natural landscape becomes a building site and a nuclear reactor is made to come forth all at once. Everything human and living is written out of this story: the bus station with its drivers and travellers, the bullock cart with its driver, the lighthouse with its operators. We are informed only about the progressive deterioration of the land, and, by inversion, the growing perfection of the site – visible at one glance – where from *nothing* would come the most modern artefact of all.

There is an uncanny symmetry between this passage and Marshall Berman's reading of modernity, beginning with Goethe's *Faust*. In Acts four and five, when Faust comes upon the sea, which he sees as a potential source of great energy which is being wasted, Berman notes: 'Suddenly the landscape around him metamorphoses into a site. [Faust] outlines great reclamation projects to harness the sea for human purposes: man-made harbours and canals that can move ships full of goods and men; dams for large-scale irrigation; green fields and forests, pastures and gardens; a vast and intensive agriculture; waterpower to attract and support emerging industries ... all this to be created from a barren wasteland where human beings have never dared to live.' [8] The only obstacle in his way are the old couple, Philemon and Baucis, who live in a small cottage on the beach. Eventually the couple are killed and their house razed. Returning to Bombay and Srinivasan's pioneer narrative, it comes as little surprise to find that the allegedly virgin land from where a reactor and all the by-products of rational modernity would emerge full-blown was similarly transformed: an entire village of 600 people, the village of Tarapur, was, in good bureaucratese, 'shifted beyond three miles prior to the operation of the reactor'.[9]

The violence scripted into the 'tragedy of development' narrative outlined in Berman's reading is typical of the Enlightenment's belief in science and progress, and, by the same token, its suppression of the human and social. Goethe's original insight, the need to fuse 'the affinity between the cultural idea of *self*-development and the real social movement toward *economic* development', captures the core of the Nehruvian project: to bring people's minds and their landscape into harmony through the imposition of large-scale industry and modern technique. The violence that is inscribed into a transformation of this kind is never spoken of by the makers of development. But it is there. In the case of atomic energy, it is manifest in 'shifting' villages, harassing journalists, trying to get academics fired, rejecting calls for testing of water-tables for radioactive leaks, using unprotected villagers as casual labour for cleaning up radioactive spills, and denying the extent of radiation-related illnesses in the communities around their reactor sites.[10] But above all, the use of the might of the state is a sign that the hegemony it sought, the transformation of people's minds, has not taken root. This brings us to secrecy.

We have seen the play of secrecy from the outset. Secrecy was written into the fabric of the atomic energy programme through the atomic energy acts and other ordinances, ostensibly because atomic energy was a substance prized by unnamed foreign agencies, but in fact to shield many activities from the eyes of the Indian public and their representatives. Secrecy would be used to prevent other scientists from working on atomic energy, and would be used to hide the state of progress within the atomic energy programme. Secrecy would be useful in order to negotiate with competing foreign agencies to get the best deal for the Indian programme. But secrecy is also a part of the scientific enterprise. For scientists seeking to be the first to come up with a discovery, it is commonplace to conceal techniques, strategies, data, experimental materials and instruments from rival labs, even as it is not uncommon to use forms of scientific espionage in order to determine what other labs or scientists are up to. Secrecy is so ingrained in the modern scientific enterprise that it is hardly commented upon unless someone, usually an outsider, draws attention to it.[11]

Secrecy takes all these forms, and one more, which is foundational. Secrecy is a boundary-producing mechanism, an instrument of modern discipline. Rather than simply seeing it as a furtive condition that keeps information privileged or hidden, it can act to produce a violent rupture between inside and outside, between a space that is privileged and that which is profane. The imposition of secrecy allows the unambiguous definition of what is 'inside' and what is 'outside', what is modern and what is not. Secrecy helps to produce and monitor formal lines of transgression. For the Indian atomic energy programme, struggling under the weight of its modernist project of total transformation, the unsightly and unseemly presence of premodern and irrational India was a constant sign that their project was not complete, and generated the anxiety that it never would be. From the outset, but especially as the ability to keep a proper distance between the modern and the premodern became more and more limited, as it became more and more difficult to assert with authority that the modern was in fact so, they took recourse to the force of the state in order to police and maintain the difference they needed so badly. To hold on to this difference was crucial for the atomic scientists. Secrecy, in this form, produces and maintains the fiction that there is an unbridgeable difference between the premodern and the modern. The boundary-producing mechanism we usually associate with secrecy works to keep the outside at bay. But this may not be sufficient in this context, for it presupposes that we already know that what is inside is valuable, and what it outside is not. More effective in this case is to invert the agency: secrecy *constitutes* the inside as valuable and devalues the outside. Secrecy, in other words, becomes a necessary condition for the maintenance of the difference between the modern and everything else. Without secrecy, the singularity of the postcolonial project would become difficult to maintain for those practising, and with most invested in, its performance, and under those circumstances there would be no project at all.

POSTSCRIPT

If the notion of a state fetish is undermined by its conditions of production – scientists who cannot become industrial engineers – while secrecy is the means by which the eroding difference of the postcolonial is shored up, it does not take much to realise that these are unstable relations. The signs of collapse of the postcolonial project are made manifest by the 1974 underground 'peaceful' nuclear explosion, a would-be fetish that became a pure sign. We are reminded that, 'Mrs Gandhi decreed that the experiment should be carried out on schedule for the simple reason that India required such a demonstration'.[12] For Mrs Gandhi, this 'experiment' may have been less an announcement to the world of India's new bellicose status than a reminder to a domestic audience that India's state institutions were capable of scientific and technological achievement of a high order. By semantic relay, she may have hoped to suggest that the promise of a scientific modernity was still the privileged means for the making of a postcolonial state. But it was too late for that. Given the ever-present ambivalence between development and security within the modern state's postcolonial project, a demonstration for national development could no longer be differentiated from a demonstration for national security. Indira Gandhi may have wanted to reaffirm development as the focus of the state's purpose, but she could not control the flow of representations that made this event the proof of the move to national security. The tension of straddling the pacific/military divide had been resolved in favour of the latter, historically more familiar, stance. The 1974 explosion was the demonstration for which 'India' had unconsciously been waiting since 1948 and the formal announcement of the creation of an atomic energy programme.

Following the PNE of 1974 it slowly began to dawn on the atomic energy establishment and the political leadership what they had demonstrated and what its implications were. This event had moved them from a mythic space of non-alignment and peaceful co-existence into an everyday realm of naturalised fear, threat, danger and insecurity. The more this political class protested that the nuclear explosion was peaceful, the more it was assumed by those outside that it was not. Faced with this discursive cul-de-sac, the national security community had no choice but to believe that it was true. They began to re-imagine the history of the Indian nuclear programme to fit these 'facts', they began to build long- and short-range rockets and ballistic missiles, and they began to change the state's self-representation. The conditions of secrecy that enveloped the scientific project are now more familiar: this is secrecy for national security, the naturalised condition of exclusion that is intrinsic to the modern state and normalised in contemporary international society. Ideological sustenance could now be drawn from the dominant discourse of International Relations, the currency and speech of inter-state interaction. The apparatus of the national security state began to take shape on the ground. Finally, in 1998, the state's rhetoric caught up when India conducted a new round of tests and officially announced it was a nuclear weapons state.

India's position at the Comprehensive Test Ban Treaty talks, once seen as out of character, should now come as no surprise. Following the 1974 peaceful nuclear explosion, an event whose signification lay wholly within the realm of national security, the postcolonial project of development collapsed into a project of national security. Refusing to sign this treaty for reasons of 'sovereignty' and 'national self interest' is completely consistent with the dominant discourse of political realism, of the search for security of the state in an anarchic realm. This was the fallout of the original postcolonial project – while the peaceful nuclear explosion certainly demonstrated the possibility of an 'India', it produced an India remade for the times, more in line with the rest of the world and its paranoias, less committed to retaining its distinction and the options that it had once articulated. Under the weight of a nuclear explosion, singularity fused into identity.

The Indian atomic energy programme continues to be out of time. Even as the Indian state has now abjured its original position on the peaceful uses of atomic energy and accepted fully the anarchic norms of the international system, the world has not remained in the same place. International ideas about nuclear power have come full circle. Atomic energy no longer has the significance it once had. A country acquires neither international respect nor prestige by developing, or continuing to hold, nuclear weapons. The latest movement against nuclear weapons is not led by the superpowers eager to monopolise atomic energy for themselves and to prevent other countries from obtaining them, but rather by non-nuclear countries. International public opinion, to the extent that there is such a thing, is now where India was nearly half a century ago. But India has moved on from its once lofty, idealistic standpoint. India has demanded its right to become a nuclear power just when the atomic age has come to an end, and thus remains an outsider, a spoiler, but for reasons completely opposed to its original purpose.

NOTES

1. Michael Taussig, '*Maleficium*: State Fetishism', in Emily Apter and William Pietz, eds., *Fetishism as Cultural Discourse* (Ithaca: Cornell University Press, 1993), pp. 217–50.

2. Laura Mulvey, 'Preface', in *Fetishism and Curiosity* (Bloomington: Indiana University Press for the British Film Institute, 1996), p. xiv.

3. Cf. Martin Heidegger, 'The Question Concerning Technology', in *The Question Concerning Technology and other essays*, trans. William Lovitt (New York: Harper Torchbooks, 1977).

4. See the essay by architect Helmut Bartsch in 'Inauguration of New Buildings' (Bombay: Tata Institute of Fundamental Research, 1962).

5. Thomas R. Metcalf, *An Imperial Vision: Indian Architecture and Britain's Raj* (Berkeley: University of California Press, 1989), p. 93.

6. Metcalf, *An Imperial Vision*, p. 96.

7. M.R. Srinivasan, 'An Intermezzo', in *Selected Lectures of Dr M.R. Srinivasan* (Bombay: Department of Atomic Energy for the Nuclear Power Corporation of India, n.d.), p. 6.

8. Marshall Berman, *All That is Solid Melts into Air* (New York: Simon and Schuster, 1982).

9. P. Abraham, D. Pattnaik, and S.D. Soman, 'Safety experience in the operation of a BWR reactor in India', IAEA/SM-169/26, n. d., p. 2. Victor Gilinsky Papers, Box 211, HI, Stanford, Calif.

10. See the documentation in Dhirendra Sharma, ed., *The Indian Atom: Power and Proliferation* (Delhi: Philosophy and Social Action, 1986); the work of Praful Bidwai in the *Times of India*, Bombay and elsewhere; recent articles by Rita Chinai referenced in my 'Science and Power in the Postcolonial State', *Alternatives*, Spring 1996.

11. Cf. Bruno Latour, *Science in Action: How to Follow Scientists and Engineers through Laboratories* (Cambridge, Mass.: Harvard University Press, 1986).

12. P. Abraham, D. Pattnaik, and S.D. Soman, 'Safety experience', p. 89.

BIBLIOGRAPHY

I. PUBLISHED BOOKS AND ARTICLES

Abraham, Itty, 'Science and power in the postcolonial state', *Alternatives*, 21, 3 (July–September 1996).

Abraham, Itty, 'Towards a reflexive South Asian security studies', in Weinbaum and Kumar, *South Asia Approaches the Millenium*.

Abraham, Itty, 'Civilian Scientists and Military Technologies: India's "Strategic Enclave" ', *Armed Forces and Society* (Winter 1992).

Agarwala, A.N., and S.P. Singh, eds., *The Economics of Underdevelopment* (New York: Oxford University Press, 1963).

Ahmed, Aijaz, *In Theory: Classes, Nations, Literatures* (London: Verso, 1992).

Ajwani, SH., 'Thorium Cycle', *Nuclear India*, vol. 4, 8 (April 1966).

Anderson, Benedict O'G., *Imagined Communities: Reflections on the growth and spread of nationalism*, expanded edition, (London: Verso, 1991).

Anderson, Robert, *Building Scientific Institutions in India: Bhabha and Saha* (Montreal: Center for Developing Area Studies, 1975).

Anderson, Robert, 'Growing Science in India – 2: Homi J. Bhabha', *Science Today* (Bombay), November 1976.

Apter, Emily, and William Pietz, eds., *Fetishism as Cultural Discourse* (Ithaca: Cornell University Press, 1993).

Aronowitz, Stanley, Barbara Martinsons and Michael Menser, eds., *Technoscience and Cyberculture* (New York: Routledge 1996).

Bardhan, Pranab, *The Political Economy of Development in India* (Delhi: Oxford University Press, 1984).

Barthes, Roland, *Mythologies* (New York: Farrar, Strauss, and Giroux, 1973).

Basalla, George, 'The Spread of Western Science', *Science*, 156 (May 1967).

Berman, Marshall, *All That is Solid Melts into Air* (New York: Simon and Schuster, 1982).

Bernstein, Barton J., 'The Quest for Security: American foreign policy and international control of atomic energy, 1942–1946', *Journal of American History*, 60, (March 1974).

Bhabha, Homi J., and W. Heitler, 'The passage of fast electrons and the theory of cosmic ray showers', *Proceedings of the Royal Society*, 159A (1937).

Bhabha, Homi J., 'On the penetrating component of cosmic radiation', *Proceedings of the Royal Society*, 164A (1938).

Bhabha, Homi J., 'The role of atomic power in India and its immediate possibilities', paper presented at the first international conference on the peaceful uses of atomic energy, Geneva, August 1955. Reprinted in Jain, *Nuclear India*, vol. 2.

Bhabha, Homi K., 'Interrogating Identity: The Postcolonial Prerogative', in Goldberg, *Anatomy of Racism*.

Bhabha, Homi K., 'The Commitment to Theory', in Pines and Willemen, *Questions of Third Cinema*.

Bidwai, Praful, and Achin Vanaik, 'Testing Times: The global stake in a nuclear test ban' (Uppsala: Dag Hammarsköld Foundation, 1996).

Bothwell, Robert, *Nucleus: The History of Atomic Energy of Canada Limited* (Toronto: University of Toronto Press, 1988).

Broughton, John, 'The Bomb's Eye View: Smart weapons and military TV', in Aronowitz et al., *Technoscience and Cyberculture*.

Buchan, A., ed., *A World of Nuclear Powers* (New York: Prentice Hall, 1966).

Campbell, David, *Writing Security: United States Foreign Policy and the politics of identity* (Minneapolis: University of Minnesota Press, 1992).

Casimir, Hendrik, *Haphazard Reality: Half a century of science* (New York: Harper and Row, 1983).

Chambers, Iain, and Lidia Curti, eds, *The Postcolonial Question: Common Skies, Divided Horizons* (London: Routledge, 1996).

Chatterjee, Partha, *Nationalist Thought and the Colonial World: A derivative discourse?* (London: Zed Books, 1987).

Chatterjee, Partha, *The Nation and Its Fragments: Colonial and postcolonial histories* (Princeton: Princeton University Press, 1993).

Chaudhuri, Pramit, *The Indian Economy: Poverty and Development* (Bombay: Vikas, 1978).

Chenery, Hollis, et al., *Redistribution with Growth* (Oxford: Oxford University Press, 1974).

Chilton, Paul, 'Nukespeak: nuclear languauge, culture and propoganda', in *Nukespeak: The media and the bomb* (London: Comedia, 1982).

Chomsky, Noam, *Deterring Democracy* (London: Verso, 1992).

Cortright, David, and Amitabh Mattoo, eds, *India and the Bomb: Public Opinion and Nuclear Options* (Notre Dame, Ind: University of Notre Dame Press, 1996).

Dickson, David, *The New Politics of Science* (Chicago: University of Chicago Press, 1984).

Dirlik, Arif, 'The postcolonial aura: Third world criticism in the age of global capitalism', *Cultural Critique* (Winter 1992).

Dixit, Abha, 'Status Quo: Maintaining nuclear ambiguity', in Cortright and Mattoo, *India and the Bomb*.

Dutt, Som, 'India and the Bomb', *Adelphi Papers*, no. 30 (London: IISS, November 1966).

Edelman, Murray, *Political Language: Words that succeed, policies that fail* (Orlando, Fla: Academic Press, 1977).

Elsasser, Walter M., *Memoirs of a Physicist in the Atomic Age* (New York: Science History Publications, 1978).

Fermi, Laura, *Atoms in the Family* (Albuquerque: University of New Mexico Press, 1954).

Foucault, Michel, *Discipline and Punish: Birth of the Prison*, trans. Alan Sheridan (New York: Vintage, 1979).

Frankel, Francine, *India's Political Economy, 1947–1977* (Princeton: Princeton University Press, 1978).

Frisch, Otto R., *What Little I Remember* (Cambridge: Cambridge University Press, 1979).

Galison, Peter, and Bruce Hevly, eds, *Big Science: The growth of large scale research* (Stanford: Stanford University Press, 1992).

George, T. J. S., *Krishna Menon: A biography* (Bombay: Jaico Publishing House, 1966).

Gilpin, Robert, *The Political Economy of International Relations* (Princeton: Princeton University Press, 1987).

Goldberg, David, ed., *Anatomy of Racism* (Minneapolis: University of Minnesota Press, 1990).

Goldschmidt, Bertrand, *The Atomic Complex* (La Grange Park, Ill.: American Nuclear Society, 1982).

Goldschmidt, Bertrand, *Atomic Rivals* (New Brunswick: Rutgers University Press, 1990).

Gowing, Margaret, *Independence and Deterrence: Britain and Atomic Energy, 1945–1952*, vol. 1, 'Policy Making' (New York: St. Martin's Press, [1964] 1974).

Gupta, Anirudha, 'A Brahmanic Framework of Power in South Asia?' *Economic and Political Weekly*, 7 April 1990.

Gupta, Sisir, 'The Indian Dilemma', in Buchan, *A World of Nuclear Powers*.

Hagerty, Devin, 'Nuclear Deterrence in South Asia: The 1990 Indo-Pakistani Crisis', *International Security*, 20, 3, (Winter 1995–96).

Hall, Stuart, 'When was the "postcolonial": Thinking at the limit', in Chambers and Curti, *The Postcolonial Question*.

Harding, Sandra, ed., *The 'Racial' Economy of Science: Toward a democratic future* (Bloomington: Indiana University Press, 1993).

Harvey, David, *The Condition of Postmodernity* (Oxford: Blackwell, 1989).

Hart, David, *Nuclear Power in India: A comparative analysis* (London: George Allen and Unwin, 1983).

Hecht, Gabrielle, 'Political Designs: Nuclear Reactors and National Policy in Postwar France', *Technology and Culture*, 35, 4 (1994).

Hecht, Gabrielle, 'Peasants, Engineers, and Atomic Cathedrals: Narrating modernization in postwar provincial France', (forthcoming in *French Historical Studies*).

Helmreich, Jonathan E., *Gathering Rare Ores: The diplomacy of uranium acquisition, 1943–1954* (Princeton: Princeton University Press, 1986).

Hersey, John, *Hiroshima* (New York: Vintage [1946], 1985).

Hirschman, Albert O, *The Strategy of Economic Development* (New Haven: Yale University Press [1958], 1961).

Holloway, David, *Stalin and the Bomb: The Soviet Union and Atomic Energy, 1939–1956* (New Haven: Yale University Press, 1994).

'Inauguration of New Buildings' (Bombay: Tata Institute of Fundamental Research, 1962).

Infield, Leopold, *Why I left Canada: Reflections on Science and Politics* (Montreal: McGill–Queen's University Press, 1978).

Jaggi, O. P., *History of Science, Technology, and Medicine in India*, vol. 9, 'Science In Modern India' (Delhi: Atma Ram and Sons, 1984).

Jain, J. P., ed., *Nuclear India*, vols. 1–2 (New Delhi: Radiant Publishers, 1974).

Jeffrey, Robin, 'The Prime Minister and the Ruling Party', in Manor, *Nehru to the Nineties*.

Jessop, Bob, *State Theory: Putting capitalist states in their place* (University Park: Penn State Press, 1990).

Joshi, Padmanabh K., ed., *Vikram Sarabhai: The Man and the Vision* (Ahmedabad: Mapin Publishing, 1992).

Jungk, Robert, *Brighter than a Thousand Suns* (New York: Harcourt, Brace, Jovanovitch, 1956).

Kapur, Ashok, *India's Nuclear Option: Atomic diplomacy and decision-making* (New York: Praeger, 1976).

Kaviraj, Sudipta, 'Indira Gandhi and Indian Politics', *Economic and Political Weekly*, vol. XXI, 38–39, 20–27 September 1986.

Kevles, Daniel, *The Physicists: The history of a scientific community in modern America*, reprint ed., (Cambridge, Mass.: Harvard University Press, 1995).

Klein, Bradley, *Strategic Studies and World Order: The global politics of deterrence* (Cambridge: Cambridge University Press, 1994).

Knorr-Cetina, Karin, and M. J. Milkay, eds., *Perspectives on the Social Study of Science* (London: Sage, 1983).

Krishna, Raj, 'India and the Bomb', *India Quarterly* (Delhi), May 1965.

Krishna, Sankaran, *Postcolonial Insecurities: India, Sri Lanka and the Question of Eelam*, (Minneapolis: University of Minnesota Press, forthcoming).

Kumar, Deepak, *Science and the Raj: 1857–1905* (Delhi: Oxford University Press, 1995).

Kuznets, Simon, 'Underdeveloped countries and the pre-industrial phase in the advanced countries', in Agarwala and Singh, *Economics of Underdevelopment*.

Latour, Bruno, 'Give me a laboratory and I will raise the world', in Knorr-Cetina and Milkay, *Science Observed*.

Latour, Bruno, *Science in Action: How to follow scientists and engineers through society* (Cambridge, Mass.: Harvard University Press, 1987).

Lefort, Claude, *The Political Forms of Modern Society: Bureaucracy, democracy, totalitarianism*, translated by John B. Thompson (Cambridge, Mass.: MIT Press, 1986).

Lewis, John, and Xue Litai, *China and the Bomb* (Stanford: Stanford University Press, 1988).

Lippman, Walter, *U.S. Foreign Policy: Shield of the Republic* (Boston: Little, Brown, 1943).

Manor, James, ed., *Nehru to the Nineties* (Delhi: Viking, 1994).

Marshall, W., ed., *Nuclear Power Technology*, vol. 1, 'Reactor Technology' (Oxford: Clarendon Press, 1983).

Menon, M.G.K., 'Homi Jehangir Bhabha, 1909–1966' (London: Royal Institution of Great Britain, 1967).

Menon, Ritu, and Kamla Bhasin, 'Recovery, Rupture, Resistance: Indian state and abduction of women during Partition', *Economic and Political Weekly*, Annual Review of Women Studies, 24 April 1993.

Metcalf, Thomas R., *An Imperial Vision: Indian Architecture and Britain's Raj* (Berkeley: University of California Press, 1989).

Monthly Public Opinion Surveys, vol. 19, no. 9 (June 1974).

Morehouse, Ward, *Science in India*, Administrative Staff College of India (ASCI) Occasional Papers (Hyderabad, 1971).

Mulvey, Laura, *Fetishism and Curiosity* (Bloomington: Indiana University Press for the British Film Institute, 1996).

Nandy, Ashis, *Alternative Sciences: Creativity and authenticity in two Indian scientists* (Delhi: Allied, 1980).

Nandy, Ashis, ed., *Science, Hegemony, and Violence* (Delhi: Oxford University Press, 1988).

Opinion (Delhi), vol. 7, no. 3, May 1966.

Peierls, Rudolph, *Bird of Passage: Recollections of a physicist* (Princeton: Princeton University Press, 1985).

Penny, [Lord] 'Homi Jehangir Bhabha, 1909–1966', *Biographical Memoirs of Fellows of the Royal Society*, vol. 13 (London: The Royal Society, 1967).

Peters, Bernard, 'The Primary Cosmic Radiation', Presidential Address of the Physics Section, Indian Science Congress, Agra, 1956. *Science and Culture*, vol. 21, no. 10 (April 1956).

Peters, Bernard, 'Bhabha and Cosmic Rays', *Science Reporter* (New Delhi), vol. 3, no. 10 (October 1966).

Pietz, William, 'Fetishism and Materialism', in Apter and Pietz, *Fetishism as Cultural Discourse*.

Pines, Jim, and Paul Willemen, eds., *Questions of Third Cinema* (London: BFI Publishers, 1989).

Potter, David C., *India's Political Administrators: From ICS to IAS* (Delhi: Oxford University Press, 1996).

Poulantzas, Nicos, *Political Power and Social Classes* (London: New Left Books, 1973).

Poulantzas, Nicos, *State, Power, Socialism* (London: New Left Books, 1978).

Prakash, Gyan, 'The Modern Nation's Return in the Archaic', *Critical Inquiry*, vol. 23, no. 3 (Spring 1997), pp. 536–56.

Pye, Lucien, *Aspects of Political Development* (Boston: Little, Brown, 1966).

Rajan, M.S., *Non-alignment: India and the future* (Mysore: University of Mysore Press, 1970).

Ramanna, Raja, *Years of Pilgrimage* (Delhi: Viking, 1991).

Reid, Escott, *Envoy to Nehru* (Delhi: Oxford University Press, 1981).

Rostow, W.W., 'The Takeoff into Sustained Growth', *Economic Journal*, vol. 66 (March 1956).

Rhodes, Robert, *The Making of the Atomic Bomb* (New York: Simon and Schuster, 1986).

Rudolph, Lloyd I., and Susanne H. Rudolph, *In Pursuit of Lakshmi: The political economy of the Indian state* (Chicago: University of Chicago Press, 1987).

Sagan, Scott, 'Why do states build nuclear weapons: Three models in search of a bomb', *International Security*, 21, 6 (Winter 1996/97).

Schrooer, Dietrich, *Science, Technology and the Nuclear Arms Race* (New York: John Wiley, 1984).

Seminar (Delhi), no. 83 (July 1966).

Sen Gupta, Bhabani, *Nuclear Weapons: Policy Options for India* (Center for Policy Research/New Delhi: Sage 1983).

Sethna, H. N., and S. N. Srinivasan, 'Operating experience with the fuel reprocessing plant at Trombay', *Nuclear Engineering* (Chemical Engineering Progress Symposium series), vol. 65, 94, (1967).

Shapin, Steven, *The Social History of Truth* (Chicago: University of Chicago Press, 1994).

Shapiro, Michael, 'Warring Bodies and Bodies Politic: Tribal Warriors vs. State Soldiers', in Shapiro and Alker, *Challenging Boundaries*.

Shapiro, Michael J., and Hayward R. Alker, eds., *Challenging Boundaries* (Minneapolis: University of Minnesota Press, 1996).

Sharma, Dhirendra, *India's Nuclear Estate* (Delhi: Lancers, 1983).

Sharma, Dhirendra, *The Indian Atom: Power and Proliferation* (New Delhi: Philosophy and Social Action, 1986).

Singer, Han, 'The Mechanics of Economic Development', *Indian Economic Review* (August 1952).

Singh, Sampooran, *India and the Nuclear Bomb* (Delhi: S. Chand and Co., 1971).

Singh, Virendra, 'H.J. Bhabha: His contribution to theoretical physics', in Sreekantan et al., *Homi Jehangir Bhabha*.

Sreekantan, B.V., Virendra Singh, and B.M. Udgaonkar, eds., *Homi Jehangir Bhabha: Collected Scientific Papers* (Bombay: Tata Institute of Fundamental Research, 1985).

Sreekantan, B.V., 'H.J. Bhabha: His contributions to cosmic ray physics', in Sreekantan et al., *Homi Jehangir Bhabha*.

Srinivasan, M.R., 'An Intermezzo', *Selected Lectures of Dr. M. R. Srinivasan* (Bombay: Department of Atomic Energy, n.d.).

Subramaniam, C. R., *India and the Computer* (Delhi: Oxford University Press, 1994).

Tata Institute of Fundamental Research, 1945–1970 (Bombay: TIFR, n.d.).

Taussig, Michael, '*Maleficium*: State Fetishism', in Apter and Pietz, *Fetishism as Cultural Discourse*.

Thapar, Raj, *All These Years* (Delhi: Penguin, 1991).

'The Architects of Nuclear India', special issue of *Nuclear India*, vol. 26 (October 1989).

Thomas, Raju, *Indian Security Policy* (Princeton: Princeton University Press, 1988).

Udgaonkar, B.M., '"Growing Science" – from Bhabha's writings', *Science Today* (Bombay), October 1984.

Vanaik, Achin, *The Painful Transition: Bourgeois Democracy in India* (London: Verso, 1990).

Venkataraman, G., *Journey Into Light: Life and Science of C. V. Raman* (Delhi: Penguin, 1994).

Venkateshwaran, A.L., *Defence Organisation in India* (New Delhi: Publications Division, Government of India, 1967).

Viner, Jacob, 'The Economics of Development', in Agarwala and Singh, *The Economics of Underdevelopment* (New York: Oxford University Press, 1963).

Virilio, Paul, *Speed and Politics* (New York: Semiotext(e), 1986).

Visvanathan, Shiv, 'Atomic Physics: The career of an imagination', in Nandy, *Science, Hegemony, and Violence*.

Visvanathan, Shiv, 'On the Annals of the Laboratory State', in Nandy, *Science, Hegemony, and Violence*.

Wali, Kameshwar S., *Chandra: A biography of S. Chandrasekhar* (New Delhi: Penguin, 1991).

Walker, R.B.J., *Inside/Outside: International Relations as Political Theory* (Cambridge: Cambridge University Press, 1993).

Waltz, Kenneth N., *Theory of International Politics* (Reading, Mass.: Addison Wesley, 1979).

Weart, Spencer R., *Nuclear Fear: A history of images* (Cambridge, Mass.: Harvard University Press, 1988).

Weber, Max, 'Politics as a Vocation', in *From Max Weber: Essays in Sociology*, trans. and edited by H.H. Gerth and C. Wright Mills (New York: Oxford University Press, 1958).

Weinbaum, M.G., and Chetan Kumar, eds, *South Asia Approaches the Millenium: Reexamining National Security* (Boulder: Westview, 1995).

Winner, Langdon, *The Whale and the Reactor* (Chicago: University of Chicago Press, 1984).

II. GOVERNMENT DOCUMENTS, UNPUBLISHED MATERIALS, PERSONAL PAPERS

Canada

Iris Lonergun, 'The negotiations between Canada and India for the supply of the NRX nuclear research reactor, 1955–1956: A case study of participatory internationalism', unpublished MA thesis, Carleton University, Ottawa, August 1989.

India

Atomic Energy and Space Research: A profile for the decade, 1970–1980 (Bombay: Atomic Energy Commission, 1970).

Constituent Assembly of India (Legislative) Debates.

Indian Industrial Commission, *Report*, 1916–1918 (Calcutta: Superintendent of Government Printing, 1918).

Lok Sabha Debates.

Meghnad Saha Papers, Nehru Memorial Museum and Library, New Delhi.

Minoo Masani, 'The challenge of the Chinese Bomb', ICWA lecture, 8 December 1964 (mimeo).

Nuclear India, Department of Atomic Energy, Bombay.

Selected Works of Jawaharlal Nehru, Second Series, vols. 1–2, 4–5 (Delhi: Jawaharlal Nehru Memorial Fund).

TIFR File, Tata Archives, Bombay.

UK

Atomic Energy Files, Public Records Office, Kew Gardens.

P.M.S. Blackett Papers, Royal Society of Great Britain, London.

Hill, A.V., 'Scientific Research in India', Tracts/695, (London: Royal Society, 1944). L/P&S Files. India Office Library, London.

USA

Abraham, Itty, 'Stepping Back from the Nuclear Threshold? Latin America and South Asia', Occasional Paper Series no. 15, Henry A. Stimson Center, Washington, DC.

'Analysis of six issues about nuclear capabilities of India, Iraq, Libya, and Pakistan', Report prepared for the US Senate Foreign Relations sub-committee on Arms Control, Oceans, International Operations, and Environment (Washington, DC: January 1982).

Foreign Relations of the United States (Washington, DC: US Department of State).

History of Quantum Physics Project, Niels Bohr Library, American Institute of Physics, New York [now College Park, Maryland].

Victor Gilinsky Papers, Hoover Institution, Stanford, Calif.

Gupta, Vipin, and Frank Pabian, 'Investigating the Allegations of Indian Nuclear Test Preparations in the Rajasthan Desert', mimeo (July 1996). Reprinted from http://www.cmc.sandia.gov/issues/papers/gupta1

Ernest O. Lawrence Papers, Bancroft Library, University of California, Berkeley.

Robert LeBaron Papers, Hoover Institution, Stanford, Calif.

Office of Technology Assessment (OTA), 'Nuclear Proliferation and Safeguards', Main Report, PB–275–843, US Department of Commerce, Washington, DC (June 1977).

Isidor I. Rabi Papers, Manuscripts Division, Library of Congress, Washington, DC.

South Asia folder, Nuclear non-proliferation documents, National Security Archives, Washington, DC.

State Department/Atomic Energy (S/AE) Files, US National Archives, Washington, DC.

III. NEWSPAPERS, JOURNALS, AND MAGAZINES

The Hindu (Madras)
Morning Standard (Bombay)
New York Times (New York)
Science and Culture (Calcutta)
Statesman (New Delhi)
The Telegraph (Calcutta)
Times of India (New Delhi)

INDEX